# SOCIAL POLICY IN THE
# MODERN WORLD

# SOCIAL POLICY
## IN THE
# MODERN WORLD

## A Comparative Text

Michael Hill

Blackwell
Publishing

BLACKWELL PUBLISHING

350 Main Street, Malden, MA 02148–5020, USA
9600 Garsington Road, Oxford OX4 2DQ, UK
550 Swanston Street, Carlton, Victoria 3053, Australia

First published 2006 by Blackwell Publishing Ltd

2    2007

*Library of Congress Cataloging-in-Publication Data*

Hill, Michael J. (Michael James), 1937–
    Social policy in the modern world : a comparative text / Michael Hill.
        p. cm.
    Includes bibliographical references and index.
    ISBN-13: 978-1-4051-2723-3 (hardback : alk. paper)
    ISBN-10: 1-4051-2723-6 (hardback : alk. paper)
    ISBN-13: 978-1-4051-2724-0 (pbk. : alk. paper)
    ISBN-10: 1-4051-2724-4 (pbk. : alk. paper)   1. Social planning—Cross-
cultural studies.   2. Public welfare—Cross-cultural studies.   3. Social
policy—Cross-cultural studies.   4. Social security—Cross-cultural
studies.   I. Title.
    HN20.H55 2006
    320.6–dc22

                                                            2005025957

A catalogue record for this title is available from the British Library.

Set in 10/12.5pt Palatino
by Graphicraft Ltd, Hong Kong
Printed and bound in Singapore
by C.O.S. Printers Pte Ltd

The publisher's policy is to use permanent paper from mills that operate
a sustainable forestry policy, and which has been manufactured from
pulp processed using acid-free and elementary chlorine-free practices.
Furthermore, the publisher ensures that the text paper and cover board
used have met acceptable environmental accreditation standards.

For further information on
Blackwell Publishing, visit our website:
www.blackwellpublishing.com

# CONTENTS

# TABLES

Much of the underlying data used in these tables were originally published by the OECD. However, their reproduction in this book does
not necessarily reflect the official views of the OECD or the governments of its member countries.

# PREFACE

The most important acknowledgement is to Margaret May. This book originated in discussions with her about the production of a joint book on comparative social policy. She was fully involved in the original planning of it and then unfortunately had to drop out because of the many pressures emanating from the establishment of the London Metropolitan University. Happily she agreed to contribute a chapter (on employment policy) and to provide advice to me during the production of the book. She has given me splendid support throughout the project, based on her extensive experience of teaching comparative social policy.

Back in 1996 I published a book called *Comparative Social Policy: A Comparative Analysis*. However, since then, the study of comparative social policy has advanced enormously so this book, while it carries forward some of the features of that original book, is radically different. I have benefited from the many new books and articles and from using my original book when teaching students at Goldsmiths College and in various countries in the world. I have found it particularly valuable to discuss many of my ideas with scholars from East Asia (particularly Sammy Chiu, Yuen-Wen Ku, Tetsuo Ogawa, Victor Wong and Chack-kie Wong) where a lively interest in this topic has developed.

I am grateful to Justin Vaughan and Ben Thatcher of Blackwell Publishing for their support on this project, to Jolyon Phillips for his efficient editorial work on the typescript, and to the anonymous advisers who were consulted.

This book is dedicated to my wife Betty, who keeps urging me to take it easy but understands my continued commitment to academic work.

M.H.

# PART ONE

# GENERALISATIONS

# CHAPTER 1

# INTRODUCING THE COMPARATIVE STUDY OF SOCIAL POLICY

## Introduction to the Book

This book explores similarities and differences between countries in the way in which they approach social policy, both by looking at the broad characteristics of those policies and by examining variations in the ways in which some key issues of universal importance for social welfare are handled in different countries. It differs from those textbooks which combine overview chapters with examination of a selection of specific countries in more detail (e.g. Alcock and Craig, 2001; Cochrane, Clarke and Gerwirtz, 2001) in that discussion is organised by policy area or theme. Hence in principle the countries covered comprise all the countries of the world, though none are examined in any detail. In practice, however, much of the discussion compares only some of the countries of the world, with an emphasis on the more developed ones. There are two crucial reasons for this. First, social policy as a form of public policy (see discussion below) is almost totally absent in a large number of countries in the world, largely the poorer ones. Obviously this is not to say that these countries have no social welfare problems, but rather that the state plays very little role in providing solutions to them. Second, it is also true of more or less the same sample of countries that there is a lack of reliable data on those social policies that do exist. The approach adopted in the book is not to completely ignore these countries but to provide comments and comparative material where appropriate and available.

Hence it is, with these small exceptions, what are often described in shorthand terms as the **OECD** (Organisation for Economic Cooperation and Development) countries (see the discussion of OECD statistics below) whose policies get most of the attention in this book. Additionally, three countries that are not OECD members but which are highly developed and for which there are data available – Singapore, Hong Kong and Taiwan – do get attention from time to time. Finally, even within the OECD group of countries, two small countries (Iceland and Luxembourg) have been left out merely to keep the discussion simple and the tables short.

In this introductory chapter I argue that any approach to comparative social policy needs to take into account issues about defining social policy, recognising the way in which assumptions about alternative roles for individuals, families, communities, markets and the state may be embodied in alternative approaches to the topic. I then go on to examine the various data sources available for comparison and the way in which studies have been set up to secure new data. Without going too deeply into overall questions about the methodology of social science, I will discuss some of the issues concerning data interpretation and the use of quantitative and qualitative data in comparative studies.

The next chapter reviews the development of comparative theory and shows how regime theory has now become the dominant approach. This has replaced earlier theory that emphasised 'convergence': how as nations developed, their social policies became more similar. This was challenged by evidence showing that this process is only occurring to a limited extent. Instead, regime theory suggests that there are distinct 'families' of nations whose social policies share certain distinctive characteristics. The strengths and weaknesses of this approach are reviewed, as are suggested variations from the original regime model formulated by Gøsta Esping-Andersen. Throughout the rest of the book I will make reference to regime theory, illustrating further where it helps analysis, where alternative formulations of it may be preferable and where it is inapplicable.

Chapter 3 explores ways in which the mainstream emphasis on the characteristics of policies in comparative analysis may need to be modified by taking into account aspects of the policy process, particularly how policies are funded and delivered.

There then follows the second part of the book (chapters 4–8) in which specific policy *areas* are examined. In this chapter some comments will be made about the difficulties in delineating social policy. The choice of policy areas is necessarily arbitrary, but influenced by the choices made in other books and in the mainstream teaching of social policy. Here individual chapters deal with:

- social security (chapter 4);
- employment policy (chapter 5);
- health services (chapter 6);
- social care (chapter 7);
- education (chapter 8).

Topics that have been omitted include housing (though some references are made to housing support in chapter 4), environment protection and transport. In all these policy areas the comparative literature is rather limited.

The third part of the book explores social policy *issues* comparatively. In chapter 9, taking the traditional concerns about citizenship and universalism in the social policy literature as the starting point, I will argue that it is important to explore whether social policies reduce those socio-economic divisions, are relatively neutral in respect of them or even perhaps increase them. Comparative data about redistribution and the relief of poverty will also be explored.

The next two chapters carry on the analysis started in chapter 9, exploring the impact of social policy on divisions based on gender or ethnicity. Chapter 10 reviews the extensive comparative literature on the impact of state social policy on families and on the way social policy impacts on women. Chapter 11 explores issues about how social policies affect ethnic minorities and about the implications of migration for social policy.

In some respects chapter 12 can be seen as a continuation of the exploration of the social divisions theme in terms of age divisions. However, issues about social policies for elderly people dominate much of the contemporary social policy agenda, with the ageing of societies being seen as a problematic development. This therefore dominates the discussion in this chapter. I will argue that the analysis of the impact of ageing societies should not be seen as a universally impending 'explosion' of a demographic 'time-bomb' but as involving the very complex evolution of transfer relationships between the generations in different ways in different societies.

Chapter 13 brings the overall survey of social policy in the world today to a conclusion through the exploration of the impact of global forces – seen as economic, political and cultural – on social policy. The arguments for and against the importance of globalism are reviewed, followed by a discussion of the particular ways in which global influences are important for social policy. This returns to the theme of 'convergence', since globalist theory often suggests that national social policies will become similar. It will be argued that whilst it is certainly the case that ideas about policy travel rapidly round the world, and that accordingly there are policy exchanges and even 'fashions' in new ideas, the outcome is not necessarily convergence in the way in which the more determinist of the globalism theories suggest.

## What is Social Policy?

In order to understand what is involved in comparing social policies it is important to step back from two often taken for granted assumptions:

- that social policies are specific actions designed to promote welfare;
- that such actions are necessarily state actions.

Both of these assumptions embody essential truths about the activities to be explored in this book; however they can be very misleading if they are not placed in a wider understanding of human welfare and the role of the state.

Readers should try for a moment to put aside their assumptions about what this book is about and ask themselves two related questions.

- What do I understand by my own welfare or well-being?
- Upon what and who does that welfare depend?

Answers to the first of these questions are likely to include such things as not being hungry or cold or unwell, but may well go on from these to wider considerations about what may contribute to a sense of well-being – participation in social life, involvement in activities that may provide emotional or intellectual stimulation, even sexual activities. A number of writers have sought to identify a set of human needs (see Doyal and Gough, 1991), recognising difficulties in separating needs from wants and suggesting that there may be some senses in which more or less basic needs can be identified or even that there may be a sort of hierarchy from essential concerns with maintaining bodily integrity to forms of self-actualisation. In this discussion there is no intention to go into the arguments that obviously arise about which needs must be met and which may be more appropriately described as 'wants'. However, it must not be forgotten that much evaluation of social policy, and accordingly much comparison, centres around questions about the adequacy of contributions to welfare. In addressing contributions to welfare it must not be forgotten therefore that answers to questions about what welfare is will be varied, and will indicate that it is a vague and elastic concept.

Answers to the second question, upon what or who does your welfare depend, will be much more complex. People just about to read a book that they know will have a great deal to say about state policy may well start by identifying the state as a source of their welfare. But introspection, unbiased by this situation, may equally well produce answers like:

- myself, meaning my work, my savings, my self-care;
- my family;
- my friends;
- my community, meaning not only neighbours but the organisations to which I belong.

For many of us welfare depends upon a complex mix, with the state perhaps playing an overarching role (regulating and providing support when other systems fail) rather than a very explicit direct one. To make analysis even more difficult, however, the sources of welfare identified here may equally be sources of diswelfare (the state, the family, étc.); even we ourselves may be sources of harm to ourselves.

Just as the issues about the definition of welfare (and the related question of need) are topics of dispute so, perhaps even more saliently, there are controversies about the different contributions to welfare. This is most particularly evident in the arguments about the appropriate role of the state on the one hand and the individual on the other.

So let us now return to the first of those taken for granted assumptions: that social policies are specific actions designed to promote welfare. To what extent can we expect to be able to identify a specific category of actions in this way, when welfare is complex and is promoted in diverse ways? In conventional discussions of policy a distinction is often made between economic policy and social policy. However, if welfare particularly depends on work and economic policies create work, then those are the most important policies for the promotion of welfare. In fact, the distinction between economic policy and social policy is often based on a particular set of assumptions about the working of markets that suggest that the free play of economic forces creates diswelfares which social policies then need to correct. However, these are peculiar, rather ideologically loaded, assumptions which are partially true at particular times in particular places. They may be challenged both by the denial that untrammelled market forces create diswelfare (a position taken by some classical economic thinkers) and by the assertion that economic policies may be developed that manage markets in ways that promote welfare.

Hence we need to analyse all courses of action taken or not taken (we return to the latter below) in terms of effects which seem in common-sense terms to be social effects or influences on welfare. For example, much management of the economy focuses on rates of inflation or unemployment. These are not just statistics but evidence of effects that increase or decrease welfare (reduce or increase the real incomes of those on fixed forms of remuneration, throw some people out of work or get them into work, and so on) (see chapter 5). Similarly, changes to transportation systems cannot be seen as merely adjustments to economic infrastructure, since they convey benefits and disbenefits. And so we may go on.

Another problem with any emphasis on a straightforward connection between social policies and the advancement of welfare is that such propositions seem to highlight benign intentions. Social policies may enhance welfare but they may equally enhance diswelfare (or of course there is a neutral position where they do neither). Even more problematical is the fact that statements about the enhancement of welfare may confuse intentions and effects. It is essential not to assume that policies will have particular effects just because policy-makers say they will have them.

How then can we compare social policy if we cannot readily define it? We have essentially two choices. One is to try to compare the sources of welfare and diswelfare in different societies. But this implies a very wide activity: trying to bring together the multiple influences on social well-being. The other, adopted in this book, is to confine attention to a limited number of policy areas, conventionally defined as 'social policy', recognising that their particular hallmark seems to have been efforts to advance human welfare. At this stage the reader may well ask 'If that is where you were heading anyway, why go in for the rather difficult argument about welfare you have just concluded?' The answer to this is to stress the extent to which what is being adopted is merely a pragmatic solution to the problem of defining social policy, and that therefore it is very important for readers to recognise that when we compare societies the policies examined (1) may or may not enhance welfare and (2) may or may not be dwarfed in importance by other policies. Let us look beyond those generalisations by considering a society where conventional 'social policy' development has been limited but substantial welfare advance has occurred, Taiwan. This country has relatively low levels of poverty and has (at least until recently) had low levels of inequality. It has experienced a dramatic fall in premature death, lifting it distinctively into the group of privileged societies in this respect. The advancement of Taiwan has occurred primarily because of strong state-led economic development. Until very recently the society has enjoyed very full employment. As it has developed, governments have paid more attention to infrastructure developments – improvements to the environment and to transportation (both road and rail) – than to social policy ones. Furthermore, such social policy development as has occurred has not been particularly egalitarian: there has been a strong emphasis on education rather than any more directly ameliorative policies, health insurance has involved high levels of cost sharing, and the social security structures that have been most developed take care of soldiers, civil servants and teachers.

However, looking at specific state policies, in the case of a society like Taiwan, will not tell the whole story about welfare in that society relative to others. There are issues about family life and about demography that need attention too. It is argued that in Taiwan the Confucian extended family is itself an important protector of individuals, income transfers within extended families being very important. At the same time the changing nature of such families, in the context of low birth and death rates and high levels of occupational and geographical mobility, needs attention.

This leads to the other issue about the definition of social policy, the widespread assumption that social policy actions are necessarily state actions. The concept of 'policy' is identified in Chambers dictionary as 'a course of action, especially one based on some declared and respected principle'. At the same time the *Oxford English Dictionary* identifies as 'the chief living sense' of the word policy 'A course of action adopted and pursued by a government, party, ruler, statesman . . .'. So policies may be identified as purposive action, but such action is recognised as a particular characteristic of state action. Returning to our sources of welfare, while we recognise state action as particularly significant we may ourselves adopt policies which influence our welfare, as may our families and our communities. We could digress here into some quite complex issues of political anthropology about the extent to which families and communities preceded states as social organisations.

However, an acknowledgement of policy as a course of action must include the possibility that systematic inaction occurs. Students of power (see Lukes, 2004; Hay, 2002, chapter 5) have drawn attention to the importance of non-decisions, in which the emergence of issues onto the public agenda has been actively prevented or implicitly inhibited. A particularly misleading model of public policy processes, linked to economic analyses that see market processes as natural, involves seeing social policies as interventions which divert systems from their normal course. The reality is that the ways in which human life, including economic life, is organised depends on a framework of laws, conventions and customary procedures which themselves have implications for the benefits or disbenefits that occur. There is no starting point at a state of nature. Holding to particular arrangements on the grounds that it is problematical to meddle with markets may have distinct consequences for human welfare. Significantly a branch of economics, appropriately called welfare economics, concerns itself with diswelfares that flow from some kinds of market arrangements (and accordingly with the exploration of issues and problems about markets that are seen as justifying state intervention).

As with the definition of social policy, it is true to say that this book pays particular attention to the role of the state as an agent of social policy. However, in this case it is important not to be misled by the either/or arguments of political philosophy into disregarding the extent to which state social policy may involve direct action to support or enhance the roles of the other actors. States adopt policies to influence the roles of families and communities. Even in respect of individual self-help, states are never entirely neutral but rather support some roles and proscribe others. An emphasis on specific areas of social policy highlights issue about the provision of benefits and services. It is then important not to forget the extent to which states operate as regulators rather than as direct providers, influencing what we can do and what others can do for or to us.

## Comparison in Social Policy

Margaret May puts the basic case for comparative study in these terms:

> The study of welfare provision inevitably involves some form of comparison between current practice and past or alternative ways of meeting need or improving existing policies. Such comparison may not always be explicit . . . but they are central to a discipline geared to evaluating welfare arrangements. (May, in Alcock, Erskine and May, 2003, p. 17)

This implies both a practical and an intellectual case for comparative studies. The practical one is that policy evaluation and improvement requires to be grounded in a recognition of alternative ways of doing things and a capacity therefore to learn form the experience of others.

The intellectual one is embodied in a classic argument for comparison in the social sciences by the famous French sociologist Emile Durkheim:

> We have only one way of demonstrating that one phenomenon is the cause of another. That is to compare the cases where they are both simultaneously present or absent, so as to discover whether the variations they display in these different combinations of circumstances provide evidence that one depends on the other. (Durkheim, 1982, p. 141)

May's general statement embraces several variants of comparison:

- comparison within one country at different points in time;
- comparison between different parts of the same country;
- comparison between countries.

This book is about the last of those three, though elements of the other two surface from time to time in the discussion: the first in relation to different rates of change in different countries, the second where questions need to be raised about whether statements about a country as a whole may not apply to some parts of it.

In the first part of this chapter I have suggested that the determinants of human welfare depend on the roles played by the state, the market, the family and so on. In which case the study of social policy must require the application of ideas, theories and concepts derived from a range of academic disciplines, including particularly sociology, political science and economics. These ideas, theories and concepts involve propositions about what promotes (or undermines) welfare which, though they may only be applied in a static way to one society at one point in time, often claim some measure of universality. Many statements about power or how markets work or the roles of families are often offered as generalisations about all human societies. Their claims to universality need testing. Conversely, statements that purport to apply to only one society need to be challenged in search of reasons why they are cast in such narrow terms.

The first of these points may seem more obvious than the second. Any expectation that a 'market' or a 'family', for example, behaves in similar ways in different societies requires further examination. Any theory embodying deterministic propositions about influences on social policy suggests that countries with similar characteristics will tend to have similar policies. Many forms of Marxist theory suggest that policy similarities will arise at similar stages in the development of capitalism; more general theories of socio-economic development embody comparable propositions whilst many forms of globalist theory suggest widespread uniformities in responses to issues, particularly those with economic implications, across nations.

Equally, statements that seem to rest upon, or take for granted, the idea that one country's policies are unique products of its cultural and institutional characteristics needs to be examined. Although it is often easier to show that systems diverge rather than converge, there is nevertheless an implication in theories stressing uniqueness that requires comparison to demonstrate they are right.

Comparative work is vital for the wider understanding of social policy if we do not want propositions to be seen as merely observations about specific occurrences in a particular place and even at a particular point in time. As social policy is an applied discipline, it is appropriate to note observations on the case for comparison made in one of the disciplines on which it draws. A leading textbook on comparative politics echoes the quotation from the sociologist Durkheim set out above: 'Comparison is the methodological core of the scientific study of politics. Comparative analysis helps us develop explanations and test theories of the way in which political processes work' (Almond, Powell, Strøm and Dalton, 2004, p. 31).

It is appropriate however to pause a moment to consider that word 'scientific' in this context. There is no wish to explore here the difficult philosophical arguments about whether social behaviour can be studied scientifically, and what methodological conclusions flow from views taken on that subject. But it is important to state that the view taken in this book is that comparison can be something more than the setting down side by side of statements that in society $x$ they do this and in society $y$ they do that (something that characterised some of the early work on comparative social policy; see Rodgers, Greve and Morgan, 1968; Kaim-Caudle, 1973). Consequently, forms of systematic comparison will be adopted that aim to lead to generalisations which, whilst not offered as 'universal laws' of social policy, can be open to some form of testing. In this sense, in a discipline in which opportunities for experimental studies are very rare, systematic comparison does provide for a form of quasi-experimentation important when policies have unexpected consequences, or policy borrowing occurs, in which questions can be raised about differences between national contexts which will affect outcomes.

Inasmuch as I am asserting here that systematic comparison is possible, another issue also needs to be mentioned: the extent to which comparison is quantitative. The stance taken in this book is a pragmatic one. As soon as comparison moves beyond a very small number of cases, it necessarily becomes implicitly if not explicitly comparative:

individual cases get sorted into separate boxes as examples of 'type 1', 'type 2', 'type 3', and so on. In many cases that sorting needs further justification: if we say 'type 1' contains countries that have high levels of $x$ and low levels of $y$ whereas 'type 2' has different features, then our notions of what 'high' or 'low' mean are open to challenge, to which we can respond much better if there are numbers we can quote.

In other words comparisons involving a number of different cases work much better if there are numerical indices that can be used. On the other hand, there are many important and interesting differences between societies for which numerical indices are not available. Those indices that can be used may well tell us very little about key phenomena. Indeed they may well obscure rather than illuminate key differences. Furthermore, two observers allegedly counting the same thing may actually be counting very different things, particularly if they are in different countries with different cultures and different institutions.

There is here then a dilemma for comparative studies. Close-grained qualitative comparisons between social policy systems start to get into difficulties if more than two countries are compared. We find few efforts at systematic qualitative studies going beyond the comparison of five or six nations. There are qualitative databases containing information about more nations than this (e.g. the European Union's MISSOC information system and the US Social Security Administration's *Social Security Programs Throughout the World*), but they are in the same category as the early academic studies in which descriptive material is placed side by side. They require further work to turn them into sources for generalisations about social policy, work in which the summing activity described above becomes necessary. The alternative is quantitative studies in which broad statistical comparisons are made, with questions about the reliability of the statistics or the compatibility of data sources often pushed into the background.

The argument between quantitative and qualitative methods is ultimately a sterile one since there is a case to be made that use of either (or both) depends on what you are trying to do, on the situation and on the data available. There may also often be a case for combining both, using qualitative methods to explore more deeply puzzles thrown up by quantitative comparison. A qualitative focus on unusual cases may be appropriate. Throughout this book examples will be found of nations with characteristics that do not seen to fit the quantitative generalisations, nations that seems to have developed rather distinctive approaches to policy problems. Moving to and fro between quantitative and qualitative methods may be a fruitful way of exploring issues.

These observations on generalisation and quantification broadly sum up the approach to be adopted in this book. The stress on pragmatism is important. In the case of this account, the commitment to an over-view of comparative social policy on a world scale leads to a heavy dependence on quantitative material, much of it crude in character. Fine-grained analysis of a qualitative kind is limited both by the relative absence of such studies and by the difficulties in integration into a short book taking a world view of findings from comparisons between just two (or slightly more) countries.

## Sources of Comparative Data

The most important data source for this book is the OECD, an organisa-tion now of thirty member countries drawn from the more economically advanced countries of the world. It is often colloquially described as the 'rich nations club'. Its membership is growing steadily. South Korea, Mexico and some of the former Soviet bloc nations now members of the European Union (Czech Republic, Hungary, Poland and the Slovak Republic) are comparatively new members. It collects information on a regular basis from its members, producing key expenditure statistics on an annual basis. Its social expenditure database yields a considerable amount of information on the divisions between different kinds of expenditure in different nations. The broad social policy expenditure figures quoted in chapter 2 and elsewhere come from this database, with education added in for the purposes of this book. OECD also produces regular reports on topics it is concerned about, for example issues about ageing and social policy, about health inequalities and about variations in educational performance have been given attention.

As far as the analysis of social policy is concerned, the OECD is a key source for almost all the nations with high incomes, in terms of **gross domestic product (GDP)** per head, and therefore almost all the nations with large public social policy sectors. Many key expenditure statistics are expressed as percentages of GDP per head, since this represents the most straightforward way of achieving comparability.

Clearly, while many of the issues to be explored in this book involve these large spenders, OECD data does not give an adequate picture of social policy in the world as a whole. In various places therefore the OECD data are supplemented by data from various United Nations organisations, particularly the World Health Organisation.

There is an additional source of comparative statistics for members of the European Union (EU), particularly deriving from the work of the EU's data collection agency (Eurostat). An annual report titled *The Social Situation in the European Union* contains a great deal of comparative data, though what it has to say about the nations that joined the EU in 2004 is still limited. This report draws on a range of survey material, collected directly by Eurostat or produced by other EU-supported bodies such as the European Community Household Panel and the European Foundation for Living and Working Conditions.

There is also an international project supported partly by the Luxembourg government and partly by research institutes from participating countries, the Luxembourg Income Survey (LIS), which brings together data on a comparable basis from national household income surveys. This information is valuable for the light it throws on the distributional impact of social policy, but assembling it and getting it into usable forms is a slow process and accordingly much of the data is rather dated.

There have been a number of specific international studies of education, notably the work of the International Association for the Evaluation of Education Achievement and the International School Effectiveness Research Project (see Teddlie and Reynolds, 2000), together with the Programme for International Student Assessment commissioned by the OECD (see www.pisa.oecd.org).

Beyond these sources much of the rest of the work that is quoted in this book relies upon rather small-scale efforts to assemble information from sources within individual countries.

Some comments in the last section suggested that making comparisons between countries requires a willingness to use the data available without worrying too much about the difficulties that might have been encountered in trying to assemble that material. Inasmuch as there is heavy use made of OECD data, it is important to bear in mind that the OECD puts a great deal of effort into trying to minimise these problems. Expenditure data are probably the most reliable, except that situations in which there are both central and local spenders within a country may be a source of problems. Trying to estimate private expenditure, for example on health, social care and education, is more difficult. However, social policy performance needs to be explored in terms of **'outputs'** (what services are actually offered) and **'outcomes'** (results, like reduction of poverty or illness, or illiteracy) as well as in terms of expenditure **'inputs'**. There is a need to see amounts spent as 'inputs' as having a relatively direct influence upon 'outputs' but an indirect and complex influence upon 'outcomes'. The relationship between 'inputs' and 'outputs' is influenced by the efficiency with which resources are used, with a crucial consideration being the extent to which rewards for staff delivering the service is a primary cost. The relationship between 'outputs' and 'outcomes' depends on the extent to which services actually deliver the additions to welfare attributed to them, in a context in which many other things (not only other policies but wider social and environmental factors) also have an influence. Hence when we try to compare countries we have to bear in mind that the indices often easiest to acquire, i.e. on 'inputs', may tell us very little about what actually happens. Output data may be more helpful, but it is outcomes that really matter. But then the problem with outcome data is that the variations between countries which are identified may have very little to do with policy factors, but may be the product of influences that are not easy to bring within policy control. These issues are important for the analysis of all policies, but particularly important for comparison of different services.

Even if a variable is a rather poor indicator, it may nevertheless throw up important questions when used comparatively. Take, for example, the issue of poverty. There is a great deal of controversy about how best to measure this; for international comparative purposes the index commonly used is the percentage of the population with incomes below 50 or 60 per cent of the mean or median income. Obviously this means that in aggregate the poor in rich countries will be richer than the poor in poorer countries. Additionally, incomes may be assessed in different ways in different countries, particularly where it is difficult to disaggregate individuals from the households in which they live. However, if one of your main concerns (as is the case in this book) is to compare countries in terms of the extent to which specific interventions reduce poverty (to compare pre-tax and transfer incomes with post-tax and transfer ones), then the lack of comparability in the original poverty measures may not matter so much. A similar point may be made about the use of another even more questionable set of comparative statistics, those on educational performance.

## Conclusions

This chapter started with a discussion of what is meant by 'social policy'. Whilst the book is concerned with the examination of policies where a public-sector element is very important, it was considered important to warn against three common fallacies:

- that our welfare is only promoted by state social policies;
- that an easy line can be drawn between social policies and other public policies;
- that social policies (however defined) necessarily promote welfare.

All these points imply that examining social policy, and particularly looking at it comparatively, requires an awareness of the complex ways in which the actions of individuals in the marketplace, the behaviour of families (and sometimes communities) and the roles played by the state interact.

The chapter goes on to examine what is involved in comparison of social policy, suggesting that there are important connections between the efforts to study social policy systematically, informed by the mainstream social sciences, and the case for comparison. Any generalisation about social policy needs to be seen as located in a specific place and time, and therefore either related to other generalisations about other places or times or needing to have its claims to uniqueness tested. Hence alongside more pragmatic justifications for the comparative study of social policy, there are important questions about setting specific observations in a wider context.

This discussion led on to some consideration of the use of quantitative data in the making of comparisons, arguing that the case for this must be seen to be a pragmatic one, based on the difficulties to be faced when one is trying to make comparisons between a significant number of different countries. It was recognised that the use of quantitative data requires a willingness to try to compare even when the quality of the data available is limited and masks many interesting issues. This led to an examination of the main quantitative sources to be used in this book.

This introductory discussion has been designed to set the scene for the book as a whole. This was described at the beginning of the chapter. The aim throughout the book is to link its three parts. The arguments for comparative generalisations explored in the first part are tested in relation to specific policy areas in the second part, whilst the themes in the last part must be seen as not only drawing upon but also playing an important role in the development of comparative theory.

## GUIDE TO FURTHER READING

Since this is an introductory chapter, in many respects the rest of the book is 'further reading'. However, there are some other introductions to comparative studies that readers may want to consult. Margaret May's 'The role of comparative study' is one chapter in the first part of *The Student's Companion to Social Policy* (Alcock et al., 2003) which contains a number of essays on 'What is social policy?' Kennett's *Comparative Social Policy* (2001) explores questions about approaches to social policy and includes a chapter that gives some attention to data sources and methodological questions. Issues about data and methods are also explored in *Comparative Social Policy* (Clasen, 1999), particularly in Mabbett and Bolderson's chapter.

The following websites may be useful for the book as a whole (specific website recommendations are not included at the end of individual chapters):

- www.sheffield.ac.uk/socst/ICSP (a comparative network established by the British Social Policy Association)
- www.espanet.org (a Europe-wide organisation of social policy researchers)
- www.oecd.org (OECD)
- www.who.int (World Health Organisation)
- www.unstats.un.org/unsd (United Nations)
- www.worldbank.org
- www.ilo.org (International Labour Organisation)
- www.issa.org (International Social Security Association)
- www.lisproject.org (Luxembourg Income Study)
- www.pisa.oecd.org

# CHAPTER 2

# COMPARATIVE THEORY

## Introduction: Identifying the Issues

The basic question to be addressed in this chapter is 'How does social policy in different nations differ and are there ways of explaining these differences?' Variations in public expenditure can be readily identified but it is more difficult to interpret these differences. Early attempts to explore them tended to concentrate on what developed nations had in common, and tended to predict **convergence** as a consequence of shared social, economic and political development trends. This was then challenged by theories that suggested nations at similar levels of prosperity might nevertheless be developing very different approaches to social policy. From this observation have emerged efforts to develop typologies, dominated by one particular approach: Gøsta Esping-Andersen's **regime theory**. The discussion in this chapter will thus lead up to an examination of this theory, some of the main reservations about it and to comparative approaches that build upon it.

It was noted in the last chapter that the OECD statistics give a reasonably comprehensive picture of social policy expenditure in the developed world. It is appropriate therefore to start with this in order to form a context for a discussion of comparative theory, since it gives a good idea of the overall variation that is the starting point for theoretical explanations. From this we can move on to questions that go beyond the picture they provide. Table 2.1 lists the OECD member states (excluding a few small ones and ones for which no data are available) in order of social expenditure as a percentage of GDP, and includes data which enables that expenditure to be related to the overall prosperity of each country.

Examination of the first column indicates that there are marked differences between nations in their levels of public social expenditure, but with a tendency for the European (particularly northern European)

**Table 2.1** Social expenditure (including education) in OECD countries as a percentage of GDP, 2001

| Country | Public social expenditure (including education) as percentage of GDP[a] | GDP per head in $US (using purchasing power parities)[b] |
|---|---|---|
| Denmark | 35.7 | 29,800 |
| Sweden | 35.2 | 28,100 |
| France | 34.2 | 27,800 |
| Belgium | 32.3 | 28,400 |
| Germany | 31.7 | 26,300 |
| Switzerland | 31.7 | 30,400 |
| Austria | 31.4 | 28,500 |
| Finland | 30.3 | 27,400 |
| Norway | 29.7 | 36,100 |
| Italy | 28.9 | 26,100 |
| Poland | 28.2 | 11,500 |
| Greece | 28.0 | 19,500 |
| Netherlands | 26.7 | 29,100 |
| Portugal | 26.7 | 18,400 |
| UK | 25.3 | 29,000 |
| Hungary | 24.5 | 14,600 |
| New Zealand | 24.3 | 22,800 |
| Czech Republic | 24.2 | 16,700 |
| Spain | 23.9 | 23,200 |
| Canada | 23.0 | 31,000 |
| Australia | 22.6 | 28,500 |
| Slovak Republic | 21.9 | 13,000 |
| Japan | 20.4 | 28,000 |
| USA | 19.6 | 37,600 |
| Ireland | 17.9 | 33,200 |
| Mexico | 15.5 | 9,400 |
| South Korea | 10.4 | 20,300 |

[a] *Source*: calculated from OECD (2004e), a social expenditure database that includes 'Old age, Survivors, Incapacity-related benefits, Health, Family, Active labour market programmes, Unemployment, Housing, and Other Social Policy Areas', with figures on education added from OECD (2004a).
[b] *Source*: data from OECD (2004c) (data for 2003).

nations to be near the top of the list and countries from the rest of the world to be towards the bottom. The highest non-European nation is New Zealand in nineteenth place and it has only two European nations below it: the Slovak Republic and Ireland.

The second column sets out a measure of the comparative prosperity of the nations listed. The relationship between national prosperity and social policy expenditure may be seen as likely to be affected by two conflicting influences. On the one hand there seems good reason to suggest that public social policy is something that only well-off nations can afford. On the other hand, the richer a nation becomes, the easier it may be for it to achieve some minimum standards of public social provision. The data suggest in fact quite a strong association between national prosperity and social expenditure, but with some significant deviant nations. First, there is a group of nations that come quite high on the list despite low levels of GDP per head: Greece, Poland, Portugal, Hungary, Czech Republic. It is worth noting that these are all members of the post-2004 EU, with three of them amongst the countries that joined that year. Such nations may have experienced particularly strong pressures to raise their social expenditure levels despite low levels of overall prosperity. The second group of nations is perhaps more significant in that it comprises prosperous nations with low levels of public social expenditure: Canada, Japan, USA, Ireland and South Korea. However, these can be divided between two that are relative newcomers to the very rich group (Ireland and South Korea) and the rest.

Clearly, a discussion about comparisons between nations that limits itself to the OECD members is incomplete. Outside this group, however, the accumulation of relatively reliable comparative data is difficult. Such data as there is does nevertheless give support to the view that in many respects public social expenditure is a 'luxury' largely confined to the better-off nations of the world. Gough and Wood (2004, p. 41) suggest an average figure of total domestic expenditure around 9 per cent of GDP in the rest of the world, ranging between figures as low as 2 or 3 per cent in Indonesia and Nigeria and 13 or 14 per cent in South Africa and Argentina. If the actual levels of national income are then considered (as shown for a sample of nations in table 2.2), it will be recognised that public social policy will be very low indeed in many countries.

Returning to the OECD data, what has been demonstrated is that any notion that there is a general link between social expenditure and national prosperity has to take into account some very important exceptions, particularly the USA and Japan. In fact it seems that the distinction between northern Europe and the rest of the world is more significant than any pattern based on levels of prosperity. Furthermore, even within northern Europe it may be remarked that the UK and the Netherlands differ considerably from some nations which they might be expected to resemble.

**Table 2.2** Gross annual national income per head for various countries, 2000

| Country | Gross annual national income per head ($US) |
|---|---|
| Argentina | 7460 |
| Bangladesh | 370 |
| Brazil | 3580 |
| China | 840 |
| Ghana | 340 |
| India | 450 |
| Indonesia | 570 |
| Iran | 1680 |
| Jamaica | 2610 |
| Mozambique | 210 |
| Pakistan | 440 |
| Russian Federation | 1660 |
| Saudi Arabia | 7320 |
| South Africa | 3020 |
| Tunisia | 2100 |
| Ukraine | 700 |
| Zimbabwe | 460 |

*Source*: data from World Bank (2002).

Of course these are very crude comparisons based on aggregate public social expenditure. Later chapters will return to data on expenditure on social transfers, on health and on education, for example, which bring out rather different contrasts between nations. Beyond that there are important questions to be asked about:

• how this public money is spent;
• the relationship between public and private expenditure;
• differences between nations in the extent to which poverty is effectively reduced by public expenditure.

Bearing these considerations in mind, it is appropriate to shift attention here to efforts to develop theoretical approaches to comparisons between nations. Whilst these tend to depend heavily on data sources like that offered by OECD, they do at the same time try to go beyond the sorts of crude comparisons offered here. Broadly, there has been a shift in comparative work from generalisations about worldwide trends to identification of 'families' of nation states ('regime types').

# The Origins of Comparative Theory

May stresses that

> Historically the starting point for comparative analysis was the observa-
> tion that in the decades after the Second World War many countries,
> especially those of the industrialised West experienced a massive
> expansion in publicly financed and delivered welfare. (May in Alcock
> et al., 2003, p. 17)

This observation initially focused attention on the idea that, notwithstanding differences between nations (like those set out in table 2.1),
there was steady evolution towards fully developed welfare systems,
or 'welfare states'. Differences could be seen as consequences of earlier
or later starting dates for this process or perhaps of differences in the
speed of development.

One explanation widely offered for this growth was that there was
increasing awareness of social problems and a commitment to search
for solutions. There was certainly an element in the teaching of social
history, at least in the UK, which presented social policy development
in this way. Such a perspective was connected with a tradition of
historiography that stressed the growth of enlightenment.

Another approach sharing that sort of optimism, but more grounded
in political analysis and still finding echoes in contemporary theory,
stresses the role of democratisation. The British sociologist Marshall
(1963) saw the quest for 'social rights' as following on from the development of civil and political rights. Where the optimism of the first
approach stressed awareness and altruism in society, indeed perhaps
principally amongst elites, Marshall saw progress coming from the
expectations of democratic political movements.

However, much early comparative work took a rather different view,
seeing social policy growth as a product of social change in which
the evolving relationship between economic market systems and the
state was the important driving force (Wilensky and Lebaux, 1965).
Industrialisation was seen as the generator of distributional changes
in society and a source of demands for new ways of handling labour
as 'a factor in production' (Rimlinger, 1971). Mishra describes the way
this was related by these theorists to social policy as follows:

> With further socio-economic advance, leading to the industrial society,
> institutional specialisation develops further. So does mobility – both
> geographical and occupational. The extended family and the local com-
> munity weaken as collectivities. . . . More specialised structures arise to

cope with the growing volume of welfare functions. (Mishra, 1977, pp. 57–8)

The initial steps here were seen as comprising (1) development of welfare activities by enterprises and (2) development of voluntary organisations (both of an egalitarian cooperative kind and charities). In order to then explain why the state becomes involved, arguments from welfare economics were applied. Firms recognised that to try to cope with issues about the education and the health and welfare of their workforce imposed costs that could make them uncompetitive with others who did less. As far as education and training were concerned, they might suffer from poaching of trained labour by others. Voluntary organisations faced other kinds of 'free rider' problems since the benefits of their activities extend indirectly to the whole community. Moreover, they found that many of the problems they set out to solve were too big for them. Hence, there was an increased tendency to look to the state as a means of enforcing the 'socialisation' of the costs, sharing them more widely through society.

There is also a **Marxist** version of the above argument. It has been most forcefully put by O'Connor (1973) but also by others such as Gough (1979) and Ginsburg (1992). This sees industrial capital as facing two kinds of problems. One of these is that set out above, that the efficient operation of capitalism requires attention to be given to the maintenance of a fit and trained labour supply. It is in the interest of individual capitalists that the cost of doing this should be 'collectivised', i.e. taken on by society as a whole. This function is most readily performed by the only overarching body, the state. The other problem facing capital is unrest in a society in which employment is insecure, rewards are low and the old and sick are particularly vulnerable. Marxist theory postulates that capitalism needs a 'reserve army of labour' and that workers are regarded by capitalists as 'factors' of production to be employed as cheaply as possible, with no regard to their nuclear or extended family responsibilities. These are inherent characteristics of capitalism for Marx, which will contribute to its ultimate downfall. However, if the state can deal with some of these problems, without at the same time undermining the basic economic relationship between capital and labour, then the otherwise gradually accumulating discontent about the system can be reduced.

Both the non-Marxist and the Marxist theory are largely **functionalist** in character. It is argued that these developments are the necessary consequences of industrialisation. These approaches have been attacked as deterministic, paying little attention to the choices made by actors or to variations in response from place to place (Ashford, 1986). Nevertheless, these theories contributed to generalisations about welfare development, taking the discussion away from naive emphases on 'progress' or the growth of compassion. They also offered an approach for explaining the roles of some unlikely actors in the growth of social policy (like, for example, the conservative Prussian Chancellor Bismarck; see Clasen and Freeman, 1994).

Industrialisation was of course recognised as making an important contribution to increases in the standard of living. High levels of personal income may make it possible for the state to raise high levels of taxes to pay for social policies. Some exponents of the modernisation thesis went on to consider the demographic effects of industrialisation, urbanisation and high levels of income (e.g. Wilensky, 1975), these effects being lowered birth rates and raised life expectations at the end of life. The second of these, particularly when associated with an earlier fall in the birth rate to limit the size of the prime age population relative to the elderly, can be seen as important for social policy expenditure (an issue followed up in chapter 12).

These emphases on modernisation were challenged by others who either sought to examine the quantitative evidence more carefully, recognising that there was no simple correlation between, for example, social expenditure and national prosperity (Flora and Heidenheimer, 1981; Pampel and Williamson, 1989), or who sought to add qualitative considerations (Higgins, 1981; Jones, 1985; Ashford, 1986; Flora, 1986; Dixon and Scheurell, 1989; Baldwin, 1990; Ginsburg, 1992; Gould, 1993). These studies, particularly the latter group, recognised that even if there were broad general influences to which countries were responding, there was a diversity of ways of doing this. This diversity might arise because of the varying strength of the influences on social policy development from country to country. Hence attention shifted very much to issues about diversity, stimulated by the increased recognition of the complex influences on policy change and also perhaps by the evidence that the convergence predicted by some of the earlier theorists was not occurring.

## Approaches to Comparative Theory: An Overview

Comparative theory can be seen to involve four alternative approaches.

1 Determinist approaches: these see economic conditions as determining social policy (with this category may be bracketed those theories

that stress developmental processes in social policy history in individual countries and contemporary theories that stress the dominant impact of global economic forces).

2 Political approaches: these share some of the assumptions of the determinists but argue that the specific politics of individual countries have an impact on policies (crucial here is the argument that **social democratic** movements have had a distinct effect on social policy developments in some countries).

3 Cultural approaches: these often build upon the ideas of the previous two approaches but stress the social rather than the political characteristics of societies. These will include issues about values and ideologies, including religious beliefs.

4 **Institutional** approaches: the emphasis here is on the extent to which current responses depend on the institutions that shape and structure any policy developments. This approach also tends to involve historical analysis, and has obviously to deal with the 'chicken and egg' problem about where the configurations deemed so important in the present came from in the first place. This sort of approach tends to emphasise policy 'pathways', raising difficult questions about the circumstances under which new developments may divert from those pathways.

While much of the history of comparative studies has involved arguments between advocates of these different approaches, it is unrealistic to believe in only one of them. There is probably a need to use most or all of them together. Of course, the argument must then be about the weight to be given to each of them in any comparative explanation. The development of this subject has tended to show evolution from the first to the fourth, with new theorists building on the simpler theories that preceded them.

As has been noted, early determinist theory was challenged by scholars who felt dissatisfied with the high level of generality in these studies. A particular concern was to explore the extent that 'politics matters', looking at political inputs including ideologies (Rimlinger, 1971; Castles, 1982). Since orientation to welfare seemed to distinguish parties of the Left from those of the Right it was obviously relevant to ask whether this had any real effect. The most influential work on this theme is Esping-Andersen's *Three Worlds of Welfare Capitalism* (1990). Esping-Andersen's approach has come to dominate contemporary comparative work. Hence it needs separate attention here. Later, when the discussion moves on to criticisms (or modifications) of Esping-Andersen's work, it will be seen that the third and fourth types of explanation outlined above (cultural and institutional approaches) have been brought into play.

## Esping-Andersen's Regime Model

The origins of the idea that types of welfare systems might be distinguished lie in work by Titmuss (1974, reproduced in Alcock, Glennerster, Oakley and Sinfield, 2001) which suggests that three models may be distinguished.

1 The institutional redistributive model, providing services 'outside the market on the principle of need' (Alcock et al., 2001, p. 181).
2 The industrial achievement model, which holds that 'social needs should be met on the basis of merit, work performance and productivity' (ibid.).
3 The residual welfare model, which sees the private market and the family as the main sources of welfare with the state only coming into play temporarily when these institutions break down.

Taking his lead from these ideas, Esping-Andersen's approach to comparative analysis is rooted in the notion that some social policy systems may reflect and contribute to social solidarity. Its derives also from work which has seen social policy development as an important elements in the alleged 'truce' between capital and labour within democratic societies, in which social policies may be concessions to the latter that contribute to the preservation of the capitalist order. The concept of **'decommodification'** is used by Esping-Andersen to suggest that some policy systems achieve **universalism**, where all sections of society are treated alike. Decommodification is used to describe the extent to which individuals' social entitlements are relatively independent of their positions in the labour market.

Esping-Andersen identifies what he describes as three regime types.

1 The ' "liberal" welfare state, in which **means-tested** assistance, modest universal transfers, or modest social-insurance plans predominate' (Esping-Andersen,1990, p. 26). This indicates low levels of decommodification. The word 'liberal' in the definition refers to liberal economic ideas, which see the free market as the ideal device for allocating life chances, with the primary role of the state being to enhance economic efficiency. Esping-Andersen puts Australia, the USA, New Zealand, Canada, Ireland and the UK in this category.

2 Nations which Esping-Andersen labels as '**conservative**', where it was state-led development that was very important for the evolution of social policy institutions. In these societies neither strong pro-market ideologies nor democratic movements were important for this development. Instead, in these nations a strong state sought to incorporate interest groups to ensure their support for the regime. The consequence was welfare systems in which 'the preservation of status differentials' is more important than either 'the liberal obsession with market efficiency' or 'the granting of social rights' (ibid., p. 27). This second category includes Italy, Japan, France, Germany, Finland, Switzerland, Austria, Belgium and the Netherlands.
3 Countries 'in which the principles of universalism and de-commodification of social rights was extended also to the middle classes'; in these places 'the social democrats pursued a welfare state that would promote an equality of the highest standards' (ibid., p. 27). This involves a clear willingness to work 'outside the market'. Denmark, Norway and Sweden are the nations in this category.

The decommodified systems of Scandinavia are thus contrasted with conservative and liberal systems that more clearly reflect labour market divisions and market ideologies. These are attempts to classify national systems as a whole; the inclusiveness of the Scandinavian systems is seen relative to other systems. But it is important to bear in mind that in this approach the nations in the 'conservative' group are not simply identified as middle ones, with levels of spending between the other two. They may indeed be high spenders, the key point being that such spending will tend to be distributed proportionately across the socio-economic spectrum in ways likely to reflect Titmuss's idea of 'merit, work performance and productivity'.

The method Esping-Andersen adopted to develop his regime model involved comparative statistical analysis of the extent to which some key social security benefits delivered extensive social support without making **labour market participation** a crucial qualifying condition. Decommodification is thus a variable, systems being placed along a commodification/decommodification continuum.

Esping-Andersen justifies his approach in two ways. First he argues against the 'simple class mobilisation theory of welfare state development' in which welfare development can be seen as coming from the growth of demands by less advantaged people through emergent democratic political process. Instead he sets out a more complex theory that can be seen to be built upon that idea. He presents a picture of regime development in which historical forces are interactive. Political coalition formation is seen as contributing in distinctive ways to 'the institutionalisation of class preferences and political behaviour' (Esping-Andersen, 1990, p. 32). In a rather difficult empirical chapter, Esping-Andersen explores the influence of independent variables (namely a measure of the share of Left parties in government, a measure of the share of Catholic parties and 'absolutism' alongside measures of GDP per head and GDP growth) and shows that these political variables have a key influence on the dependent variable, decommodification. This part of his enterprise may thus be seen as focusing on the explanation of regime difference. The theory suggests, in Arts and Gelissen's words, alternative 'regime-types, each organized according to its own discrete logic of organization, stratification and societal integration' (Arts and Gelissen, 2002, p. 139).

Second, Esping-Andersen makes claims for the predictive capacity of his model. He argues that 'a theory that seeks to explain welfare-state growth should also be able to understand its retrenchment and decline' (Esping-Andersen, 1990, p. 32). This is a challenge he takes up very positively in his later work, emphasising differences in the ways the different regimes have responded to global economic challenges in his contributions to *Welfare States in Transition* (Esping-Andersen, 1996), and giving attention to issues about family arrangements (neglected in his 1990 work) to predict responses to demographic change and increasing female labour market participation in *Social Foundations of Post-industrial Economies* (1999) and exploring future scenarios in *Why We Need a New Welfare State* (2002).

## Bonoli's Argument that Esping-Andersen Confuses Issues about System Generosity with Ones about Redistribution

Perhaps the main theoretical challenge to Esping-Andersen's typology has been from the argument that he tends to run together a distinction between national income maintenance systems in terms of levels of expenditure with one in terms of the nature of the redistributive system used (Bonoli, 1997). Bonoli labels the second dimension by using the names of two of the key 'founding fathers' of state social policy. One of them, Bismarck (a nineteenth-century German), is seen as the key figure for the development of the conservative regimes, devising along relatively strict insurance lines a system where what people get out heavily depends on what they put in. The other, Beveridge (a British policy adviser influential in the first half of the twentieth century), also advocated the use of **social insurance** but in a way that paid much more attention to 'need'. A key point here is that Beveridge can be seen as an influential figure for both the minimal approach embodied in the use of insurance principles by the liberal regimes and for the generous but need-oriented approach of the social democratic regimes.

Hence Bonoli offers a two-dimensional classification of European welfare states that arrives at a four-category typology combining a distinction between the extent to which benefits are financed by contributions (Bismarck approach) or not (Beveridge approach) with levels of generosity. Hence the Bismarck group divides along broadly north–south lines with much lower levels of benefits in the latter; on the other side, contributions are seen of relatively low importance in both the Scandinavian and the UK and Irish systems but the benefits provided are much higher in the former case.

## A 'Radical' or 'Targeted' Regime Type: Arguments Developed from Castles and Mitchell's Critiques of the Placing of Australasia in Esping-Andersen's Theory

Esping-Andersen's underlying explanatory approach involves the suggestion that decommodification has been a goal of social democratic parties. Esping-Andersen thus correlates the strength of social democrat support in various countries with decommodification. This is a proposition that is challenged in Castles and Mitchell's work (see Castles, 1985; Castles and Mitchell, 1992). In describing Australia and New Zealand as perhaps belonging to a 'fourth world of welfare capitalism', Castles and Mitchell draw attention to the fact that political activity from the 'left' may have been directed, in those countries, not so much into the pursuit of equalisation through social policy as into the achievement of equality in pre-tax, pre-transfer incomes.

Hence Castles and Mitchell challenge 'the expenditure-based orthodoxy that more social spending is the only route to greater income distribution' (Castles and Mitchell, 1992). Castles' earlier work had drawn attention to the particular emphasis in Australian and New Zealand Labour politics on protecting wage levels (Castles, 1985). Castles and Mitchell make a second point, again about Australia but also with relevance for the UK, that the Esping-Andersen approach disregards the potential for income-related benefits to make a very 'effective' contribution to redistribution. Australian income maintenance is almost entirely means-tested, using an approach which does not simply concentrate on redistribution to the very poor.

Mitchell (1991) brings to the argument an interest in exploring the relationships between income differences in societies *before* government interventions and *after* them, suggesting that it is the size of the 'gap' between rich and poor and the extent to which policies close that gap that needs to be the object of attention rather than simply aggregate expenditure. She goes on to examine income transfer policies in terms of their contribution to both the reduction of inequality and the eradication of poverty; these are alternative social policy goals that need to be interpreted in their wider political contexts. She also compares income transfer systems in terms of efficiency (the relationship between outputs and inputs) and effectiveness (the actual redistributive achievement of systems).

This work, and that of Mitchell in particular, is important for raising questions beyond the issues about Australasia, about the wide range of influences on incomes, and the variety of policy options available to political actors who want the state to try to change income distribution. Arts and Gelissen, in their survey of alternatives to the Esping-Andersen model, identify an additional category that some authors have identified from within the 'liberal' regime group, termed 'radical' (see Kangas, 1994) or 'targeted' (Korpi and Palme, 1998). Its characteristic is an absence of social insurance but some evidence of the use of means-tests to effect substantial redistribution. Australia and New Zealand are put in this category, and some writers add the UK (Castles and Mitchell) and Ireland (Kangas).

## Issues about Family Policy and Familist Ideologies

Esping-Andersen's strong emphasis on mainstream political processes has been challenged by those who see other ideologies and sources of power as important for the determination of income maintenance policies. Particularly important in this respect have been writers who have been concerned about the lack of analysis of relationships between men and women, and of family ideologies, in Esping-Andersen's work. There is now a considerable literature on this subject. Key contributions are edited collections by Sainsbury (1994) and Lewis (1993, 1997a), monographs by O'Connor (1996) and Sainsbury (1996), and articles by Lewis (1992, 1997b), Orloff (1993) and Sainsbury (1993). They remind us that the 'solidarity' of the Swedish model rests on an expectation that there will be high labour market participation by women; given the expectations about work imposed by the social security system, this may be coerced participation (perhaps most evident in nations where the rise of female labour market participation has been recent, such as the Netherlands and the UK). It is also often participation in the least advantaged parts of the labour market (where work is insecure and poorly paid). Consequently, wherever benefit entitlements are influenced by contribution amounts, women get less (overall).

However, the feminist work also draws attention to the importance of familist ideologies in influencing the politics of social security and determining the expectations embedded within it. Attention has been drawn to the extent to which there is a Roman Catholic and/or southern European (see also Siaroff in Sainsbury, 1994; Ferrara, 1996) approach to the design of social security, which alternatively can be seen as either more 'protective' of the housewife outside the labour market or as increasing her 'dependency' within the family. Ferrara argues that the income maintenance systems of the southern European countries are fragmented and ineffective and often characterised by 'clientilism' in which political patronage is important. His view is supported by others. It is implicit in Bonoli's approach described above but also in regime categorisations developed by Leibfried (1992) and Trifilletti (1999). The case for a 'fourth world' in southern Europe is a strong one.

The literature on female welfare also suggests that there is a need to consider, alongside issues about the working of the income mainte- nance system, questions about provision for child care (Ungerson, 1995, 2000; Daly, 2000; Daly and Rake, 2003) and about the expectations of the roles that women (and perhaps men) play in the care of sick and disabled adults. Here are areas of social life where there are political choices being made about (1) the role the state will play and (2) the extent such a role will involve either the provision of care or the provision of cash benefits to enable people to buy care. The answers to these questions have, in practice, considerable implications for the labour market participation of women. The high participation of women in the Scandinavian labour market has been partly generated by a willingness of the state to pay women to carry out caring tasks that elsewhere have to be carried out by (generally female) parents and relatives themselves. Chapter 10 returns to these themes.

## The Applicability of Esping-Andersen's Work to East Asia

Another theme about family ideologies is raised in the literature about the East Asian countries. Here the theoretical question is whether the highly industrialised eastern economies (Japan, South Korea, Taiwan, Singapore, Hong Kong) can be fitted into Esping-Andersen's typology, at least as later 'arrivals'. There does seem to be a case for seeing the first three in this list (the other two have perhaps been too influenced by British colonial policies) as joining Esping-Andersen's 'corporatist-statist' group. This is a view that has been given support in Ramesh's (2004) examination of social policy in the last four of the five nations listed above.

An alternative is to see them as having features that are more specifically eastern, which explains areas of limited development. The main argument along these lines has been the suggestion that Confucian family ideologies lead to a greater delegation of welfare responsibilities to the family and extended family (Jones, 1993). The problems about this argument are that (1) in any underdeveloped income maintenance system the family will *faute de mieux* have to take on greater responsibilities, and (2) the use of Confucian ideologies as a justification for inaction by the political elite is not evidence that political demands can and will be damped down in this way in the absence of evidence of the acceptance of that reasoning by the people.

Kwon (1997) seems to take a relatively agnostic stand on these issues. However, he does point out another dimension in the policy processes in South Korea and Taiwan, the importance of state-led policies initiated in an era of authoritarian government. The groups who first secured social protection in these societies were the military and civil servants. Measures to extend some insurance-based benefits to industrial workers followed next. Securing the support of the emergent industrial 'working class' was important for the state-led growth that has been seen as so significant in these societies (Ku, 1997; Kwon, 1999). More universalistic policies only really got on to the political agenda with the coming of democracy.

At the same time Castles and Mitchell's argument about other ways in which states may promote social welfare may also be relevant for these societies. Over much of the period between the Second World War and the severe financial crisis that shook East Asia in 1997, these societies experienced substantial growth with minimal unemployment. Hence inasmuch as governments secured social support, they did it through their success in generating rapid income growth for the majority of the people. Data showing relatively low income inequality in South Korea and Taiwan offer additional evidence in support of this proposition (Ramesh, 2004, pp. 21–2).

Holliday has developed an alternative approach to the analysis of the special characteristics of East Asian societies, describing them as belonging to a 'regime' type characterised by 'productivist welfare capitalism' (Holliday, 2000, 2005), in which the orientation towards growth has been of key importance for social policy development. This point is relevant beyond East Asia inasmuch as it is increasingly argued that global economic forces make it increasingly difficult to defend the 'social democratic' version of the 'truce between capital and labour' or to extend it to later developing welfare systems. There are grounds for arguing that the 'liberal' regimes in Esping-Andersen's theory are also 'productivist', although Holliday suggests that the state has taken a more positive role in East Asian societies: 'In a productivist state, the perceived necessity of building a society capable of driving forward growth generates some clear tasks for social policy, led by education but also taking in other sectors' (Holliday, 2005, p. 148). While Holliday is making some important links here with discussions of these societies as exemplars of state-led growth (Lau, 1986), it is worth noting that in emphasising education policy he is citing a policy area not considered by Esping-Andersen in his formulation of regime theory.

An important reservation about the suggestions that East Asian societies are following a trajectory not envisaged in Esping-Andersen's theory is that it is important in comparative studies not to lose sight of the extent to which policy learning takes place over time and between nations. The newly industrialised Asian economies have the opportunity to observe the strengths and weaknesses of the policies adopted earlier in time and to learn from them selectively. They have, inevitably, been drawn into the new global debate about the economic costs of generous welfare benefit systems and have wanted to draw their own conclusions. Croissant's view on this is interesting:

> Thus, it is not surprising that the discussion of an 'Asian model' as an alternative to the 'Western-style' welfare state is losing much of its attractiveness. In some Asian countries, the debate about reform of the welfare system is already increasingly shaped by European models. Political elites and social activists seek answers for the social problems of their countries in the experiences of the European and Anglo-American welfare regimes. No longer does the liberal model of the American marginal welfare state dominate these debates. Particularly for health and pensions, European models of the 'conservative welfare state' are influential. There is growing discussion of universal, contribution-funded pension and health insurance systems, of universal unemployment insurance in Taiwan and South Korea, as well as of a tax-financed, British national health service model in Thailand. (Croissant, 2004, pp. 520–1)

## An Ethnocentric Model?

There is another kind of contribution to the debate about East Asia that goes further than the various rather specific contributions discussed above (with their questions about whether nations can be slotted into the Esping-Andersen model or whether there is another kind of regime). This is an argument that the whole regime approach embodies 'Western' ethnocentric assumptions about the role of the state and about welfare development as a product of what has been described above as the 'truce' between capital and labour (see Walker and Wong, 2004). It does seem odd that an elaborate debate has developed about what is happening in a number of (relatively) small East Asian states whilst China goes almost unmentioned. Walker and Wong's view on this is that China:

> lacks a western-style political democracy and is not a fully capitalist economy. In spite of these two institutional 'anomalies' from the perspective of the Western construction, it had managed and is still able to provide sufficient social protection to its urban population, albeit with enormous difficulties at the present moment. Back in the pre-reform era, comprehensive welfare was provided through the 'work-units' (that is, state-owned enterprises, government bureaux and so on) which could mirror the central idea of 'from cradle to grave' welfare of the classic perception of the idealized Western welfare state (Walker and Wong, 1996). Even in its reform era, the Chinese Government has made tremendous efforts to institutionalize social protection for its urban population. For example, a poverty line, with its accompanying benefit provisions, was first promulgated in 1993 in Shanghai and now covers all urban areas. Despite these advances China was and is not currently perceived as crossing the threshold of the welfare state group. (Walker and Wong, 2004, p. 124)

Clearly their reference to the earlier model of work-unit based welfare (also sometimes called the 'iron rice bowl', see Leung, 1994) reminds us that once the Soviet Union (and perhaps its satellites) offered a similar challenge to comparative theorists. Now perhaps only Cuba and North Korea remain as societies that may claim to follow that model. An interesting point here for the Esping-Andersen approach is whether these cases represented extreme commodification or extreme decommodification: the former inasmuch as the key link was with work, the latter inasmuch as work unit protection extended to families.

As China (and the former Soviet countries) move away from the work-based welfare model the question is to what extent they are developing their own unique adaptations. Alternatively, Russia may be seen as moving into the 'liberal' camp, while in Eastern Europe there is a struggle going on between the liberal model (sold forcefully by bodies like the World Bank; see Deacon, 1997) and the conservative one. There is some evidence that Chinese choices involve a mixture of the two: social insurance for state employees, 'liberal' developments in relation to private enterprise and a continuing residual system in the countryside (which may be called liberal but is perhaps better seen in terms of the Western situation before the twentieth century).

Perhaps the key point about Walker and Wong's challenge is, apart from the obvious that regime theory is mostly expounded and contested in English by scholars influenced by traditional arguments about the state, that advice to societies developing welfare institutions from outside comes largely from two traditions represented by two of Esping-Andersen's regime types: the conservative and the liberal (the social democratic model being largely seen as a lost cause in the contemporary political climate).

Walker and Wong's challenge should also remind us that the efforts to classify welfare regimes exclude very large parts of the world, including the whole of the Islamic world, India, Africa and (to some extent) Latin America. Gough and Wood (and their associates) (2004) have engaged in a bold attempt to deal with this problem. They explore ways to analyse welfare systems (including of course their absence) in the poorer countries of the world. They take as their starting point Esping-Andersen's regime theory, noting that whilst the original concern was with explaining 'welfare state regimes', this shifts in Esping-Andersen's later work (1999) into the simpler form 'welfare regimes'. They argue that Esping-Andersen is generalising about societies with two crucial characteristics: the presence of predominantly capitalist employment and a democratic nation state. Hence the significance of the idea of the welfare state as a product of state intervention to secure a 'truce'. Thus for Gough and Wood it is important to see welfare *state* regimes as one 'family' of welfare regimes in a world in which there are others, where the above defining characteristics are not present. These others are identified as 'informal security regimes', in which families and communities may play key roles as providers of welfare, and 'insecurity regimes', in which even these do not provide effective welfare. Consequently, regime theory is used by Gough and Wood and extended in important ways to contribute to the analysis of welfare worldwide.

Important elements in Gough and Wood's analysis of regimes include exploration of the implications of an absence of secure formal employment, of states that function ineffectively or even exploitatively, of weak or absent communities and even of families that do not protect their members. Attention is also given to various respects in which welfare outcomes depend heavily on actions outside the regimes, not just the impact of global capitalism and of aid via governments and non-governmental organisations but also of the extent to which welfare in many societies depends upon contributions from family members living and working elsewhere in the world.

A chapter in Gough and Wood (2004) by Barrientos explores the way in which Latin American regimes have shifted from being rudi-mentary conservative ones (within the Esping-Andersen 'family' of regimes) to liberal ones. However, this is still very much within the original regime theory paradigm, as is the book's discussion of East Asia. Other chapters go beyond, particularly one by Bevan on Southern Africa that analyses the desperate social insecurity in so many of the societies in this region.

Gough and Wood thus both offer suggestions on how regime theory may be extended and highlight some of the problems about the original theory. Their concerns with the interconnectedness of systems, both because of multinational economic activities and because of remittances from workers abroad and international aid, offer a quite new perspective on comparative analysis. Yet still their analysis does not extend to China or India or most of the Islamic world. However, they offer tools for the use of those who want to go further, deriving them from the regime theory paradigm.

## The Use of a Typology?

A typology, regime theory, has been presented as advancing a sup-erior approach to the analysis of welfare state development compared with theories that postulate uniform or unidimensional processes. However, there is clearly an alternative response to the inadequacies of global generalisations. This is to stress the unique characteristics of each individual system. Much early writing on comparative social policy did just that. Moreover, to go in that direction need not imply a postmodernist reluctance to theorise. Comparisons may be made between detailed developments in individual countries, developing 'middle range' theories. There is a good case to be made for this approach, recognising that social policy 'systems' are complex mixtures of policies that may bear relatively little relationship to each other (see Kasza, 2002). In many places later in this book more limited comparative remarks will be made that cannot be located within any overarching theory.

Arts and Gelissen (2002) provide, in their state-of-the-art report on regime theory, a valuable discussion of reasons to be cautious about the use of a typology for theory development. Their starting position is as follows:

> Do typologies based on ideal-types have theoretical and empirical value...? The conclusion emerging from the philosophy of science literature is clear: not if **ideal types** are goals in themselves, but only if they are a means to a goal; namely, the representation of a reality, which cannot yet be described using laws (Klant, 1984). This means that typologies are only fruitful to an empirical science that is still in its infancy. In contrast, a mature empirical science emphasizes the construction of theories and not the formulation of typologies. (Arts and Gelissen, 2002, pp. 138–9)

They not surprisingly see the 'sociology of welfare states' as in its infancy. We could move on from this point to question the feasibility of the evolution of a topic of this kind to the maturity envisaged by Arts and Gelissen, engaging with the debate about the inherent limits to generalisation within the social sciences. But rather than do this it is better to consider one of the justifications for typologising that Arts and Gelissen acknowledge as valid: that it is 'a means to an end – explanation – and not an end in itself'.

## ✳ Using Regime Theory Today

While the roots of regime theory lie in a concern to delineate differences in the politics of welfare, modern usage focuses much more on the extent to which it is possible to characterise as opposed to explain social policy systems, with the implication that issues about explanatory power are now more about explaining responses to new developments rather than origins. The original issues about the politics of welfare are still explored, particularly in terms of the extent to which particular arrangements have support coalitions that protect them. This is particularly salient in the work of Pierson (1994, 2001). Another related approach stresses the importance of institutional pathways, as in Taylor-Gooby (2001, 2002).

Since much of the contemporary controversy about welfare policies is about the applicability of strongly market-oriented approaches, there may be a case for a simple dichotomy. In this respect it is often easier to draw a line between the liberal systems and the rest than between the social democratic and conservative regimes. The advocates of the social democratic approach are in many respects marginalised today, and that therefore inasmuch as dissemination of models of social policy is occurring the 'battle lines' are between the liberal and the conservative approaches. It can be added that the social democratic regimes are all in small countries.

This alternative way of considering social policy systems has much in common with Hall and Soskice's (2001) classification of varieties of capitalism. They distinguish between 'liberal market economies' and 'coordinated market economies'. In the former:

> firms coordinate their activities primarily via hierarchies and competitive market arrangements. . . . Market relationships are characterized by the arm's-length exchange of goods or services in a context of competition and formal contracting. In response to the price signals generated by such markets, the actors adjust their willingness to supply and demand goods or services, often on the basis of the marginal calculations stressed by neoclassical economics. (Hall and Soskice, 2001, p. 8)

In the 'coordinated market economies' by contrast:

> firms depend more heavily on non-market relationships to coordinate their endeavors with other actors and to construct their core competencies. These non-market modes of coordination generally entail more extensive relational or incomplete contracting, network monitoring based on the exchange of private information inside networks, and more reliance on collaborative, as opposed to competitive, relationships to build the competencies of the firm . . . economies are more often the result of strategic interaction among firms and other actors. (ibid.)

The state is crucially a more active partner, linking with a range of interest groups (in the way described in Esping-Andersen's description of the conservative regime).

However, many scholars resist any reduction of the regime categories to two; rather they extend Esping-Andersen's three to four. An important twenty-first century example of this is the recent work of Castles, who only explicitly differs from Esping-Andersen in emphasising the separate character of the southern group within Europe and being wary of outlier cases, in his case Switzerland and Japan. He writes of four 'family of nations' groupings 'designed to capture affinities and commonalities arising from history, geography, language and culture' (Castles, 2004, p. 26). These families are (1) Scandinavian,

(2) western European, (3) southern European and (4) the English-speaking nations.

## Conclusions

The chapter started by noting diversity as summarised by comparative expenditure statistics. It went on to show that early efforts at comparative generalisation gave rather more attention to common trends than to diversity. The theoretical work that really marks the shift away from this approach is Esping-Andersen's stress on the idea of different regimes. The initial contribution by Esping-Andersen was examined, and then the ideas of some of his main critics were explored.

It has been suggested that 'regime theory' in some form is the dominant approach to social policy comparison. Esping-Andersen's original work has been an enormous influence. To dissent from the view that there are in various senses 'families' of social policy systems can only imply a wish to either stress the uniqueness of systems or to confine oneself to limited comparisons of specific aspects of social policy.

Yet in many respects these 'families' can still be identified in terms of the simple differences in levels of expenditure set out in table 2.1. In this sense regime theory does not supply a new set of figures to replace the simple ones, but rather offers an approach for explaining gross differences between nations. There remains therefore a need to ask: why typologise? It may just be an academic game, of no wider significance. It is important therefore not to lose sight of Esping-Andersen's argument that his regime theory is designed to highlight the dynamics of social policy systems past, present and future. This seems a good reason not to depart too radically from his carefully theorised model or to ensure that when we do so we have good reasons based on the identification of an alternative dynamic, not just observations that some systems are different.

The arguments about the limits of Esping-Andersen's model are important in themselves for comparative analysis inasmuch as they highlight different process in the ever-changing world of social policy. In this respect a rough and ready but well-theorised taxonomy is useful precisely because it highlights the complex nature of differences between societies.

Hence much modern theory follows Esping-Andersen's general perspective: that different economic, political and institutional arrangements generate rather different approaches to social policy and that countries can to some extent be clustered as kinds of 'regimes' sharing characteristics. The view taken in this book is thus that there is (1) a case for a fourth regime embracing those nations in southern Europe and East Asia where the family is still required to play a very salient role in social policy, and (2) there is merit in Gough and Wood's argument that when we look outside the developed societies it is appropriate to identify regimes with low levels of security in which the state plays a minimal role (dividing these perhaps between those where families are still important and those where any form of social protection is minimal).

Any mapping of regimes will show some countries to be towards the margins of the type. At this point it is appropriate to reiterate Arts and Gelissen's warning against typology development without any intention to generate theory. Looking at regime theory with this in mind, what may seem at first glance to be a rather surprising point can be made. This is that the very fact that there are marginal or hard-to-classify cases contributes towards, rather than undermines, the development of hypotheses about the development of welfare states. These cases provoke questions about the limits of the arguments used to explain the 'core' cases and draw attention to the way in which welfare system development is a dynamic and contested process. There is perhaps an analogy here with the development of taxonomies within the biological sciences. Hard-to-classify cases assist with the delineation of evolutionary processes in that field. Over time, as the pressures on countries, from within and from the rest of the world, change so their key policies may change.

The study of 'marginal' nations in relation to regime typologies may be useful inasmuch as the definitions of the typologies embody theories about social policy system dynamics. It has been acknowledged also that the modelling of regime types depends on the use of a limited number of available comparative variables. Alternative variables are likely to lead to alternative classifications (see Arts and Gelissen, 2002, tables 2 and 3). While Esping-Andersen moves away from the use of the very general expenditure variables set out in the OECD statistics at the beginning of this chapter, he is still very dependent on data that explore differences between countries in the main element of social policy expenditure, mainstream income maintenance expenditure. Hence some of his severest critics have been people who are more interested in other areas of social expenditure, such as health or social care expenditure (see, for example, Antonnen and Sipilä, 1996; Kautto, 2002; Bambra, 2005a,b). Hence later chapters of this book, in looking at different policies, will identify challenges to regime theory that either reconfigure regimes differently for different policy areas or reject it altogether as unusable for comparative purposes in respect of specific policies or policy issues.

### GUIDE TO FURTHER READING

The best accounts of social policy development up to Esping-Andersen are chapter 1 of Norman Ginsburg's *Divisions of Welfare* (1992) and Pete Alcock's 'The comparative context' in Alcock and Craig (2001). Of course, Esping-Andersen's original exposition of regime theory (1990) is the first place anyone who wants to understand his approach better should go, together with the restatement of the perspective in the *Social Foundations of Post-industrial Economies* (1999). For an overview of critiques of regime theory, the article by Arts and Gelissen (2002) is essential reading. Castles (2004) is valuable in offering a related and more up-to-date data analysis exercise with much in common with Esping-Andersen's original one.

It is difficult to single out a limited number of recommendations from the large number of books and articles that criticise Esping-Andersen's handling of the gender dimension. A comprehensive overview of this approach can be found in O'Connor (1996); otherwise, the edited volume by Sainsbury (1994) and her subsequent book (1996) are particularly recommended. Other crucial sources for divergences from, or critiques of, Esping-Andersen are Castles and Mitchell (1992), Bonoli (1997) and Korpi and Palme (1998). Ramesh (2004) (particularly his first chapter) and Croissant (2004) are good up-to-date sources for examination of the issues about the locating of East Asian societies.

# CHAPTER 3

*Cdn soc wf policy*

# POLICY PROCESSES

## Introduction: Identifying the Issues

The last chapter argued that whilst regime theory remains the most satisfactory overarching theoretical approach to comparative social policy analysis, it tends to involve a high level of generalisation by combining a diverse range of countries in a necessarily limited number of regime types. It is then the case that any attempt to look more deeply at the characteristics of policies, and the way they are developing, in specific countries requires attention to be given to constitutional, institutional and cultural factors. There are two important issues here: how social policy is financed and how it is delivered.

The following themes will be explored in this chapter, with suggestions on how they either emerge in comparative work or (more likely) might be considered.

- The need to look at the constitution of the input side of policy (how it is financed).
- The relevance of the 'mixed economy of welfare', with its related concerns with privatisation, the roles of communities and the roles of families.
- Centralisation and localism, with an excursion into issues about federalism.
- Models of policy delivery as explored in terms of hierarchies, markets and networks.
- Issues about rights and discretion.

It will be recognised that these issues overlap in places, and that in some cases there are also substantial links with the general concerns about what systems provide, as explored in the last chapter.

## The Financing of Social Policy

The broad figures on social policy expenditure set out in table 2.1 suggested substantial differences between nations in the amounts of GDP they spend on public social policies. Given that later in the book (particularly chapter 13) we will be exploring arguments that global processes are restricting areas of policy choice for nations and thus engendering convergence, and that social policy expansion is made difficult or impossible for individual nations (either directly because of the requirements of international competition or indirectly because of political difficulties in increasing or decreasing expenditure), it is important to note just how widely nations vary in the extent, and ways, in which they fund social policies.

There are then some wider questions about the relationship between taxes and benefits as far as individuals are concerned. Concessions within tax systems based on assumptions that certain needs should be taken into account in the determination of tax levels have much in common with social security benefits, except that they tend to be targeted towards the better off (if for no other reason than you have to be a potential tax-payer to gain these benefits). The emergence of forms of negative income tax or **tax credits**, which may extend these benefits below the tax threshold, further complicates this subject.

These issues lead to wider ones about the way people pay for social policies; it is possible that in situations where the public contribution is low, private contributions may be high. Questions also need to be explored about the extent to which social security contributions or even mandatory savings really differ from tax payments. There are some particular issues here about the roles of employers as providers of benefits. In this sense any discussion of the *real* cost of welfare must not focus only on the public costs; accordingly, it may be that some of the contrasts between nations are not really about what levels of welfare people expect but about how they expect (or are required) to pay for them.

The starting point for this discussion involves returning to the comparative data reported in table 2.1, bearing in mind that as well as examining social policy in relation to GDP it is also necessary to look at it in the context of national public expenditure as a whole. Thus table 3.1 relates social expenditure to overall public expenditure. It retains the ordering of countries in the previous table, from the highest to the lowest proportionate spenders on social policy, but adds columns representing (1) overall public expenditure as a percentage of GDP and (2) social expenditure as a percentage of public expenditure.

**Table 3.1** Public social expenditure in its public expenditure context

| Country | Public social expenditure (including education) as percentage of GDP | Public expenditure as percentage of GDP | Social expenditure (including education) as percentage of public expenditure |
|---|---|---|---|
| Denmark | 35.7 | 55.8 | 64 |
| Sweden | 35.2 | 58.3 | 60 |
| France | 34.2 | 53.5 | 64 |
| Belgium | 32.3 | 50.5 | 64 |
| Germany | 31.7 | 48.5 | 65 |
| Austria | 31.4 | 51.3 | 61 |
| Finland | 30.3 | 50.1 | 60 |
| Norway | 29.7 | 47.5 | 63 |
| Italy | 28.9 | 48.0 | 60 |
| Greece | 28.0 | 46.8 | 60 |
| Netherlands | 26.7 | 47.5 | 56 |
| Portugal | 26.7 | 45.9 | 58 |
| UK | 25.3 | 40.7 | 62 |
| Hungary | 24.5 | 52.7 | 46 |
| New Zealand | 24.3 | 41.8 | 58 |
| Czech Republic | 24.2 | 49.9 | 48 |
| Spain | 23.9 | 39.9 | 60 |
| Canada | 23.0 | 41.7 | 55 |
| Australia | 22.6 | 37.9 | 60 |
| Slovak Republic | 21.9 | 51.0 | 43 |
| Japan | 20.4 | 38.2 | 53 |
| USA | 19.6 | 35.7 | 55 |
| Ireland | 17.9 | 33.3 | 54 |
| South Korea | 10.4 | 27.5 | 38 |

The comparison overall is between 2001 social expenditure and 2002 public expenditure, but the difference this makes is marginal. However, there are no directly comparable overall expenditure data available for Poland, Switzerland and Mexico to relate to the figures in table 2.1 for these countries, so they have been excluded.

*Source*: data on social and education expenditure as in table 2.1. Public expenditure data from OECD (2004d).

Table 3.1 suggests a general tendency for lower social policy spenders to use a lower proportion of overall public expenditure on social
policy. Clearly there are two things mixed together here: variations in
public spending and variations in social expenditure. We see evidence
of what may be called national 'choice' in respect of both levels of
spending and of allocations of the budget between social policies
and other policies. Within the high social spenders of northern and
western Europe there is remarkable uniformity, with social expenditure
around 60 per cent of overall public expenditure. The Netherlands is
an exception as a relatively low social spender relative to its public
expenditure, while interestingly the UK spends a rather high proportion
of its public budget on social policy. Proportionately lower spending
is apparent amongst a group of countries that may be identified as
having developing social policy systems: the former Eastern bloc countries, some of the southern European countries (though not Greece)
and Korea. Japan together with some of the countries Esping-Andersen
describes as 'liberal' (except Australia and the UK) feature as proportionately low social policy spenders despite being amongst the
richer nations.

Within overall expenditure it needs to be borne in mind that as
far as social security expenditure is concerned governments do not
so much spend as **transfer** money from contributors to beneficiaries
(incurring administrative costs in the process, though these are marginal
relative to the benefits). This is an important distinction for the examination of the implications of levels of government spending. For example,
any arguments about excessive government expenditure need to bear
in mind that governments do not 'consume' this money; similarly, any
arguments about taxation tolerance within the electorate must consider
whether insurance contributions are perceived as taxation. Table 3.2
highlights the varied role of social security transfers in public social
expenditure, listing the countries from the highest social spender to
the lowest.

The nations to highlight in this table are the extreme cases. Obviously
Mexico is an example of a nation where social security is scarcely
established, and whilst it is in the OECD group of nations it has much
in common with many nations outside the relatively rich OECD 'club'.
Perhaps the most interesting cases in table 3.2 are the USA and Korea,
where we may deduce that social expenditure would be remarkably
low but for social transfers. It is also interesting to note Australia, the
Netherlands and Switzerland as nations where social expenditure is
relatively high despite relatively low social security expenditure levels,
all countries with well-funded health-care systems.

**Table 3.2** Social security transfers as a percentage of social expenditure and social security contributions as a percentage of GDP

| Country | Social security as percentage of total public social expenditure | Social contributions as percentage of GDP | Percentage of social security expenditure funded by contributions |
|---|---|---|---|
| Denmark | 60 | 2.2 | 13 |
| Sweden | 61 | 15.3 | 87 |
| France | 63 | 16.3 | 91 |
| Germany | 71 | 14.6 | 75 |
| Belgium | 71 | 14.4 | 89 |
| Switzerland | 42 | 7.8 | 71 |
| Austria | 72 | 14.9 | 80 |
| Finland | 68 | 12.4 | 74 |
| Italy | 70 | 12.2 | 82 |
| Greece | 67 | 11.4 | 70 |
| Norway | 62 | 8.9 | 60 |
| Poland | 77 | 10.2 | 58 |
| Netherlands | 54 | 14.2 | 83 |
| UK | 62 | 6.3 | 47 |
| Portugal | 62 | 9.1 | 70 |
| Hungary | 68 | 11.6 | 85 |
| Czech Republic | 66 | 17.1 | 77 |
| Spain | 63 | 12.6 | 98 |
| New Zealand | 68 | 0 | 0 |
| Australia | 48 | 0 | 0 |
| Slovak Republic | 66 | 14.4 | 82 |
| Canada | 60 | 13.0 | 82 |
| Japan | 64 | 10.3 | 94 |
| USA | 82 | 7.1 | 59 |
| Ireland | 61 | 8.9 | 94 |
| Mexico | 14 | 3.2 | 53 |
| South Korea | 74 | 5.0 | 90 |

*Source*: data on social contributions from OECD (2003). Social security as percentage of total social policy expenditure taken from table 4.1; note definition of social expenditure used there.

The last column in table 3.2 throws light on how social transfers are funded. There is a large group of nations where social insurance contributions are a very significant source of social transfer funds. In a number of cases (France, Spain, Japan, Ireland, Korea), social transfers are hardly a charge on any other form of taxation at all. At the other extreme, there are two nations without any form of social insurance contribution (Australia and New Zealand) and the curious case of Denmark, where a very generous social insurance system is nevertheless only marginally funded by contributions.

Social security contributions often come from employers as well as employees. In the EU, employers' contributions range from a low of about 9 per cent of expenditure in Denmark to a high of about 52 per cent in Spain, with an average across the fifteen nations of the pre-2004 EU of about 38 per cent (European Commission, 2004). Exceptionally, employers may be the sole contributors to the costs of some part of the social security scheme (unemployment insurance in the USA, family allowances in France and Belgium).

Rather than looking at employers' contributions in relation to social transfer contributions as a whole, it is perhaps more appropriate (given that there are countries like Denmark where the state contribution is very large) to look at them in comparison with employees' contributions. We then find, across the EU countries discussed in the last paragraph, that they exceed employees' contributions in all the countries except Denmark and the Netherlands and are more than double the latter in Belgium, Finland and Italy (ibid.).

Employers' social insurance contributions are a form of tax on the size of the workforce for an employer. This may thus be a factor, at the margin, in choices about the extent to which tasks should be performed in capital-intensive as opposed to labour-intensive ways. In some countries (e.g. Belgium) this connection has led to deliberate manipulation of levels of employers' contributions as an economy management tool in order to try to influence levels of unemployment or inflation. OECD has seen this as one of a number of issues about the **real cost** of labour, which may hamper efforts to reduce unemployment (OECD, 1994c).

If social security contributions need to be seen rather differently from direct government expenditure, it is appropriate to look at their size in relation to other taxation. Table 3.3 provides comparative information on the relative shares of various forms of taxation.

The last column in table 3.3 is derived from the others, showing all taxes unaccounted for. The assumption is that as far as citizens are concerned these are broadly speaking **'indirect taxes'**. It may be

**Table 3.3** Contributions to revenue of various forms of taxation

| Country | Personal income taxes (%) | Social contributions (%) | All other taxes (%) |
|---|---|---|---|
| Australia | 57 | 0 | 43 |
| Austria | 28 | 34 | 38 |
| Belgium | 39 | 31 | 30 |
| Canada | 49 | 14 | 37 |
| Czech Republic | 23 | 44 | 33 |
| Denmark | 59 | 5 | 36 |
| Finland | 43 | 26 | 31 |
| France | 25 | 36 | 39 |
| Germany | 30 | 39 | 31 |
| Greece | 28 | 30 | 42 |
| Hungary | 24 | 29 | 47 |
| Ireland | 43 | 14 | 43 |
| Italy | 33 | 29 | 38 |
| Japan | 34 | 37 | 29 |
| Korea | 28 | 17 | 55 |
| Mexico | 27 | 16 | 57 |
| Netherlands | 25 | 39 | 36 |
| New Zealand | 59 | 0 | 41 |
| Norway | 41 | 23 | 36 |
| Poland | 30 | 29 | 41 |
| Portugal | 30 | 26 | 44 |
| Slovak Republic | 21 | 41 | 38 |
| Spain | 28 | 35 | 37 |
| Sweden | 43 | 28 | 29 |
| Switzerland | 39 | 34 | 27 |
| UK | 39 | 16 | 45 |
| USA | 51 | 23 | 26 |

*Source*: data from OECD (2003).

suggested that tax impact awareness will be least in those countries where the combination of personal income tax and social security contributions is lowest and most where it is highest. However, as indicated already there is a difficult question to answer about the extent to which social security contributions are seen as taxes. Furthermore, something that cannot be teased out from these figures is the extent to which social security contributions are charges on employers as opposed to employees.

One possibility here is that expenditure will be less where tax has more direct impact on individuals; if they are more aware of their tax burden, citizens may be more likely to oppose expenditure. The two countries without social security contributions (Australia and New Zealand) and the one with very low contributions (Denmark) obviously come out as very clear examples of countries where tax awareness is particularly likely to be high. However, to these we may add Canada, Ireland and the USA. Interestingly, we have again a grouping of all Esping-Andersen's 'liberal' regimes except the UK but with the addition of one of his social democratic regimes (Denmark). To these may be added a rather diverse group of countries where individuals seem particularly likely to be aware of the impact of the personal tax/social insurance combination: Belgium, Czech Republic, Finland, Germany, Japan, Sweden, Switzerland. However, in some of these (notably Belgium and Finland, see above) the role of employers' contributions may mitigate this. All this adds up to no obvious support for a hypothesis about the relationship between visible tax impact and expenditure, either negative or positive.

However, what is quite invisible when we look at national tax burdens is the way tax is distributed relative to incomes. The key issue here is the extent to which tax is either 'progressive' (concentrated on people with high incomes) or 'regressive' (extending down to people relatively low in the income distribution). On the whole the very big social policy spenders also have high top tax rates. However, data on top tax rates does no tell us very much. There are related issues about the lower tax rates used, and about the 'banding' rules used for different income levels. Furthermore, analysis of this issue needs to be carried out alongside consideration of the redistributive effects of social policies. Chapter 9 returns to some of these issues.

Nevertheless, generalised data on tax rates hides something very important. This is that tax reliefs are important in many countries, enabling tax-payers to pay less than might appear to be the case. A famous essay by Titmuss (1958, pp. 44–50) highlighted what he called 'fiscal welfare policies' providing similar benefits to the more readily identified social security benefits and recognising 'dependent needs'. This theme has been developed by Sinfield, first in relation to the UK (1978) and more recently in comparative work with Kvist (Kvist and Sinfield, 1997) of 'tax benefit', describing 'the advantages which result from the workings of tax systems, whether they are officially recognised as tax expenditures or not' (Sinfield, 1998, p. 115). Sinfield quotes research by Greve (1994) which suggests that tax benefit is over 10 per cent of public expenditure in many countries. At the time of Greve's survey in the early 1990s it was 37 per cent of public expenditure in Finland, 26 per cent in Denmark, 23 per cent in Ireland, 22 per cent in the UK and 16 per cent in the USA. Amongst the countries surveyed it was only very low in Germany, Austria and Sweden (though Sinfield suggests there may be a classification problem in respect of the first named). It may be noted in passing that here is a distribution of countries that would not be predicted by regime theory. This approach to welfare might be expected of the liberal regimes, but in this case there are two social democratic countries at the top of the list.

Titmuss's original essay (and Sinfield's amplification of it) went beyond 'fiscal welfare' to define another hidden area of social welfare called 'occupational welfare'. This involves the provision of social benefits to employees by their employers, something that might perhaps be classified merely as private welfare (alongside the other sources of welfare explored in chapter 1) but for the fact that this very often thrives because the state is willing to disregard it when it considers either the accounts of employers or the benefits derived by their employees. When this topic is viewed comparatively it can be found that there are significant variations between countries in the ways in which taxation authorities will treat employers' contributions to private pensions or health care or education. Whilst there is a lack of sustained comparative analysis of this complex issue, it is recognised that tolerance of these forms of expenditure is an important feature of the American social policy system (with distributional consequences of an inegalitarian kind inasmuch as higher-paid workers benefit more from these contributions). This leads us on therefore to a discussion of identifiable differences in respect of private social welfare expenditures.

There are only two items of private expenditure readily identifiable from the OECD database: health and education. However, there are also some data available on private pension investment, which is worth noting in this context (given the massive importance of pension expenditure for social expenditure). An examination of the data on private health and education expenditure (see chapters 6 and 8) suggests that this has a small impact on the 'league table' of social spending. It tends to compress the distribution of the very high spenders at the top of the table a little and it lifts the richer nations that are towards the bottom of the public expenditure table (broadly, as might be expected, the nations in Esping-Andersen's 'liberal' regime group plus Switzerland). These nations also figure very significantly (along with the Netherlands) amongst the countries with large private pension schemes. As far as the discussion in the previous section is concerned it is appropriate to mention that after examining the rather limited OECD data on tax concessions to pension contributions, Sinfield (2000) notes relatively high levels in the UK, Ireland, Netherlands, Australia and the USA (listing these countries from the highest contributor, as a percentage of GDP, downwards).

There is thus some suggestion that the real cost of welfare is rather higher than suggested in some of the nations that are in relatively low places in the 'league table' of public spenders, and that if it was possible to develop a usable indicator of the impact of private pension systems on citizens this might reinforce that view.

## The Mixed Economy of Welfare

The above discussion of the private financing of social policy suggests a need to explore rather more what is called the **mixed economy of welfare**, namely 'a shorthand descriptor of the combination of ways in which benefits and services can be provided and funded. These include the public sector, the private and voluntary sectors and informal care' (Alcock et al., 2002, pp. 149–50). The concept of mixed economy of welfare embodies a common-sense notion explored in chapter 1: that our welfare depends on a mixture of ourselves, our families, our neighbours, our communities, our access to opportunities to obtain and spend money and the state. A particular aspect of this mix lies in the distinction between who pays for particular services and who provides them.

Regime theory is clearly concerned with this mix in relation to the question of who pays, dealing as it does with the contributions of the state, the market and the family to welfare. What it does not do is give direct attention to the issues about who provides. However, the issue is present in an indirect way in Esping-Andersen's emphasis on the way in which 'corporatism' plays a role in the conservative regime. He does not bring it out very clearly but what this implies in several of the states within this regime group (particularly France and Germany) is the direct involvement of organisations of employers and employees in the administration of social insurance. This has been noted as a key feature of many of the central European 'conservative regimes', contributing to the insulation of insurance systems from state interference and to the status distinctions between different funds which reduce the redistributive potential of some of these systems. Note for example the following point about the French system:

All schemes are administered by different funds (caisses) at national, regional and local level, and staff are neither paid by state, nor under its authority. Each caisse is headed by a governing board comprising representatives of employers and employees. (Palier in Clasen, 1997)

This, as Béland (2001) has noted, can give these interest groups positions in which they may influence (or of course veto) policy change.

A now dated view of the nature of social policy development entailed an assumption that it involved steady growth of the role of the state, which was increasingly both payer and provider. This view has been directly challenged by critiques of the state as provider. Often these are of course linked, particularly in 'new right' rhetoric, with arguments against the state role as payer too. But the interesting feature of modern discussions of the welfare state has been a recognition, by those who support an active state role as well as by those who oppose it (e.g. Donnison, 1982; Deakin, 1994), of the defects of the state as a delivery agent. At the same time it has been recognised that many long-standing arrangements for the delivery of social policy involve partnerships between the state and other organisations, in which the latter play key roles in delivery. Much of the modern literature on alternative 'provider' models for state benefits and services examines two options: the private market and voluntary organisations. To these must be added situations where, although the state is in the first place the provider, what it provides is cash, which individuals or families may then use to purchase services directly or absorb into the family budget.

The way in which the three models of provision can occur in relation to the same social policy area is well illustrated by the example of a topic not examined in more detail in this book: social housing. The state may be a direct provider of housing. It may subsidise housing provision by voluntary organisations or private (for profit) companies. It may regulate housing provision that, to an extent, forces private providers to subsidise tenants by preventing them realising full market gains from the activity. Or it may provide benefits which subsidise tenants, enabling them to pay rents they could otherwise not afford. In this last case, the subsidy is normally explicitly linked to proof that a rent is being paid, but the logic of this solution may extend to the inclusion of the expectation of rent costs within assumptions of what is a necessary basic income.

The issues about alternative providers will loom large in the three chapters of this book that deal with health, social care and education. In the field of social care they are particularly prominent, in all the forms outlined here, and interact in complicated ways with the issues about who pays.

As far as voluntary organisations are concerned, are there also grounds for expecting the use of 'intervening' voluntary organisations in the conservative regimes inasmuch as there has been a strong cultural commitment to the delegation of care tasks to local organisations, particularly to faith-based organisations, as embodied in Catholic social theory? Case study evidence, for example on Germany and Austria, supports this. Conversely, the strong state tradition in Scandinavia has been seen as inhibiting voluntary action. However, there is evidence from Sweden that refutes this hypothesis (Lundström and Svedberg, 2003), the social democratic tradition involving high participatory norms. Also many of the liberal societies have strong traditions of voluntary organisation (not least the USA). Studies by Anheier and Salamon (2001) explore these issues, but face difficulties about how exactly to identify a strong voluntary sector (in terms of levels of volunteering or in terms of the incidence of voluntary organisations). Volunteering is shown to be high in much of northern Europe and in the USA but low in southern Europe and Japan. Overall, comparative studies of volunteerism are at an early stage and there is an absence of studies that make direct connections between comparative social policy and the comparative analyses of the voluntary sector.

Perhaps a more promising line is to focus explicitly on the expectations of family roles, recognising the extent to which there may be a logical evolution in those countries with strong traditions of family care, from situations in which the family both pays and provides to one in which the state offers various forms of cash support to the family. These issues about care will be explored further in chapter 7. In health it seem unlikely that the Esping-Andersen model helps with the analysis of provider arrangements. More crucial may be the way in which the funding mechanism – **direct tax** funding versus insurance provision – encourages or discourages direct provision. We look further at this in chapter 6. In education, strong market ideologies may also have an influence over models of provision where the state is payer, but concerns about accommodating religious differences seem also likely to be important. We return to this in chapter 8.

## Centralisation, Localism and Federalism

There is an inherent tension within social policy about the extent to which optimising policy to individual needs seems to call for decision-making at the lowest (i.e. most local) possible level, whereas **'territorial justice'** within a nation state (or even more universal entity; we will return to this) requires that citizens in different places are treated broadly the same. The need to have regard to the latter increases in importance wherever citizens freely and regularly cross boundary lines between local units of government, and particularly where they may easily seek services across a boundary (a school or a hospital for example) without even moving.

De Swaan (1988) suggests that nation states come under pressure to centralise control over services as people are able to move and expectations of services rise. He thus sees the widespread tendency for income maintenance to be nationalised as a consequence of the way in which any locality that took a hard line in relation to the provision of relief would tend to export its poor to other areas, which would then be forced to toughen up their own stances in self-defence. Such a process forces central action inasmuch as the state is not prepared to accept the general immiseration of the poor. Such a nationalisation process is then reinforced by the extent to which the poor are seen as dangerous, the spreaders of disease or the perpetrators of crime.

The comparative question is therefore whether there may be differences between societies in the extent to which social policy is centralised, with the subsequent question as to whether there are societies in which generalisations about their systems will be undermined by local variations. As far as the nationalisation of poor relief is concerned, it is interesting to note that there are some surprising examples of societies in which high levels of discretion are left to the local level. However, it is suggested that in several cases this occurs against a background of very comprehensive social insurance measures so that social assistance is a 'last resort' for a minority. Conversely, strong nationalisation of social assistance has been observed where it plays a more central role (as in Australia and the UK). This is explored further in chapter 4.

The examination of territorial inequalities may produce more challenging results if other social policies are examined. The geography of health inequality has been substantially studied (see Boyle, Curtis, Graham and Moore, 2004). Whilst in many respect these inequalities are reflections of the geographical location of deprived groups of citizens, including particularly ethnic minorities, they do pose questions about the adequacy of local policies and accordingly challenge any model of nation states, like the regime one, that does not look below these large aggregates.

It is important to bear in mind that alongside relatively simple central–local divisions in some societies there are federal ones, in which the respective roles of national units and some more local ones are enshrined in a constitution (USA, Canada, Australia, Germany, Switzerland, etc.). The impact of **federalism** on social policy has been given comparatively little attention. However, Obinger, Leibfried and Castles (2005) have reviewed previous studies, explored deductions about the impact of federalism based on policy theory and carried out their own case studies in the countries listed above. They note a prevailing assumption that federalism impedes social policy development, and therefore a related assumption that it may now also impede retrenchment. This assumption is supported by theoretical propositions about the greater difficulties in assembling policy change coalitions in the context of the more complex institutional arrangements in federal states. However, Obinger and his colleagues also note alternative propositions about the opportunities federal structures may give to individual units to engage in policy innovation that may challenge policy stability in the federation as a whole.

The implications of the competing theories and evidence is that there is a need to look beyond the simple federal–unitary state distinction to consider the institutional arrangements in any specific federal system and the ways in which taxing and spending arrangements are distributed between the levels. This is a consideration that also applies to central–local arrangements in non-federal systems.

In most countries some taxation is raised by the lower tier of a federal system and/or by local governments. Equally, some social expenditure is at these levels too. In the examination of this it is generally not possible to make a clear-cut distinction giving separate attention to local expenditure or specific local services. Considerations of national politics and national identity, and concerns about the 'territorial' injustice that follow from letting localities, whether rich or poor, solve their own problems, have led to the development of some very complex financial exchanges between levels of government, accompanied by central intervention, into the way money is used at the local level. Hence the statistics need interpreting with some care (the key source is Joumard and Kongsrud, 2003). They, at least on initial inspection, give a much greater impression of local autonomy than is in fact the case.

The USA and Canada stand out as federal systems where the lower-tier units raise substantial parts of their income, though the situation in Canada varies very substantially from province to province. The other federal states have much in common with many of the unitary states. There is a group that raises significant amounts of income at the local level, including federal Germany and unitary Denmark,

Ireland and Sweden. There is then a group of states that raises relatively little at the local level, including one federal state (Belgium), France, the Netherlands and, above all, Greece and the UK.

In all the countries examined by Joumard and Kongsrud, with the exception of the USA, more is spent at the local level than is raised at that level. In a large number of nations there is a very substantial amount of devolved spending of nationally raised revenues (particularly in Belgium, Denmark and the Netherlands). However, these statistics tell us nothing at all about the extent to which fiscal equalisation is being practised within these countries to iron out territorial inequalities in respect of either income-raising capacity or need.

Education is a strong component in local expenditure in most countries. On the other hand, there are wide variations in the extent to which health expenditure appears within local expenditure, from the low figures for unified national systems such as the UK to high levels in Norway, Sweden and Ireland. Variations in the figures for 'social security and welfare' are substantial, and hard to explain without looking at systems in detail (ibid.).

In some of the federations there has been a tendency (particularly in the older federal states) for social policy to be regarded as a responsibility of the sub-national levels. Clearly, here is a situation where internal differences may be likely to reduce the validity of overall generalisations. However, two strong modern tendencies have worked against this. One is the extent to which there has been a corresponding tendency for economic matters to be the responsibility of the national level. This has meant that differences in social policy could have implications for competition between sub-national levels, inasmuch as generous policies would reduce competitiveness. The paradox here of course is that the weakest economic units are likely to be most in need of social interventions, whilst the strongest units may fear interventions they can well afford in case they undermine their comparative advantage. Hence the second modern tendency is for considerations of national solidarity to operate in the direction of the centralisation of social policy. This is surely another version of de Swaan's point, then reinforced by the extent to which international conflict strengthens the need for internal solidarity. The centralisation tendency is most evident in those federations in which some of the sub-national units are particularly weak, notably Australia and Canada.

It is interesting to reflect the extent to which the process described in the last paragraph is being reproduced in clusters of allied nations, notably the EU. Whilst this is not the place for speculation about the extent to which a 'united states of Europe' is emerging, it is worth noting that the EU is also a system in which economic integration is stronger than social policy integration. Social policies are the concern of individual nation states but where social policy differences have significant economic effects and where there is substantial migration of workers, then social policy issues are on the EU agenda (Kleinman, 2002; Taylor-Gooby, 2004a). The stronger the economic integration, the stronger the social policy integration is likely to be, despite the best efforts of those politicians who want to leave social policy issues outside the EU. In the discussion of global influences on social policy in chapter 13 this issue will be further discussed as a source of pressures towards social policy homogeneity across the EU.

## Hierarchies, Markets and Networks

Three different social policy delivery models are widely identified (see Hill and Hupe, 2002, pp. 178–9).

1 *Hierarchy*: normally involving direct service delivery by the state in which officials are required to follow rules.
2 *Markets*: delivery principles that try to ensure efficiency through enlisting self-interest and encouraging competition. This may involve actually sub-contracting services to commercial organisations, working under contract, or setting up systems in which public organisations are forced to compete with each other. Using market approaches may also involve trying to attract private services to enter into partnerships with public ones.
3 *Networks*: service delivery in which collaboration between different organisations is necessary. This approach, whilst it may be mandated hierarchically and encouraged by market-like incentive payments, depends heavily on the willingness of people in different organisations to recognise common concerns and to trust each other.

Arguments about the desirability of either hierarchies or markets are, in some respects, derived from arguments for or against the state as a provider of welfare. They are particularly closely linked with suggestions that the state is an inefficient provider. However, the issues about the roles of networks are rather different and, taken together, exploration of the trilogy raises a range of questions about different provider options for different situations. As such they connect up with the themes of localism, participation and rights explored elsewhere in this chapter.

The idea of distinguishing between these three approaches, recognising that the hierarchy model has been widely challenged, is closely linked with the notion that in the modern world we are seeing a shift from 'government' to 'governance'. The latter has been defined in a variety of ways, but the central point here is that the shift is seen as towards policy systems in which there are many actors (different parts of central governments, local governments, international organisations, voluntary organisations, private companies) working together. In these circumstances simple hierarchies and simple accountability relationships are hard to identify. Pertinently for this discussion Milward and Provan (1999, p. 3, unpublished paper) then say that:

> Governance . . . is concerned with creating the conditions for ordered rules and collective action, often including agents in the private and non-profit sectors, as well as within the public sector. The essence of governance is its focus on governing mechanisms – grants, contracts, agreements – that do not rest solely on the authority and sanctions of government.

Some writers suggest a process of system evolution from hierarchies, through markets to networks. However, it seems more appropriate to suggest that where once the hierarchical approach to policy delivery was widely accepted as desirable, it is now the case that alternatives are on the agenda. The result is that if we take an overview of the governance system in any state we will observe a mix of approaches to policy delivery. Choices between approaches will be influenced by ideology (for example the strong preference for markets amongst many politicians of the liberal Right). But they will also be influenced by the task to be performed, a point made long ago in a challenging book on organisation theory by Etzioni (1961) that suggested that there are congruent and incongruent ways of running activities (a point his book explores at length by examining the rather different ways that prisons, business firms and churches need to be run). Hence in social policy it may be argued that, for example, hierarchies are more appropriate for guaranteed social benefit delivery, transactions for simple service delivery tasks (provision of meals to house-bound people) and networks for complex personal services (integrating health and social care services).

However, the implication of this analysis for comparative studies is that while it may be argued that each mode of action may be best for some policies, actual differences in approaches to them between societies will be influenced by differences in power systems, ideologies and cultures. Again this may seem to point towards the distinctions made in regime theory, raising questions about whether liberal societies are, other things being equal, more likely to choose markets, social democratic ones hierarchy and conservative ones networks. But a more careful look at the last two suggests a need for caution: the social democratic societies have consensual features that would surely incline them towards networks, whilst some of the conservative ones have strong authoritarian features. It is one of the latter, Germany, that has been seen as the country where hierarchical **bureaucracy** was particularly developed.

There is perhaps a potential for typologising here that owes little to Esping-Andersen. It must be noted that in the exploration of forms of democracy by political scientists there has been a rather different kind of typologisation, notably Lijphart's (1999) contrast between the 'Westminster model' and the 'consensus model', distinguished by the extent to which electoral processes tend to deliver single-party government.

In the study of public administration there have been efforts to distinguish between strong and weak concepts of the 'state' (Katzenstein, 1977; Dyson, 1980) and between 'policy styles' (Richardson, 1982; Bovens, 't Hart and Peters, 2001). The latter are seen as varied, not merely on account of national differences but also because (as suggested above) of differences in the policy issues at stake. Richardson is cautious about labelling countries in terms of policy styles, and in any case this literature is most concerned with the policy-making process. A Dutch writer, Van Waarden (1999; see also Hill and Hupe, 2002, pp. 165–7), whose work is not available in English (I owe my account of this work to Peter Hupe), sees both acceptance of market ideologies and the ways in which views of the rule of law are institutionalised in different societies as important for these styles. The latter is pertinent to the discussion of rights and discretion in the next section.

The various approaches to typifying political and institutional cultures might be satisfactorily fused into a single regime-type model, but this seems unlikely. This is perhaps more easily done with comparisons of a small group of countries in respect of a limited range of policies. For example, Bahle (2003) compares system changes, influenced by movements towards privatisation and decentralisation, in the care services of England and Wales, France and Germany, concluding that variations between countries need to be explained 'partly by variations in their institutional heritage and partly by country-specific socio-political constellations and institutional innovations' (Bahle, 2003, p. 5; see also Wollmann and Schröter, 2000).

## Rights and Discretion

An important influence on what people get from social policies is the extent to which the arrangements for delivery guarantee rights or leave key decisions to the exercise of discretion by 'street-level' staff. This is an issue that it is important not to oversimplify. It needs to be recognised that it is nearly always the case that discretion is exercised within a statutory framework. Discretion is what Dworkin (1977) calls the 'hole in the donut', structured in often complex ways. Moreover, this discretion may be within a complex system of delegated power so that progressive structuring occurs down throughout a system. Hence it is important to distinguish powers delegated to a lower level of government from powers delegated to street level. There is also a need to recognise that what actually happens at street level may be a product of legitimate delegation of a decision-making power or a consequence of rule-breaking at that level. Quite a lot of discussion of street-level decision-making confuses these two, equating legitimate decision-making in complex circumstances with deliberate disregard of rules (see Hill, 2005, chapter 12).

The issues discussed above in relation to decision-making through 'networks' are relevant here. There are many issues that are most appropriately handled in a context in which flexibility is allowed at street level, enabling those delivering a policy to react to exceptional or unexpected circumstances, and to negotiate with other officials or with the recipients of the benefit or service themselves. A particular aspect of this which has been much discussed concerns professional services, with extensive expertise at street level and high levels of indeterminacy in the situations which they have to deal with.

If the main determinants of the amount of discretion accorded to street-level staff lie in the tasks they have to perform and the context in which they are operating, then the scope for comparative analysis of this phenomenon may be limited. However, as also noted with the related distinction between markets, hierarchies and networks, there may be institutional, ideological and cultural phenomena that influence the operationalisation of the rules–discretion distinction.

This issue connects with some important debates within the study of social policy, and indirectly with the notion of decommodification. Decommodification tends to imply 'universalism', services available to all regardless of labour market status. Yet such a simple equation encounters problems wherever there is a need to ration services and exercise judgement about need. It is one thing to decree that everyone over a certain age should be able to ask for a pension, quite another to take the same line in respect of health services without any objective test of need.

Rothstein (1998) offers a useful analysis of this topic, exploring what 'just institutions', universalist in character and securing universal support, have to involve. Rothstein (p. 140) asks 'What are the conditions for persuading citizens to give over their money, their time . . . and possibly themselves . . . to the state?' He identifies as crucial conditions the fairness of policy programmes, a just distribution of burdens and procedural justice in their implementation. These principles offer a rationale for universal cash benefit systems. Greater difficulties are posed by state services, particularly where rationing is practised. Here he argues that the principle of equal concern and respect should involve citizen choice wherever possible. Hence Rothstein is pointing us in two different directions on the issue of discretion. On the one hand, with the more straightforward policies, notions of rights and citizenship go together. On the other, with services where there is delegation of discretion, issues arise about the extent to which delivery matters can be directly negotiated with the people receiving them. In that context rules guaranteeing rights are not enough.

One of the most poignant of Titmuss's (1974) essays celebrating universalism concerned how, when he was dying of cancer, his access to treatment was exactly the same as anyone else, regardless of income or social status. Outpatients were treated in order of arrival. The trouble with this admirable egalitarian vision is that it conveys images of queuing and inconvenience in an overburdened National Health Service. It is not surprising that others of Titmuss's socio-economic status have warmed to the Thatcherite justification of using private medicine when necessary. There is clearly a challenge here to universalist principles, inasmuch as they have been linked with paternalism and lack of choice. This is what is offered by Rothstein. He explores how services may move away from paternalism, through the example of the transformation of authoritarian maternity services in Sweden once they were challenged by an enlightened provider and a revolt by the mothers themselves. This leads to a defence of diversity, not from a market perspective but from one which explores how the state can fund and regulate mixed, including private, services that offer citizens a measure of choice. This has to involve tackling problems of accountability at the local level, in terms of relationships between 'autonomous citizens' and 'quasi-autonomous' institutions. Choice on this scale is costly. Rothstein invokes here the principle of

**Table 3.4** Rothstein's 'pictures of the market and the state'

|                            | Market            | State           |
| -------------------------- | ----------------- | --------------- |
| Nirvana assumption         | Efficiency        | Justice         |
|                            | Freedom of choice | Democracy       |
|                            | Creativity        | Equal treatment |
| Actually existing problems | Segregation       | Bureaucracy     |
|                            | Cartel formation  | Corruption      |
|                            | Monopolies        | Queues          |

*Source*: Rothstein (1998, p. 201).

'solidaristic individualism', arguing that there can be 'mutual support' and the acceptance of costs when citizens respect each other's different demands.

Rothstein's book is interesting inasmuch as it suggests that within the social democratic model, highlighted by Esping-Andersen's regime theory, there is a tension between the implicit egalitarianism embodied in rights-based social security policies and the notion (that certainly appears in many more traditional formulations of social democratic ideology) that the democratic state knows what is best for individuals. Pro-market writers (within whose ranks Rothstein definitely does not belong) offer the alternative of the liberal model as being in this respect more 'democratic'. Rothstein encapsulates the paradox in a neat chart (see table 3.4).

What then does this excursion into some issues about the philosophy of social policy imply for comparative analysis? Surely it is that whilst it may be possible, following regime theory, to draw some conclusions about the different conditions under which citizens in different countries give support to benefit systems in terms of notions like 'decommodification' or 'universalism', this analysis does not extend in any easy way into issues about the terms and conditions of street-level delivery (particularly important for many services). That is not to say that regime theory is inapplicable, but simply that there is a need to look behind apparent guarantees of services to the ways in which they are offered. In the fields of health, social care and education, the concerns of regime theory with differences in modes of access and levels of funding are important, but so too are the more specific differences in the ways in which rationing is carried out and the ways in which professional and other street-level staff work.

## Conclusions

This chapter has explored the potential significance for comparative social policy analysis of issues about the funding of policy and issues about policy delivery. It could do no more than suggest connections between some issues and the mainstream comparative literature or indicate new forms that comparative generalisations might take. In principle, some of these other distinctions could be plotted against regime theory to achieve more all-encompassing modelling of systems. In practice, the multiplication of dimensions and the difficulties in securing satisfactory indices for such an exercise make such a development unlikely. However, many of the issues explored here need to be borne in mind as the book now proceeds to the discussion of specific policy areas and other more substantive aspects of the study of comparative social policy.

### GUIDE TO FURTHER READING

This chapter introduces issues that are given little attention in the comparative social policy literature. On the financing side, two edited books by Messere and colleagues (1998, 2003) explore comparative issues about taxation, mainly using OECD data, although they are not particularly concerned to link this to social policy. These links are explicitly made by Glennerster (2003) in a book that is principally about the UK but which makes some international comparisons. The key sources about the ways in which tax reliefs function as social benefits are Greve (1994), Kvist and Sinfield (1997) and Sinfield (1998).

Readers may be reluctant to go deep into the political science and public administration literature on which much of the rest of the chapter has drawn. My own book, *The Public Policy Process* (Hill, 2005), particularly Part 3, provides a tour through key aspects of this, whilst Hill and Hupe (2002) examines implementation theory. Rothstein (1998) raises some key questions about the alternative ways social policy impacts on, and may be influenced by, citizens.

# PART TWO

# POLICY AREAS

# CHAPTER 4

# SOCIAL SECURITY

## Introduction: Identifying the Issues

Social security is collective action to protect individuals against income deficiencies. Hence the term 'social security' refers to policies that contribute to income maintenance. The wide definition of social security has a very similar meaning to another term used in comparisons of policies in the EU, social protection.

Collective action to provide social security may be taken by a variety of social organisations, including employers, charities and voluntary organisations. In some circumstances it may even be appropriate to identify the extended family as playing this role. However, when we speak of social security systems in most societies we are speaking of systems in which the state has a dominant role. Social security entitlements may thus be seen as an addition to measures individuals may take to protect themselves.

Collective action is likely to be contingent upon identification of income deficiencies that arise because of a lack of sufficient income from paid work (because of old age, sickness or unemployment) or as a result of family transfers (because of the loss or absence of a socially prescribed breadwinner). Whilst these transfers may be seen as occasioned by the identification of poverty, this is not necessarily the case. Transfers may be regarded as needed because of a fall in income or a divergence from an otherwise expected income.

State social security measures may include:

- tax-supported contingent entitlements (such as child benefit in the UK);
- contributory social insurance benefits;
- means-tested assistance benefits (with benefits in cash or in kind);
- compulsory savings (e.g. the provident funds in Singapore and Malaysia);

- obligations upon employers (e.g. statutory sick and maternity pay in the UK);
- regulation of private measures, particularly pensions;
- laws that enable individuals to litigate for compensation for accidents, divorce, etc.;
- requirements for compulsory contributions from family members;
- assistance to individuals to accumulate assets.

To these may be added the provision of benefits by way of the tax system. These can include, as indicated in chapter 3, variations in tax according to individual needs and circumstances and 'tax credits', which involve paying people without tax obligations. In respect of these, the line between giving and taking away is blurred.

## The Dominance of Social Security within Social Policy

The introductory remarks above suggest that social security systems will tend to play a dominant role in national social policy systems, particularly in state systems. Table 4.1 provides evidence for this by comparing the OECD data for public social expenditure in various nations with those for social security transfers. It shows social security expenditure at over 60 per cent of social expenditure in all the listed countries apart from Switzerland, the Netherlands, Australia and Mexico.

Of course, hidden within these aggregate figures are wide variations in the support given to various groups. However, it is difficult to develop a table that shows this in any meaningful way for a large sample of nations. Differences are affected by the ways boundaries are drawn between different categories of benefits and services (particularly as far as support for sick and disabled people are concerned), by variations in need (particularly the variations in the numbers drawing pensions, which accounts for example for nearly half of all expenditure on social security in the EU) and by variations in levels of unemployment (which will differ even within one country according to the reference date chosen).

## Comparative Analysis of Social Security Systems: An Overview

Although overall national social security systems are likely to be complex and diverse, it is possible to identify three broad groups.

**Table 4.1** Social security transfers in the context of general social expenditure in OECD countries, 2001–2

| Country | Public social expenditure as percentage of GDP | Social security transfers as percentage of GDP | Social security as percentage of total public social expenditure |
|---|---|---|---|
| Denmark | 29.2 | 17.5 | 60 |
| Sweden | 28.9 | 17.5 | 61 |
| France | 28.5 | 18.0 | 63 |
| Germany | 27.4 | 19.4 | 71 |
| Belgium | 27.2 | 16.1 | 71 |
| Switzerland | 26.4 | 11.0 | 42 |
| Austria | 26.0 | 18.6 | 72 |
| Finland | 24.8 | 16.8 | 68 |
| Italy | 24.4 | 17.0 | 70 |
| Greece | 24.3 | 16.4 | 67 |
| Norway | 23.9 | 14.8 | 62 |
| Poland | 23.0 | 17.7 | 77 |
| Netherlands | 21.8 | 11.8 | 54 |
| UK | 21.8 | 13.5 | 62 |
| Portugal | 21.1 | 13.0 | 62 |
| Hungary | 20.1 | 13.7 | 68 |
| Czech Republic | 20.1 | 13.2 | 66 |
| Spain | 19.6 | 12.3 | 63 |
| New Zealand | 18.5 | 12.6 | 68 |
| Australia | 18.0 | 8.7 | 48 |
| Slovak Republic | 17.9 | 11.8 | 66 |
| Canada | 17.8 | 10.7 | 60 |
| Japan | 16.9 | 10.9 | 64 |
| USA | 14.8 | 12.1 | 82 |
| Ireland | 13.8 | 8.4 | 61 |
| Mexico | 11.8 | 1.7 | 14 |
| South Korea | 6.1 | 4.5 | 74 |

*Source*: public social expenditure is defined here as OECD defines it (see table 2.1), excluding education. If education expenditure were included, the figures would be around 4–5 per cent higher. The social expenditure data are for 2001 and from OECD (2004e); the social security transfer data are for 2002 and from OECD (2004d). The difference between the years will have a minimum impact on the data.

1 Systems that still emphasise self and family provision, together with the role of employment, largely confining the state role to means-tested benefits.
2 Systems in which contributory social insurance is dominant, making income maintenance entitlements heavily dependent on what the individual has been able to pay in.
3 Systems that combine the social insurance principle with a strong emphasis on social solidarity, so that there is redistribution between those easily able to contribute and those less well placed.

This categorisation broadly corresponds with Esping-Andersen's welfare regimes (discussed in chapter 2): the list above sets out versions of the liberal, conservative and social democratic models. It was noted in chapter 2 that the modelling of welfare regimes has been heavily dependent on the use of data about social security systems. Taking this fact together with the evidence on the way social security dominates social policy expenditure in most societies, it is not surprising that this equation of welfare regimes with social security systems occurs.

However, systems within actual countries are more mixed than the regime approach implies. In particular, many societies combine secure and high levels of entitlements for some groups (state employees, soldiers, males, long-term full-time employees, long-established citizens) with weak and largely means-tested provisions for others (females, casual and part-time workers, recent immigrants). There is thus a 'social division of welfare', further explored in chapters 9–11. Related to this division it is also the case that some contingencies are much better provided for than others. Broadly, income deficiency because of old age, childhood and long-term sickness and disability tends to be given more attention than that arising because of unemployment, family breakdown and short-term sickness.

## Tax-supported Contingent Entitlements

The simplest approach to the provision of income maintenance involves guaranteeing payments if specific demographic, social or health status criteria are fulfilled, without reference to contribution conditions or means-tests. The clearest example of this is the provision of cash support for children regardless of the income of their parents (child benefit).

A similar example may occur at the other end of life, when the only criteria for payment of a pension may be age, and claimants merely have to prove that they are above a qualifying age. Systems of this kind have emerged out of the extension of contributory schemes to the point where past benefit records are disregarded in the interests of the inclusion of everyone, for example pension schemes in Norway (see Hatland, 1984) and Sweden (see Gould 1993, p. 185) provide guaranteed minima in this sense. This is a manifestation of the 'solidarity' (Esping-Andersen, 1990) or 'encompassing approach' (Korpi and Palme, 1998) that has come to characterise social security policy in these countries.

In these cases very heavy demands upon the public exchequer are likely to be involved. The price of the abandonment of methods to limit the number of claims is sometimes low levels of benefit. In the child-support case, the benefit is always likely to be merely a partial state contribution to the cost of a child. The issues about child support are complex and have been explored by Bradshaw and Finch (2002), whose work will be discussed later in the chapter.

Another rather less straightforward kind of benefit in this category is the provision of assistance simply on proof of disability. Here it is important to bear in mind that, as Bolderson and Mabbett (1991) indicate in their taxonomy of types of benefits, rules may restrict entitlement by reference either to the 'cause' of the disability (war, employment, etc.) or to the demonstrable consequences of it. An examination to discriminate between claimants is performed, probably by a doctor, using a set of rules that defines levels of disability and which perhaps focuses on the consequences necessary for qualification. The British benefits designed to supplement other incomes for the severely disabled (Disability Living Allowance and Disability Working Allowance) come into this category. So does the Dutch General Disablement Benefit (AAW), but with the extra requirement that some recent labour market attachment must be proved.

In all these cases complete 'universalism' may be partly undermined by rules which confine the benefits to citizens of the country concerned. In this case migrant workers may contribute through taxes but be denied support. This is but one of a number of ways in which discrimination based on nationality or ethnicity may get built into income maintenance systems.

## Social Insurance

Social insurance, with entitlement to benefit depending upon previous contributions, occupies a central role in many of the more sophisticated income maintenance systems (see Clasen, 1997). Many countries have schemes for state pensions, protection for widows, sickness benefits and unemployment benefits developed along social insurance lines. Some countries add maternity benefits and benefits to provide for parental absence from work. However, the umbrella term 'social insurance' covers a multitude of possibilities. Some remain close to the commercial insurance ideas upon which social insurance was originally based, some even involving private but non-profit organisations in the system, for example sickness insurance in Switzerland (see Segalman, 1986) and Germany (see Clasen and Freeman, 1994).

Commercial insurance requires, if it is to remain solvent, methods to ensure that the insured contribute adequate amounts matched in various ways to the likelihood that claims will be made. A consequence of this may be the rejection of some potential customers on the grounds that they will be 'bad risks'. Social insurance departs from this hard-headed commercialism by pooling risks much more radically, recognising that this may mean that 'good risks' may subsidise 'bad risks' to a degree that would simply deter the former from purchasing a commercial insurance. Compulsory inclusion deals with that problem. At the same time, state 'underwriting' of social insurance is expected to eliminate the other commercial problem that too many 'bad risks' may bankrupt a business. In fact in many social insurance schemes, risk pooling is taken further not merely by the acceptance of redistribution between contributors but also by requirements for contributions from employers and by the financial support of schemes via contributions from the state.

On top of all this, most social insurance schemes are not actually 'funded' in the way commercial schemes must be. The fact that many social insurance schemes are in reality **'pay as you go'** schemes, in which current income funds current outgoings, has inevitably led to many specific decisions based on short-run expediency when responses are needed to exceptional demands. This issue about funding is an important one as far as pensions are concerned, where insurance benefit rights are accumulated over a very long period. It is discussed further in the following separate section on pensions.

There are some important issues about the extent to which social insurance, unlike private insurance, embodies the principle of 'solidarity'. This involves several considerations.

1 There may be three contributors to social insurance: the insured person, his or her employer and the state. The proportions may be fixed along a scale in which the input from the insured person varies from a very small to a very large proportion.

2 Contributions may be flat rate or they may be related to income (or some combination of the two).
3 'Risks' do vary. Some demands on social insurance schemes are likely to come more from the worse-off than the better-off. Likelihood of unemployment is strongly skewed towards the worse-off, whereas likelihood of sickness is similarly but less strongly skewed. Conversely, the better-off are likely to live longer and thus to make greater demands on pensions schemes.
4 This socio-economic skewing of claims may be affected by entitlements. Some benefit schemes provide flat-rate payments, others contain adjustments to take into account previous incomes. If the latter phenomenon, earning-relation, applies to schemes, then clearly the better-off claimants will, proportionately to their number of claims, take more out.

In a survey of benefits amongst the twelve EU countries in 1998, all except Ireland related short-term sickness benefits to lost earnings and all except the UK related insurance benefits to the unemployed to previous earnings (MISSOC, 1998).

To make an overall judgement about the extent to which any social insurance scheme is redistributive, there is a need to look at all the issues outlined above together. Other things being equal, a scheme with graduated contributions but flat-rate benefits will be highly redistributive. A scheme with both graduated contributions and graduated benefits will achieve a comparable rate of income replacement across the income groups. A scheme with flat-rate contributions and graduated benefits, an improbable combination, would be regressive. Again, real cases can be very complex mixes, but it is possible with reference both to these issues and to the strictness with which insurance contribution conditions are enforced to compare schemes in terms of the extent to which they embrace principles of solidarity, covering all risks and redistributing resources from those at high risk of dependence to those at low risk. Solidarity is most clearly embodied in schemes that cover the whole population and redistribute effectively as in Sweden. It is least embodied in situations in which different economic or social status groups are differently protected.

However, whilst solidarity may well equate with egalitarianism, it does not necessarily do so. An inverse social redistribution effect has already been noted, associated with longevity in the better-off. There are issues here about the form of distribution being attempted: between individuals, between generations or within individual lifetimes (see Hills, 1993, pp. 15–21). Other things that will affect the equation are the levels at which the minimum benefit is set and the extent to which the egalitarianism of a social insurance scheme is offset by incentives to the better-off to make separate provision. In the British case, the egalitarianism of a flat-rate pension scheme funded by graduated contributions is undermined by the fact that a low basic pension is supplemented by an earnings-related scheme in which incentives (including relief from contributions) are provided to better-off individuals to 'opt out' into private schemes. In contrast, in Sweden and Norway effective but graduated schemes make this a comparative rarity. Korpi and Palme use their comparative data to show a 'paradox of redistribution' in which 'encompassing social insurance institutions providing relatively high levels of income security to the middle class and high income earners tend to be more efficient than basic security and targeted programmes in reducing inequality and poverty' (Korpi and Palme, 1998, p. 17). There is a complex issue here about the way that schemes commanding universal support, because all are potential beneficiaries, may offer a better deal for the poor than more specific measures, an issue to which we will return in chapter 9.

These issues are rendered all the more important if work is not available to all who want it, or is available in part-time or temporary forms or if caring responsibilities reduce labour market participation. This is where the issues about 'solidarity', discussed earlier with reference to the work of Esping-Andersen and to feminist critiques of his work, are important. The traditional social insurance model is based on an expectation of continuous labour market participation. It needs to be radically modified if for any reason this is an unrealistic expectation.

In the course of the above discussion attention has been given in various ways to the issues about individual contribution on the one hand and state contribution on the other. But it should not be forgotten that there is generally a third contributor, an employer. Hatland suggests that historically workers' organisations have seen employer's contributions as a way of making 'capital' pay for social security but that 'today there is widespread agreement among economists that employers have plenty of opportunity to pass the costs on to others through price and wage determination' (Hatland, 1984, p. 178).

Rules about social insurance may affect employment practices. Examples of these rules include the following.

- Part-time employees doing less than a specific number of hours a week need not be insurance contributors.

- Sub-contracting of work may be encouraged by the fact that the contractor does not have any responsibility for the contributions of the consequent 'self-employed' workers.
- Contribution rules may be amongst the factors that make it cheaper to offer existing staff overtime rather than to take on new staff.
- Exceptionally, onerous rules about contributions (plus the administrative complications that accompany them) may be a factor in the evasion of requirements to register staff for tax and social insurance purposes.

As a number of these examples suggest, the issues need to be seen in a wider context. That wider context will include the fact that employers may have adopted practices, or may be required by the government to adopt practices, that extend some forms of income maintenance to their employees at a cost to their enterprise, for example sick pay and pension provisions.

## Comparing Pension Systems

An examination of the proportions of GDP spent on public pensions and the consideration of this amount relative to total public social security expenditure, as set out in table 4.2, shows an interesting contrast between nations. Whilst levels of overall social security expenditure broadly run from high northern European ones through lower levels towards the south and east and even lower levels outside Europe, this pattern is not reflected in a comparison of levels of pension expenditure despite the importance of this expenditure for social security expenditure as a whole. The last column in table 4.2 particularly brings this out. Differences again largely follow Esping-Andersen's regime categories:

- in the continental group, pension expenditure dominates social security expenditure;
- in the social democratic group, pension expenditure takes a lower place amongst a generally larger expenditure level overall;
- in the liberal group, pension expenditure is a relatively modest element in a generally more modest social security budget.

There is evidence here that pension expenditure tends to be a leading element in the less-developed welfare states tending towards the 'continental' regime category, i.e. the southern and eastern European

**Table 4.2** Expenditure on public pensions, 2000

| Country | Percentage of GDP spent on public pensions | Public pension expenditure as percentage of total public social security expenditure |
|---|---|---|
| Italy | 14.2 | 84 |
| France | 12.1 | 67 |
| Germany | 11.8 | 61 |
| Poland | 10.8 | 61 |
| Austria | 9.5 | 51 |
| Spain | 9.4 | 76 |
| Sweden | 9.2 | 53 |
| Belgium | 8.8 | 55 |
| Finland | 8.1 | 48 |
| Portugal | 8.0 | 62 |
| Japan | 7.9 | 72 |
| Czech Republic | 7.8 | 59 |
| Denmark | 6.1 | 34 |
| Canada | 5.8 | 54 |
| Netherlands | 5.2 | 44 |
| Norway | 4.9 | 33 |
| New Zealand | 4.8 | 38 |
| USA | 4.4 | 36 |
| UK | 4.3 | 32 |
| Australia | 3.0 | 34 |
| Korea | 2.1 | 47 |

*Source*: figures for expenditure on pensions are from table 2 in Casey et al. (2003). The ratio is calculated using the 2002 figures for social security expenditure quoted above; since pension costs are generally growing, this will slightly underestimate the pension proportion.

states (Italy, Spain, Portugal, Poland and the Czech Republic) and in Japan.

There are three phenomena that need to be given particular attention in an examination of differences in levels of public pension expenditure: the relative size of the elderly population, the generosity of public pensions and the levels of privatisation. In the sample of nations examined in table 4.2, the proportions of the population that are already elderly will tend to be fairly high, relative to the rest of the world, but there are some interesting contrasts to be made. Table 4.3 again lists the countries by proportion of GDP spent on public pensions, and then sets out percentages of the elderly in each and a statistic on

**Table 4.3** Expenditure on public pensions, relative size of the elderly population and relative generosity of public pensions

| Country | Percentage of GDP spent on public pensions | Percentage of population aged 65 and over | Replacement rate after tax |
|---|---|---|---|
| Italy | 14.2 | 18.2 | 97 |
| France | 12.1 | 16.2 | 77 |
| Germany | 11.8 | 18.6 | 77 |
| Poland | 10.8 | 12.9 | |
| Austria | 9.5 | 15.5 | |
| Spain | 9.4 | 16.9 | 93 |
| Sweden | 9.2 | 17.2 | 82 |
| Belgium | 8.8 | 17.0 | |
| Finland | 8.1 | 15.5 | 74 |
| Portugal | 8.0 | 16.3 | |
| Japan | 7.9 | 19.0 | 50 |
| Czech Republic | 7.8 | 16.9 | |
| Denmark | 6.1 | 14.9 | |
| Canada | 5.8 | 12.8 | 53 |
| Netherlands | 5.2 | 13.8 | 92 |
| Norway | 4.9 | 14.8 | 63 |
| New Zealand | 4.8 | 11.9 | |
| USA | 4.4 | 12.3 | 47 |
| UK | 4.3 | 15.6 | 40 |
| Australia | 3.0 | 12.8 | 57 |
| Korea | 2.1 | 8.3 | 77 |

*Source*: replacement rates from Casey et al. (2003, table A1); other data from earlier tables.

pension scheme generosity (the 'replacement rate', i.e. pension level as a percentage of average earnings).

Table 4.3 emphasises the extent to which differences between these countries are explicable more in terms of replacement rates than in terms of pension scheme generosity or the size of the pensioner population. The available data on replacement rates are limited, with no data for several of the countries. The extent to which the replacement rate figures can be used to explain expenditure is limited inasmuch as they can only relate to those who actually qualify for a state pension. Also, of course, there is a need for more information on what happens to those with pre-retirement incomes well below or well above the average. The rather surprising figures for the Netherlands give a distorted impression of what happens in that country since it is one where there is a high level of privatisation; in effect the replacement rate of public pensions is important for those of average earnings but many of those above this level are more dependent on private than on public provisions. There are high levels of private pension provisions in Australia, Canada, the Netherlands, the USA and the UK (also Ireland and Switzerland, not featured in tables 4.2 and 4.3).

The relationship between private and public pensions and concerns about the alternative forms of the latter require further consideration here, both because they affect comparisons between nations and because they are important for debates about the future of social policy (see further discussion of this in chapter 12). In all free societies individuals are free to make their own pension arrangements. Clearly, there is an issue here about whether the state should get involved in the provision of pensions for all, or at least some, of its citizens. When the state does get involved, there is a further issue about the extent it should see itself as responsible for the whole of the pension for any specific individual or whether it should only be concerned to bring the individual's income to a specific minimum level. An influential report by the World Bank (1994) argues that the state should only be directly responsible for the provision of what it calls the 'first pillar' in any pension scheme, i.e. to secure a basic minimum for its elderly citizens. The state should then take an indirect regulatory responsibility for the second private 'pillar' and accept that beyond this the third pillar should be entirely a private matter.

To understand the arguments about the appropriate respective roles of private and public provision in this area, it is necessary to explore some key issues about the alternatives on the policy agenda. The standard form of a purely private pension involves an agreement between a contributing individual and a pension provider that is no more than an undertaking to safeguard and invest savings and repay them in some form after pension age. What the individual gets out is then a product of what was put in plus whatever that money earned whilst it was invested. A key notion here is that these arrangements are characterised as 'defined contribution' pensions, 'funded' within a managed pool of investments. Where employers are involved in the provision of private pensions, they may modify the principle of 'defined contributions' by making advance commitments about what individuals may take out when they retire; in this sense they are offering 'defined benefits'. To offer defined benefits is to take a risk, in any situation in which there is still investment of contributions in a fund, that ultimately pay-out obligations will exceed the resources of the fund. In the event of bankruptcy the potential or actual pensioners will have a claim on the remaining assets that has to compete with those of other creditors. Within the world of private pensions 'defined benefit' schemes are largely confined to large and strong enterprises. In a capitalist world of rapid organisational change, commitments to pay out defined benefits are seen as increasingly problematical.

When we turn to public pensions there is an important initial point to note: that whilst in discussions like that here about overall state provision 'public' means hypothetically available to all (subject to whatever contribution or means-testing rules are applied), the state may provide special pensions for its own employees as an alternative, or additional, to general state pensions. Many of these pensions long pre-date general public pensions: many states made commitments to their employees (particularly soldiers and officials of the central state) long before they considered legislating to protect anyone else. These pensions may have many of the characteristics of ordinary private pensions, with the difference that the state is, even if there is a fund, the ultimate guarantor of the pension. It is in this area of pension provision that many of the examples of contribution-based and -funded 'defined benefit' schemes are found.

Moving on to the more general forms of public pensions, governments that set up pension schemes have to make a series of choices about how they will operate (bearing in mind the concepts applied to private arrangements). They have to decide the following.

- Will the pensions they provide be 'defined benefit' or 'defined contribution'?
- If 'defined benefit', how will that principle operate in relation to need or to contributions or to past incomes, etc.?
- If 'defined contribution', what modifications will they make to the simple operation of that principle (to take into account differences in the capacity to contribute)?
- If they decide to collect contributions, will they put these into a 'fund', and how then will they manage that fund, bearing in mind that it may make a substantial contribution to public investments?
- How will they involve the private sector in the operation of publicly mandated pensions: as the operators of the public system, as sources of supplementary pensions, etc.?

Reference has already been made to a World Bank report that expressed a distinct preference for a combination of minimal state-guaranteed pensions (limiting pensions either through the operation of a relatively small-scale contributory defined benefit system or through means-testing) and funded private pensions mandated by governments (and thus implicitly regulated and perhaps underwritten by them). The reality worldwide is rather different. Broadly speaking, the following systems can be identified.

- Defined benefit schemes that provide high replacement rates from contributions that are nevertheless not funded (widely described as 'pay as you go' schemes). These schemes have been characteristic of continental European countries, hence the high expenditures noted in table 4.2.
- Defined benefit schemes that provide modest replacement rates in a context in which there is encouragement of private provision. The two prime examples of this are the social insurance schemes in the USA and the UK. These are also 'pay as you go'; this may be asserted despite the fact that the size of the so-called fund has been a long-standing preoccupation in pension politics in the USA since it has never been allowed to develop a surplus for investment by the state.
- Defined benefit schemes without contributions and with availability regulated by means-tests. The best example of this kind of scheme can be found in Australia, though it may be argued that the UK scheme is evolving in the same direction.
- Defined contribution schemes in which the state has developed a funding system. The main examples of this are the 'provident funds' of Singapore and Malaysia, though there are also some modern imitators.
- Defined contribution schemes in which there is a requirement for compulsory contributions to private sector-managed schemes. This widely advocated type has only really been developed effectively in Chile, and as a supplementary measure in Australia.

No effort has been made to place each of the countries discussed in this book into these categories, since there are many hybrid forms. For example, Sweden has recently added a defined contribution element to its long-standing defined benefit system, and as noted above the UK state system seems to be evolving from a contribution-based one to a means-test-based one.

It must also be noted that as well as actual schemes that cross the public–private boundary, some governments provide tax concessions to the contributors to, or the organisations that manage, private pensions. Governments also often choose to regulate private schemes in various ways. A crucial issue here concerns 'portability', mechanisms to enable individuals to transfer (or at least protect) pension rights when they change jobs. Regulations may deal with this issue, and it may be noted that the more effectively private schemes are 'self-standing', with funds kept separate from the accounts of the employers, the easier it is to deal with this issue. Issues may arise about the extent to which, having set private schemes within a regulatory framework, governments are regarded as having obligations when schemes fail.

The curious puzzle about the evolution of pension systems worldwide has been the way in which, taking their model from the private insurance industry, there has been a strong tendency to develop social insurance systems in which risk pooling (thus shifting away from making entitlement dependent only on contributions) has been dominant yet these have not (despite much early rhetoric about that intention) involved significant funding. Public accounting practice often maintains an illusion of funding by producing social insurance fund accounts showing income and outgoings. Sometimes this is seen as going further and offering coverage against expected deficits. This may be seen as having 'symbolic' importance, encouraging the view that contributions are being paid for a specific purpose. Governments may use evidence of deficiencies in the 'fund' to justify adjustments to either benefits or contributions as opposed to additional subventions from general taxation. Some countries even maintain accounts with balances that earn interest (see Hatland, 1984, p. 189 on Norway's scheme; similarly there is a trust fund for pensions in the USA).

By comparison with the world of private pensions this funding is very limited, offering no more than prudential coverage against relatively short-run predicted deficits in a context in which the central principle is pay-as-you-go. The explanation of the reluctance to go more fully down the funding road seems to lie partly in a strong tendency for governments to manage public accounts on a year-by-year basis (with of course varying levels of relatively short-term debt) but also partly in uncertainty about how to manage investments. State investments have been seen as implying forms of state socialism. The government investors of pension funds could acquire various forms of control over private enterprise. This certainly worried the politicians who developed the system in the USA in the 1930s (Blackburn, 2002, pp. 74–5). Alternatively, to bring the private sector into the public pension system without strict controls has been seen as equally problematical. The World Bank view that individuals should be compelled to contribute to private schemes seems to have been viewed with apprehension by governments otherwise strongly committed to privatisation. The key question here is: does a government that has compelled you to invest then have obligations when the investment fails?

There are related issues here about where investments should be made. Perhaps the strongest of the World Bank's arguments for the investment of pension contributions is that this will contribute to national economic growth, something of particular value in developing economies where investments are low and there are few alternative sources of them. The problem about this is that investing in a weak economy is probably not the best way of protecting pension funds on behalf of their contributors. Additionally, in an increasingly globalist economy it is not very easy to control the flow of investments and contain them in specific countries (Beattie and McGillivray, 1995).

Chapter 12 will explore further the way in which the growth in size of the elderly population has led to a worldwide review of pension systems. However, it is pertinent to point out here that when governments first design pension schemes they will have two potentially competing concerns: the needs of people already old and those of future generations of old people. From an electoral point of view the first concern will tend to be the most pressing. However, when the pioneer nations on pension provision (largely the western European ones) set up schemes, the size of the elderly population was small and their life expectancy low. Their needs could be seen as a relatively low demand on the budget, easily funded by relatively low contributions from the younger people required to join pension schemes. In contrast, pension reform (and even more significantly initial pension design in countries looking at pension schemes for the first time) now takes place in the context of large and growing elderly populations.

Bonoli and Shinkawa (2005) use the pillar model offered in the World Bank's classification system to analyse systems in terms of two dimensions. On the first pillar dimension a distinction is made between the absence of any pillar at all and then between whether or not that pillar provides subsistence benefits or substantial income replacement (at least 60 per cent of earnings). This is then cross-tabulated against the characteristics of the second pillar: voluntary and limited or widespread (and in some cases compulsory). The resulting classification identifies five alternatives:

1 non-existent first pillar and limited second pillar (Taiwan);
2 subsistence first pillar and limited second pillar (Canada, the USA and in some respects Japan);

3 subsistence first pillar and widespread second pillar (Switzerland and the UK);
4 first pillar offering substantial income replacement and a limited second pillar (France, Germany, Italy, Sweden before the 1990s, and in some respects Korea);
5 substantial first and second pillars (Sweden since the 1990s).

Hence what is offered is something more complex than that provided in Esping-Andersen's regime theory, the highlighting of subsistence-level first pillars offering a better approach than the liberal–conservative dichotomy in defining limited social insurance systems. This is argued also to be important for the exploration of the politics of reform, and the situations of the later developers of pensions systems inasmuch as this form of state provision faces less 'sustainability problems' than the more comprehensive first-pillar systems.

## Means-testing

The provision of income maintenance through schemes involving means-tests has a long history in many societies. At a simple glance this approach seems to satisfy the requirements of both a desire for equality and a commitment to efficiency – equality because means-testing is generally designed to concentrate help on those in greatest need; efficiency because such 'targeting' is designed to keep expenditure to a minimum. But a deeper examination of means-testing reveals many problems, which may undermine these two goals.

Whilst it may seem appropriate to concentrate help on those with least at any point in time, it may be regarded as very unfair that those who have squandered resources will get help whereas those who have saved or made some other kind of private provision for adversity will not. There is likely to be a 'savings trap' or 'assets trap' that will mean that all or parts of savings have to be spent before help can be received (see Walker, 2005, pp. 210–12). A recognition in society that such an effect will apply to income maintenance may actually operate as a disincentive to self-protection.

Means-tests are likely to be seen as very unfair to those who have self-provided incomes slightly above the level they guarantee. Achievement of a job paying wages at a very modest amount above that guaranteed level may come to be seen as a minute real reward when a comparison is made with the benefit available to the workless. Such an unfavourable comparison is likely to be encouraged by the unpleasant and onerous nature of many of the lowest paid jobs. This comparison problem may be avoided by provisions that enable means-tested support to taper off gradually above the guaranteed income level. However, much will then depend on the rate at which this tapering-off effect occurs. If it is rapid, then it will resemble a draconian tax on earnings. This is the phenomenon of the **'poverty trap'**, particularly noted in the UK, which has the effect of holding substantial numbers of families at income levels only a little above the level guaranteed to those out of work.

These issues are particularly salient where means-tested benefits are used to supplement low-paid or part-time work. There are important variations between nations in respect of these issues. In some societies (France and Sweden, for example) part-time work is rare; in others it is common (the UK and the Netherlands, for example). Similarly, there are important differences in the extent to which governments, or trade unions, have been prepared to accept low-wage systems. In some of those where they have been particularly prevalent (such as the USA, Canada and the UK), or where part-time work is common, a form of means-testing to subsidise work that aims to minimise these issues has been developed: tax credits. Embodied in the idea of tax credits is provision of benefits through the tax system that do not merely offset tax liabilities but may involve payment to low income people who are not required to pay any tax.

Disincentive effects will undermine the efficiency of means-testing. Together with the complexity of the rules relating to benefit deter-mination, they lead to situations in which large numbers of people entitled to help do not claim it. Walker (2005, p. 194) quotes studies of take-up showing rates around two-thirds in respect of means-tested benefits in the UK and the USA and well below half for **social assistance** in Germany.

On the other hand, means-tests also create incentives for fraud, as people may be able to conceal resources to secure help. In addition, if a small increase in income will undermine benefit entitlement, then there will be a strong incentive to conceal it. These issues about fraud then feed into administrative concerns. If an application for help requires proof that an individual has an income deficiency, lack of savings and no help from other family members, and if any payment made needs to be accurately tailored to available resources and to the family (and perhaps housing cost) commitments of the applicant, then a claim for help is likely to be complex. In these circumstances, if the scope for fraud is extensive, assessment of the claim will require a costly investigation. Once the benefit is in payment, high administrative costs are likely to continue. Changes of circumstances will necessitate reassessment and the continued risk of fraud may be deemed to necessitate surveillance procedures over the lives of beneficiaries.

The position is made more complicated by the fact that means-testing systems are likely to look at more than individual resources. Any individual application is likely to be assessed in ways which take into account the needs and resources of other family and/or household members. We return to this topic in the section on social security and the family.

The final problem with means-tests arises from the general implications of the points made so far (i.e. about disincentive effects, family obligations and administrative surveillance): that the process of obtaining and retaining help of this kind will be regarded as degrading and stigmatising to applicants. Of course this may be regarded by those not in need of help as a desirable feature of means-tested income maintenance, deterring claims to benefit, keeping costs down and counteracting the characteristics that seem to discourage self-help.

Hostility to means-testing from politically active low- to middle-income people (what used to be widely called the 'respectable working-class') has led to the creation of two-tier income maintenance systems in many countries. These involve contributory benefits to meet many contingencies, particularly those deemed to arise through no fault of the claimant (particularly worklessness as a result of sickness or old age). These are then accompanied by means-tested 'safety net schemes' for those not protected by contributory benefits. Whilst these may be seen as necessary to meet temporary deficiencies in the contributory schemes or to assist those whose rather exceptional circumstances prevent them benefiting fully from contributory schemes, there is then a tendency for them to be also seen as the appropriate form of support for less 'respectable' categories amongst those unable to secure support through the labour market, particularly the single-parent and the long-term unemployed person.

This dualism of contributory benefits underpinned by means-tested benefits is widespread. Inconsistencies may develop in an income maintenance system as a whole as a result of the operation of very different principles for the determination of benefits which are side by side. This arises particularly if the income guaranteed by a means-test is similar to that provided by contributory benefits. It creates situations in which there will be many people who, despite the fact that they have entitlements to contributory benefits, find that means-tests determine their final income. This is an effect that erodes support for the contributory principle. It engenders the possibility that individuals will see the making of contributions as unnecessary, evading them by working in the 'informal economy', on the grounds that if they lose their work the state will protect them just the same. The UK is a country where these issues have particular prominence: from the relative frugality of the insurance benefit rates, the desire to provide comprehensive protection through means-tests, the fact that the latter take into account housing costs but the former do not, the poor protection to women and the very limited insurance support for unemployed people. Many other countries have avoided such difficulties by ensuring a wider gap between contributory and means-tested benefits either through the generosity of the former (the Scandinavian countries) or the meanness of the latter (the USA).

There has been one major comparative study of means tests (Eardley, Bradshaw, Ditch, Gough and Whiteford, 1996; see also Gough, Bradshaw, Ditch, Eardley and Whiteford, 1997). It suggests that 'the careful study of means-tested benefits . . . muddles, but ultimately enriches prior comparative models of welfare systems' (Eardley et al., 1996, p. 171). The following taxonomy of types of social assistance systems is suggested (ibid., pp. 168–71).

- Selective welfare systems (Australia and New Zealand): all benefits are means-tested.
- Public assistance state (USA): there is 'an extensive set of means-tested benefits, arranged in a hierarchy of acceptability and stigma'.
- Welfare states with integrated safety nets (UK, Canada, Ireland and Germany).
- Dual social assistance (France and the Benelux countries): various categorical assistance schemes.
- Rudimentary assistance (southern Europe and Turkey): some national categorical schemes and otherwise local discretionary relief.
- Residual social assistance (the Nordic countries): social assistance marginalised by the presence of comprehensive social insurance, though it is noted that the rise of unemployment slightly increased the significance of these schemes in the 1990s.
- Highly decentralised assistance with local discretion (Austria, Switzerland): 'elements of both the Nordic and Southern European models' (ibid., p. 170).

Since this study is limited to OECD countries, it is important to note that there is a category missing, prevalent in much of the rest of the world, which may be described as 'rudimentary and often highly decentralised assistance in a context where there is no other state social security'. This emphasises a point about this classification, which renders it rather less of an alternative to Esping-Andersen's model than at first appears to be the case: that these types of social assistance are all (except the first, and to some extent the second) operating in a context of extensive social insurance. Hence the interesting issues are about how the supplementing of the latter has been conceived. Esping-Andersen's liberal states, not surprisingly, all have highly developed social assistance schemes and his 'social democratic' ones essentially marginal ones; it is the 'conservative' group that may be seen as diverse (with again some vestiges of a north–south divide within Europe).

## Benefits in Cash or in Kind

Inasmuch as social security systems are designed to provide incomes in specific contingencies, it is important to bear in mind that the provision of services contributes to social security. Indeed, in many basic poor relief systems, help is provided in kind rather than cash. But equally it needs to be borne in mind that the provision of housing, health care, social care, education, transport and even forms of entertainment at less than market cost will contribute to social security. Whilst these 'benefits' are not normally described as parts of social security systems, it is important to bear in mind that they do have an impact on, and interact with, income maintenance systems. The first three items in this list merit further comment.

Housing is a very large item in household budgets so housing subsidies may have a large impact. Moreover, in many cases housing subsidies are given not in respect of the housing occupied but are related to the resources of the household. This form of subsidy is likely to involve specific targeting through means-tests. Ball, Harloe and Martens (1988) identify the following issues about this form of subsidy.

- Benefits may not be taken up by all in need. The authors see this as depending very much on the extent to which there is stigma attached to the claiming of means-tested benefits, favourably contrasting the Netherlands and Denmark with Germany.
- Difficulties may ensue when tenants are required to make minimum payments regardless of their income. They observe that one of the cuts applied during the Reagan administration in the USA involved increasing this minimum without reference to tenants' capacity to pay.

• Schemes apply controls to prevent 'over-consumption of housing, requiring for example, that the space is closely matched to family size' (ibid., p. 71). A related issue, particularly if rents are not controlled in any way, concerns whether there should be an upper rent limit for support. If there is not, the possibility arises of collusion between landlord and tenant to maximise the benefit, in effect undermining the operation of the market. If there is one, it will be the case either that tenants have to meet a top slice themselves or that this reinforces the social segregation of the poor.

To these may be added the fact that a housing means-test contributes to the problems about the poverty trap (mentioned above).

Kemp (1990) has examined some of the variations in approaches to income-related assistance with housing costs in the UK, France, Germany and the Netherlands. Kemp's analysis shows why the poverty trap stands out as a problem for the British system, namely because of a combination of relatively full support for housing costs with a high taper rate. Contrastingly, the other systems he studied are likely to leave rent payers with high residual amounts to find from low incomes, particularly where (as in the Netherlands) there is no integration with other aspects of income maintenance.

The interaction between social security and health care is complicated by the fact that individuals who are sick are likely to need to pay for care but also suffer from loss of income. In many social insurance systems (in Germany and France for example) provision for the cost of health care and compensation for income loss are within the same system.

There are similar complications in respect of social care. This is particularly evident when individuals need to enter care homes or nursing homes. Then their care will consist of a combination of special attention in respect of their infirmities and what may be called 'hotel services'. Hence either subsidised care or further income enhancement may be necessary. It is interesting to note, therefore, the development in respect of social care of new forms of social insurance (in Germany and Japan for example).

There is also another category of social care, relevant to the previous section, namely care for children, where an additional complication arises inasmuch as this is either something that has to be paid for or something that prevents someone being a labour market participant. The most ambitious comparative work on the complexities of this issue is that done by Bradshaw (Bradshaw, Ditch, Holmes and Whiteford, 1993; Bradshaw and Finch, 2002). Bradshaw and his associates examined the 'child care package', which includes cash benefits, tax allowances, exemptions from charges and subsidies and services in kind, all of which assist parents with child-rearing costs. Whilst Bradshaw and Finch conclude that the most generous countries in respect of this child care package are those that deliver most of their value in non-income-related child benefits, nevertheless variations in benefits in accordance with income levels do complicate comparisons considerably. Hence, whilst they show Austria to offer the most generous package overall, the USA offers the best package for low-income families and the Netherlands the best for average-income families.

Bradshaw and Finch's study explores the extent to which variations in the child benefit package can be predicted from Esping-Andersen's regime types. They conclude that it cannot:

> The social democratic (Nordic) welfare states tend to come in the top half of the table but they are not the leaders and Denmark and Norway are well down the rankings. The liberal (Anglophone) welfare states are distributed throughout the rankings with the UK and Australia in the second rank. New Zealand is consistently towards the bottom of the rankings. The conservative (corporatist) countries tend to be found in the upper half of the table but the Netherlands is a big exception. Austria is something of an outlier with considerably more generous child benefit package than any other country after housing costs and services. The southern EU countries are in the bottom half of the table but spread, with Italy somewhat above the others. Japan, our only representative of the Pacific Rim/Confucian model, is found towards the bottom. (From a summary of Bradshaw and Finch, 2002)

All of the above illustrate a range of issues about the relationship between 'cash' and 'kind' in social security provision. Debates about these are not merely concerned with complications and anomalies that may arise between different aspects of social policy. They also raise important questions of principle about the extent to which individuals with identified income deficiencies should have their income enhanced, to enable them to make their own spending decisions, or have services free or at reduced costs.

## Social Security Systems, Redistribution and the Relief of Poverty

It might be expected that this chapter would give attention to a crucial outcome variable for the evaluation of social security: poverty reduction.

However, discussion of this is left to chapter 9 as this is seen as a crucial ingredient for the evaluation of the impact of social policy on social divisions.

## Social Security and the Family

Many social security systems strongly emphasise family obligations, seeing it as necessary to limit access to them unless within-family exchanges are impossible. As far as the nuclear family is concerned, widowhood for women and death of a father for children are generally seen to be a clear reason for access to benefits. When divorce or separation occurs, financial obligations between spouses (particularly those of men for women) and the obligations of both parents remain. Benefits are likely to be given as a last resort, with efforts to recover contributions from the 'absent' person. As far as extended families are concerned, similar obligations may exceptionally be identified between parents and their adult children and vice versa. These latter expectations are of limited relevance in European systems today but still important elsewhere in the world (see Eardley et al., 1996, table 3.2).

Related to these issues about families are complicated questions about whether benefits are given in respect of individuals on their own or whether, in assessing entitlements, regard is had to the location of the individual claimant within a family or household. There are several variations around this theme. They may be divided into issues about the responsibilities of the benefit claimant to provide for the needs of others and issues about the extent to which the claimant's needs may be met by others. Logically, some consistency between these two concerns might be expected. This is not necessarily the case in practice.

Logically, if children and a spouse are deemed to be the 'dependants' of a benefit claimant, then in the context of means-testing their resources will also be taken into account. However, many means-tests also take into account the resources of other household members, particularly if they are related. There are some problems about assumptions of this kind since households may be difficult to define; this is not a simple matter of residence since a variety of practices with regard to resource sharing may be found under the same roof. The alternative of regarding marriage as a key principle for determining how to treat a household is complicated by the range of relationships not involving formal marriages. Officials may have to impose simplifying rules or may be required to use their judgement, or there may be an element of negotiation between claimants and officials.

Some means-tests have regard to family obligations extending beyond the framework of the household as defined by residence in the same dwelling (e.g. the scheme operated in Taiwan may look to provisions from the parents and siblings of adult claimants even when they live elsewhere in the country).

Central here, however, are issues about the extent that the social security treatment of the family unit involves a 'male breadwinner' claimant who may then need to apply for help with the needs of his wife and children, and who can expect that the system will have some concern about their resources (see, for example, Sainsbury, 1994; O'Connor, 1996). The alternative, argued for from a feminist perspective and to some extent necessitated by new forms of family arrangements, is to see both entitlements and resources in terms of the incomes of individuals. This is evident in most social insurance systems but not in the operation of most means-tests. Obviously children complicate the equations; whilst child benefits partly deal with this, there remain problems about to whom those benefits are paid and about the extent to which the work of caring for children can be recognised as a contingency for benefit purposes. This topic is explored further in chapter 10.

## Conclusions

Comparative studies of social policy as a whole rest to a very large extent on the comparison of social security systems. This has been shown to be partly a logical consequence of the dominant role of social security transfers within many public social policy systems. However, it may also be partly because cash transfers are easier to measure and compare than many other social policy transactions.

Nevertheless, given this level of overlap it is not surprising that versions of regime theory emerge in various places in the analysis of social security. Overall, Esping-Andersen's approach does capture the essential areas of choice in relation to forms of social security, involving two considerations: the extent to which social security is redistributive and the choice between social insurance and means-testing systems. However, whilst Esping-Andersen's regime theory uses three alternatives, the use of these two distinctions implies at least four. Table 4.4 summarises this issue.

Certainly the discussion of the comparative study of social assistance in this chapter lends support to this perspective, noting how different this may be where it is the dominant social security system

**Table 4.4** A variant on Esping-Andersen's regimes suggested by
Mitchell's work (see pp. 30–1)

|                          | Low redistribution   | High redistribution      |
|--------------------------|----------------------|--------------------------|
| Social insurance dominant | Conservative regimes | Social-democratic regimes |
| Means-testing dominant   | Liberal regimes      | Radical regimes          |

as opposed to a residual safety net system. How far this argument
should be taken depends on the extent to which social assistance can
provide complication-free redistribution. The discussion of this topic
suggested that this is difficult to achieve, given the problems about assets
and poverty 'traps', family means-testing and detailed administration.

### GUIDE TO FURTHER READING

As was noted, much of the analysis of social policy regimes uses social
security data. Hence many of the reading suggestions made in chapter 2 apply
here also. Amongst these Korpi and Palme's (1998) article can be highlighted
for its detailed consideration of social security. Robert Walker's *Social Security
and Welfare* (2005) is a conceptual rather than a comparative analysis and only
uses references from a small sample of countries but offers a good exploration
of the key issues. For a specific examination of social insurance consult Clasen
(1997). Eardley et al. (1996) and Gough et al. (1997) offer good comparative
discussions on social assistance.

# CHAPTER 5

# EMPLOYMENT POLICY

## Margaret May

### Introduction: Identifying the Issues

The management of employment in the sense of formal remunerated work has long been a key issue in social policy in industrialised societies, with paid work as a major determinant of entitlement to statutory benefits and services across welfare systems. Over the last two decades it has also gained a new saliency as governments have re-centred social policies around labour market participation and presented paid work as the best form of welfare. However, outside the industrialised societies the relative absence of formal employment contracts and the existence of many forms of work within household and other communal economies means that the preoccupations with unemployment and the regulation of conditions of work explored in this chapter have to be seen in a wider setting.

For most individuals in advanced industrial societies paid work is probably the defining feature of their lives. It provides not only a livelihood but often determines their social standing and sense of personal identity. Work is where they spend most of their lives, form friendships and often meet their partners. A considerable body of evidence suggests moreover that people's employment opportunities affect their health and longevity as well as their overall quality of life and civic engagement. Correspondingly, as studies stretching back to the 1930s show, those outside the labour market may well face a downward spiral of poverty, ill-health and social marginalisation (Jahoda, Lazarsfeld and Zeisel, 1972). Unemployment also poses a potential drain on the state and local communities through lost production and tax revenues and the costs of statutory or other forms of support.

The range and effectiveness of a government's employment strategy is thus both directly and indirectly of central importance to policy analysis. It interconnects with social security, taxation, health, social care, education and the related welfare issues addressed in this book. As feminist researchers have shown, the governance of paid work also has profound repercussions not only for those in the formal labour market but also for other types of employment, whether in the **informal economy** or in unpaid domestic, caring and voluntary work.

Determining what should be considered within the ambit of employment policy, however, is highly problematic. Comparative researchers have adopted a range of approaches, themselves reflecting national variations in both its constituents and significance in different welfare systems. From the broadest standpoint it entails assessments of governments' macro-management of the economy and the extent to which they opt for interventionist or neo-liberal strategies. As with other policy areas, debates over this fundamental differentiator form the bedrock of comparative study. Detailed appraisal of the fiscal and other measures deployed by governments tends to be seen as a matter of economic policy. In terms of social policy, interest centres more on other issues.

Traditionally in developed economies attention has focused largely on unemployment and the income maintenance dilemmas it presents. Whilst this remains a key element of employment policy, the last two decades have seen a widespread shift away from 'passive' towards 'active' labour market programmes designed to contain public expenditure and speed people back into work. This development is closely linked with mounting interest in the related issue of sustaining high levels of employment more generally. Here too there are marked variations between countries and within them over time regarding the state's role and the measures used to influence entry, retention and employers' decision-making.

Historically, such interventions presupposed a gendered division of labour and conceived employment primarily in terms of men's work and breadwinning role (see chapter 10). The 'feminisation' of the workforce in western economies, along with other factors discussed below, has forced a reappraisal of inherited approaches to both labour supply and demand. It has also highlighted the issue of employee rights and the varying role of the state in regulating individual and collective relations between employers and employees. In the UK, despite interventions dating back to the early nineteenth century factory acts, these aspects have attracted little attention from policy analysts (Alcock, 2003; Hill, 2003). In the USA they remain a matter for the separate discourses of employee relations and human resource management. However, in northern and much of continental Europe workplace regulation has long been viewed as integral to welfare planning and analysis. It has also been a major area of EU action. Elsewhere, too, the issue of employee protection is inextricably fused with broader social policy concerns (ILO, 2005).

This chapter adopts this broad-based conception of employment policy. It focuses on measures to: (1) tackle unemployment, (2) influence overall employment levels, (3) influence the productivity and employability of the workforce, and (4) regulate employment and working conditions. The first two interventions entail macro- and micro-level action to influence the supply of, and demand for, labour; the other two affect recruitment and the terms of the labour contract. In practice these different realms tend to impact on each other and one question running through this chapter is the extent to which national arrangements can be characterised in terms of coherent employment regimes integrated with their broader welfare systems.

The state may shape the labour market indirectly as well as directly. As well as being responsible for legislation and regulation, modern governments are major purchasers of goods and services. Privatisation in its many guises and the spread of outsourcing and partnership arrangements with non-statutory agencies has extended this role in many countries. Public procurement policies, which often include specifications regarding employment practices, may thus impact on employment opportunities and experiences. Contemporary governments are also major employers. Their practices may affect not only the market for labour but people management strategies more widely, especially where the state implements 'best practice' and presents itself as a 'good employer' (Farnham, 1999).

Some of these practices may be developed independently by employers; others emerge as a consequence of employee or trade union pressure. More broadly, state interventions may operate alongside employer or union-sponsored action, particularly with respect to training and occupational welfare. The discussion starts with unemployment, the issue that has attracted most public and comparative interest and where debates are sharpest. Developments here have tended to shape employment policy more widely. They also exemplify the varied rationales for state intervention in the relationship between employers and employees. Historically this was often impelled more by anxieties over the threats to social order and economic inefficiencies associated with worklessness than the welfare of the unemployed. The tensions between these imperatives remain a major issue.

## Unemployment: Issues of Definition and Measurement

Like many welfare problems unemployment appears on the surface to be a straightforward phenomenon, the product of an imbalance between the supply and demand for labour. However, defining and measuring it are highly contentious processes. The indices used often vary between countries and within countries over time. They may also be subject to political manipulation, affecting headline figures and levels of public concern. This becomes clear when one examines the two main measurements used, claimant counts and labour force surveys.

The first is based on the numbers registered with employment offices or claiming unemployment benefits. The resultant data are likely to vary both between and within states according to the rules affecting registration and entitlement and the extent to which they deter or encourage 'enrolment'. One much-cited example of this can be found in the UK. In the post-war era the main indicator was of those registered as unemployed. From 1982, however, the official figures were based on the narrower measure of those receiving unemployment-related benefits. Moreover, the progressive tightening of entitlements, the spread of government training schemes and other changes during the 1980s and early 1990s meant this 'count' excluded many who were out of work but not eligible for benefits.

For many commentators, labour force survey data offer a more reliable and accurate picture. In 1998 this became the UK's 'preferred' approach, bringing it in line with other OECD countries that use the **International Labour Organisation** (ILO) definition. It defines unemployment as covering those who are out of work, want a job, have actively sought work in the previous four weeks and are available to start within two, or have accepted a job and are waiting to start in the next fortnight. This definition overcomes some of the problems noted above and facilitates cross-national comparison. But though widely used, ILO-based surveys are also open to criticism (Gregg and Wadsworth, 1998). In part this is because all those not actively seeking work are construed as economically inactive, but it is also because they rely on respondents' judgements.

Firstly, the ILO definition does not catch movements within benefit systems, such as the widespread reallocation of individuals from unemployment to disability assistance at the end of the last century. Secondly, the ways respondents are asked about their desire for work, their perception of local market conditions and other concerns may all affect the findings (Andersen and Jensen, 2002). Individuals in depressed areas may not deem themselves as 'actively' seeking work. Likewise, individuals on training programmes who want a job but are not currently seeking one do not count. This may also be true of people with caring responsibilities. In addition, the measure does not allow for those working part-time who want but cannot find full-time posts or who are in positions well below their skill levels or qualifications (phenomena that apply particularly to women). Prison inmates (a significant proportion of working age males in the USA) are also excluded, whilst there is considerable national variation in how students seeking work are recorded.

As MacKay (1999) notes there is no 'perfect' way to calibrate unemployment. Hence the standard ILO-based rate is often supplemented by a range of other indices. These include labour force participation rates (the proportion of those of working age who are in employment), inactivity rates (the proportion of those of working age who are neither in employment or included among the unemployed), and 'non-employment rates' (combining the 'inactive' and 'unemployed'). The issue of 'non' and 'under' employment is a major concern for many governments. Public discussion, however, is framed by the more visible problem of recorded unemployment.

## The Incidence of Unemployment

For comparative purposes the OECD compilations of official survey data based on the ILO definition provide the most comprehensive overview of recent trends in unemployment. Their full significance though can only be understood in terms of the proportion of the labour force affected. They clearly also need to be viewed in terms of the proportion of the working age population in employment.

Table 5.1 charts recent unemployment and economic activity rates among OECD countries. The unemployment rate shows the number of unemployed as a proportion of the civilian labour force. The latter comprises both the unemployed and those in civilian employment, defined as individuals who have worked for one hour or more in the past week (a construction of employment that is also open to question). As can be seen, there are marked differences between different societies. There are also differences over time; having escalated almost everywhere in the 1980s and early 1990s, unemployment has since fallen in many countries, but at varying rates. However, unemployment is still higher in many countries than in the previous two decades and at present some countries are facing rising unemployment, notably

**Table 5.1** Unemployment and employment rates in OECD countries, 2004

| Country | Unemployment rate[a] | Labour force participation rate[a] |
|---|---|---|
| Australia | 5.6 | 73.6 |
| Austria | 5.3 | 70.2 |
| Belgium | 7.4 | 65.3 |
| Canada | 7.2 | 78.2 |
| Czech Republic | 8.4 | 70.1 |
| Denmark | 5.3 | 80.2 |
| Finland | 8.9 | 73.8 |
| France | 9.6 | 69.5 |
| Germany | 9.9 | 72.7 |
| Greece | 10.4 | 66.5 |
| Hungary | 6.1 | 60.5 |
| Ireland | 4.4 | 68.6 |
| Italy | 8.1 | 62.5 |
| Japan | 4.9 | 72.2 |
| Korea | 3.6 | 66.0 |
| Mexico | 3.1 | 64.7 |
| Netherlands | 4.7 | 76.6 |
| New Zealand | 4.0 | 76.6 |
| Norway | 4.5 | 79.1 |
| Poland | 19.3 | 64.2 |
| Portugal | 7.0 | 72.9 |
| Slovak Republic | 18.2 | 69.7 |
| Spain | 11.0 | 69.7 |
| Sweden | 6.6 | 78.7 |
| Switzerland | 4.4 | 81.0 |
| UK | 4.7 | 76.2 |
| USA | 5.6 | 75.4 |

[a] The data are based on a labour force survey, with labour force participation rate expressed as a percentage of the working age population and the unemployment rate as a percentage of the labour force.

*Source*: data from OECD (2005a, table B, p. 240).

France and Germany. In contrast, both the UK and Australia are experiencing record-high employment levels.

Averaged over the decade, by the mid-2000s three main groupings had emerged: countries such as the UK, the USA, Sweden and the Netherlands with rates below 6 per cent; those such as Greece and the

Czech Republic with rates between 6 and 10 per cent; and those such as Spain, Italy, France, Germany and Poland with over 10 per cent (OECD, 2005a). These national variations mask significant variations within countries, for instance between western and eastern Germany or northern and southern Italy. Whatever the national or regional rate, it is clear that unemployment affects some groups more than others. Those most at risk are the low-skilled and young adults and, in some countries, women. Female unemployment rates are usually higher than men's. Yet in some countries, ranging from Sweden and the UK to Korea, they are lower (ibid.). Though rates vary, unemployment among the under-25s is a cause of concern for many societies (European Commission, 2005, p. 15). It is particularly problematic within the EU, where it averaged 18 per cent overall, rising to 25 per cent in France and Germany and to 40 per cent in some parts of Italy, Spain and Greece. There is also a close association between skill levels and the likelihood of experiencing unemployment.

Comparing and accounting for these patterns is clearly a complex task. At first glance recent trends seem to cut across regime analysis, placing the UK and Sweden for instance in the same 'league'. Political debate, however, has tended to focus on the apparent 'success' of the USA compared with the EU overall, rather than the many variations both within Europe and beyond. The aim here is to take a more nuanced approach, starting with a review of the main explanations of unemployment before considering the debates over variations in national 'performance' and the policies that may contribute to these.

## Accounting for Unemployment

At the outset it should be recognised that there is no consensus as to how unemployment can be explained. However, two broad distinctions can be drawn: between individualist and structuralist accounts and between politically dominant and more critical perspectives (the last range from radical-Marxist, feminist and anti-racist to 'green' analyses). Though these filter into mainstream debates, public discourse is dominated by the varying interpretations advanced by neo-liberal and welfare capitalist theorising. Following Bryson (2003) these are best summarised in terms of three approaches: behavioural, institutional and economic.

Behavioural explanations are essentially individualist, holding that the problem rests with the unemployed rather than broader socio-economic factors. Within this broad construction, one set of thinking views unemployment as the product of intentional work avoidance, sometimes partly attributed to over-generous state assistance (Murray, 1984; Green, 1999; Bartholomew, 2004). For policy-makers the implications are unequivocal and stretch back to the deterrent relief systems of pre- and early industrial Europe. Benefit systems should be designed to implant work obligations and pitched so as not to vitiate the returns from work.

A second stream of behavioural prescriptions takes a different tack, suggesting that work avoidance stems from the experience of unemployment itself. Employers are often reluctant to hire staff with fractured work histories, but frequent rejections are clearly demotivating. Prolonged joblessness also means skills become dated, contacts are lost and individuals slip into non-working lifestyles. This 'softer' view leads to a greater emphasis on re-employment schemes. However, the main solution again lies in behaviour-correcting benefit structures.

Institutional accounts overlap with behavioural theories in that they see state intervention as abetting rather than reducing unemployment. Exponents of this view believe government programmes are poorly aligned to employer needs and public agencies ill-equipped to deliver them. Rights-based benefit systems are alleged to operate as disincentives to re-employment and impede geographical mobility and state-run training is insufficiently targeted. In this view state action tends to sustain rather than curtail unemployment, which is best managed by private labour market filters, contingent benefit systems and minimal state interventions (Krugman, 1987).

Economic accounts offer a further range of explanations and injunctions. One such approach stems from classical economic writing that analysed labour in the same way as other commodities and saw it as subject to the same self-correcting market processes. In practice, social order and humanitarian concerns pre-empted the full application of this viewpoint. Even as it was being fashioned, nineteenth-century governments found it necessary to provide relief and other assistance for the unemployed. Other economic theorists take a different stance, arguing that labour markets operate very differently to other markets. They are marked by power imbalances between employees and employers and between employees. Workers are not standardised inputs, but enter the market with varying skills that in turn reflect differences in education and cultural as well as personal capital. They have family and community ties that may restrict mobility. Moreover, market processes mean that unemployment is often the product of factors beyond individual control as studies of different types of unemployment, frictional, cyclical and structural, make clear.

Amongst these types **frictional unemployment** has, historically, attracted most attention. It refers to the temporary unemployment resulting from time-lags and information gaps in the market as individuals search for or move jobs and employers seek new staff. In the past these asymmetries were exacerbated by localised markets, poor communications and the limited reach of private recruitment agencies. For early twentieth-century policy-makers, the solution lay in public employment exchanges. State bureaux offering free services for employers still predominate in Sweden (Wadensjo, 2002). The 1980s saw an expansion of private agencies elesewhere, particularly within the USA and the UK. Even across Europe during the 1990s public registration requirements were relaxed.

In practice the distinction between frictional and other types of unemployment may not be so clear. This is a concern voiced in many recent economic accounts. Looking at the pace and nature of recent labour market change, they suggest that the causes of unemployment are more deep seated. Key here is the extent to which unemployment is perceived in cyclical terms or as a more fundamental structural problem.

The notion of **cyclical unemployment** owes much to the work of the influential English economist Keynes (1936). He held that unemployment occurs when there is insufficient purchasing power, or demand, to stimulate production and employ all those who want work. At an individual level this is an outcome of rational responses to market changes, leading an entrepreneur faced with the rising cost of raw materials for instance to scale down. Multiplied throughout the economy such behaviour reduces the work available and the money in circulation until, eventually, individuals see opportunities for expansion and the economy recovers. In the optimism induced by the upswing individuals tend to over-stretch themselves, bringing another downward movement. For Keynes such swings were exacerbated by the short-termist, speculative operation of financial markets. Though these processes were ultimately self-correcting, he contended they could be managed by governments. By stimulating investment, consumer spending and active job creation, they could reduce unemployment; by regulating aggregate demand, they could maintain stability.

In the wake of the Second World War this reasoning gained widespread acceptance. A commitment to full employment became a political fundament in nearly all western societies and a key component of state welfare. With continuous economic growth from the 1950s Keynesian strategies seemed successful. As unemployment climbed again from the 1980s, however, other prognoses came to the fore. These emphasised the impact of structural factors. One was the increasing internationalisation of trade, which for many nullified Keynesian-style interventions (Scharpf, 2001). A second was ongoing technological change, particularly in information and communications. Tied in with these was the accelerating shift in OECD countries away from manufacturing to services and knowledge-based industries. This involved both an intensification of competition and a haemorrhaging of traditional heavy industrial work as labour-intensive production migrated to low-wage countries and manufacturing firms moved to lean production systems.

Opinion divides over the implications of this drawn-out and cross-nationally uneven process. Some emphasise the high reliance of many services on low-paid, manual, part-time, atypical and contingent labour. Others point to more generalised job insecurity and the erosion of post-war notions of lifelong full-time employment as firms respond to increased competition by down-sizing, de-layering and more flexible uses of labour (Jenkins and Sherman, 1979; Beck; 1992; Handy, 1994; Rifkin, 1995). These analyses, with their profound significance for employment policies, have gained widespread media coverage across the developed world. However, assessing the direction and nature of labour market change is complicated by the following.

- The expansion of both the service sector and non-standard working is strongly associated with the growth of female employment. Though its scale varies and full-time female employment is more common in America, France and most Nordic countries, the new part-time service jobs in Europe have been predominantly taken up by women (Sarfarti, 2002). Whether this reflects women's preferences (Hakim 2003) or their limited options in deeply gendered labour markets is hotly disputed, as are the differing pressures outside Europe (Yi and Lee, 2004).
- Economic restructuring has been characterised by both increasing concentrations of ownership in multinational and national corporations and marked growth in small and medium-sized businesses. These developments pose differing, not easily reconcilable, implications for policy-makers.

Recent research has added further layers of complexity to analyses of unemployment. Surveys in America (Cappelli, 1999), the UK (Taylor, 2002) and cross-nationally (Auer and Cazes, 2003) suggest that the scale and nature of some changes have been exaggerated. Job tenure in many countries has been stable over the last decade, whilst temporary and contingent work is little higher than in the past. Nevertheless, the landscape of employment opportunities has altered. Young peoples' transitions into work have become more drawn-out and uncertain, particularly for the low-skilled. Within-job changes appear to be accelerating, leading to a widespread sense of insecurity. Part-time, mainly female, work has become integral to many organisations and a major source of income disparities between households as well as between women and men. Furthermore, the spread of service and more particularly knowledge-intensive industries appears to be segmenting an already highly divided workforce. American and British labour markets in particular seem to be hollowing out, creating an 'hourglass economy' polarised between the high- and low-skilled (Nolan and Slater, 2003). More widely, much service employment growth has been in low-waged, highly routinised manual and back-office jobs. Many of these, it is claimed, are open to the lean production, offshoring and 'onshore-outsourcing' processes already experienced by swathes of manufacturing. They are also vulnerable to shifts in consumer demand and intensified competition (Reich, 1991, 2004).

Viewing these trends, many commentators since the 1980s have argued that unemployment is of a different order to that experienced earlier. For a substantial group it is rooted in the new forces of advanced technological change and **globalisation** (see chapter 13). In this context Keynesian-style welfarism appears less viable. Moreover, many experts hold that structural unemployment, especially in Europe, is compounded by labour market rigidities generated by welfarist interventions. Governments, it is argued, need to trade high protection for more work which, even when low-waged, offers the best form of welfare. This scenario owes much to comparisons between the higher employment delivered by America's open labour markets and those of Europe. As a substitute 'standard interpretation' of unemployment to that offered by post-war analysts (Andersen and Jensen, 2002), it has gained widespread credence amongst policy advisors. Alternatively, the problem has been seen to lie in a lack of preventative measures calling not for withdrawal but reorientation of the state towards a 'social investment strategy' (Esping-Andersen, 1996). For some it also lies in reasserting Keynesian thinking (Smith, 2005).

Beyond these explanations lies an array of 'critical perspectives' with different implications. Whilst Marxists have continued to highlight the instabilities of capitalism and the role of the reserve army of labour within it, feminist and anti-racist research has drawn attention to the operation of gendered and ethnically divided labour markets and the ways these affect employment opportunities (Daly and Rake, 2003). In arguing for sustainable economic growth, a range of green thinking has also questioned prevailing constructions of unemployment and employment and their overly economistic base (Cahill and Fitzpatrick, 2002).

## Unemployment Policies

Given these contested accounts it is not surprising that governments have adopted a mixture of remedies for unemployment. However, alternative approaches have tended to cluster, to some extent, in the ways implied by regime theory.

In dealing with unemployment governments can, as indicated above, address either labour demand or supply, or both. Recent policy in most but not all OECD countries has seen a marked swing away from post-war demand-side to supply-side interventions. Cross-nationally, governments have resorted to a number of similar strategies:

- reducing the labour pool;
- re-engineering benefit systems away from compensation to employment promotion;
- developing re-employment and placement services;
- providing in-work benefits and other support for employers.

However, they have been pursued at different speeds and in distinctive ways with differing connotations and outcomes. Attempts to reconfigure benefit schemes have also met extensive popular resistance in a number of countries, whilst others have made only marginal policy adjustments.

The initial response to the reappearance of unemployment in many countries was to minimise its impact by curbing labour supply. The two main instruments adopted were encouraging early retirement through a variety of incentives for employers and employees and a slackening of regulations regarding disability benefits. Partly in consequence the labour market participation of 55–64-year-old men fell dramatically as individuals were allowed to retire early or were diverted onto incapacity benefits (Maltby, De Vroom, Mirabile and Overbye, 2004). These policies were less pronounced in the USA and East Asia with their very different social security systems. But they too curtailed labour market entry by expanding post-school education, though this was also driven by other considerations.

Social security benefit schemes for unemployed people have from their inception varied in generosity, the balance between them and the extent to which they preserve labour market differentials. The common concern that provisions should not discourage employment, especially among the low-waged, has also been addressed in diverse ways. Generally the liberal regimes, with their heavy reliance on means-testing, have been the least munificent.

Currently, unemployment benefits throughout the OECD are being revamped. In a bid to contain rising public expenditure, claimants' entitlements are being tightened, the level and/or duration of support cut, means-testing increased and definitions of suitable job offers broadened. This process has gone furthest and fastest in the USA and the UK. Elsewhere, reflecting a less individualised conception of unemployment, the pace and scope of benefit changes have been far less harsh and hedged by other support. In corporatist Europe, particularly Germany, France and Italy, deep cuts have until recently been stalled by public disquiet. Concern over the removal of what are perceived as acquired social insurance rights and, in Germany, the structure of unemployment compensation largely accounts for this (Clasen, 2000). Nordic societies have seen more rigorous enforcement of long-standing work-seeking requirements, but still within a more generous accessible net.

Benefit curbs are commonly twinned with 'welfare to work' or 'activation' schemes to speed re-employment. Such schemes further curtail inherited contingency-based unemployment assistance by making it, in varying degrees, conditional upon participation in compulsory work-related activities. Often tailored for particular groups such as the young, these involve training, work experience, job counselling, placement assistance and other measures to improve employability. Here again, following well-publicised initiatives in various American states, liberal regimes have led the way.

Lodemel and Trickey (2001) distinguish four different approaches.

1 Unemployment support in western continental Europe, like France's insertion programmes, is primarily supportive and solidaristic.
2 Social activation measures in Nordic countries are essentially universalistic (Harrysson and Petersson, 2004).
3 American 'work-fare' and 'educ-fare' seems closer to earlier, deterrent relief systems (Piven and Cloward, 1993).
4 The UK 'new deals' are seen, along with those in Denmark and the Netherlands, as forming a fourth 'emergent' hybrid grouping.

However, this classification may not capture all the alternatives. In southern Europe more limited unemployment compensation schemes have meant conditionality has been less of an issue. Meantime, in East Asia what Kwon (2004) conceptualises as 'developmental welfare states' have been under pressure to extend social rights whilst maintaining work requirements and their 'productivist' agendas (Holliday and Wilding, 2003).

Like the variations in benefit arrangements, these permutations of Esping-Andersen's typology are complicated by disparities in other measures to secure labour market attachment. France, Belgium, Portugal, the Netherlands and Germany for instance have introduced subsidies lowering employers' social contributions. Many governments provide assistance with the costs of starting work. The USA, Canada, the UK, France and New Zealand have developed tax credits (see chapter 4, p. 84) designed to 'make work pay' by supplementing the incomes of those on low wages. By widening the gap between earnings and replacement incomes, these get round the disincentives associated with many benefit systems. Though redistributive in that they raise the net pay of the working poor, such 'sweeteners' raise a number of concerns. Earnings 'top ups' also carry the very real danger of sedimenting a low-wage 'junk jobs' sector with few inducements for employers to innovate. In addition, subsidised may displace non-subsidised work rather than increasing the job pool. There are also some problems about the means-testing associated with them, which were explored in chapter 4.

The effectiveness of American-style workfare is also open to question. For its advocates there are many advantages, some political rather than socio-economic (Harrysson and Petersson, 2004), because the scheme:

- addresses budgetary constraints;
- assures voters that the unemployed are being assisted into work and not idling at tax-payers' expense;
- prevents benefit abuse;
- improves the supply of labour;
- directly benefits recipients who can therefore be legitimately expected to participate in programmes they might not otherwise pursue.

Given the diversity of interventions subsumed under the notions of workfare and activation policies more generally, it is difficult to assess their impact on unemployment levels. Despite a number of favourable evaluations, falling unemployment may be more to do with a buoyant macro-economic environment. Most programmes have had more success in securing entry into work than labour market attachment, with the 'easy' rather than the 'hard to place', and in areas of low rather than high concentrations of joblessness (Clasen and van Oorschot, 2002). There is also concern that re-employment is commonly in low-paid insecure positions with limited opportunities for advancement. In a less benign climate the overall effect may be increased 'churning' and competition at the lower end of the labour market. In turn this may depress already low wages and encourage the use of temporary and part-time contracts to the detriment of those in work.

## Influencing Overall Employment

Before discussing the measures open to government, it is important to recall the disputes between neo-liberal and other conceptions of market operations and note that these have been played out differently. The post-war settlement in northern and western Europe was premised on the belief that governments should and could intervene to redress market failures and promote social justice. Securing full employment is integral to this and is still largely adhered to. In the UK, however, this commitment was abandoned by the neo-liberal Thatcher government. More recently, the Labour administration has committed itself to a 'modern definition', i.e. 'equal employment opportunity for all' (HM Treasury, 2004, p. 71), a pledge discussed below. Elsewhere approaches have varied. In Eastern Europe, in the past economic planning started with specifying desired levels of work as against market unpredictabilities. Workforce planning is also a key element in socio-economic policy in Korea and other East Asian states and central to their 'catch-up' strategies. In America, state interventions to influence employment levels are ostensibly left to the market. Nevertheless, governments here as elsewhere continue to use a range of tools to shape the economy and hence levels of employment.

### Influencing the demand for labour

In considering measures to influence the demand for labour, it is difficult to disentangle social from economic policy and measures targeted at unemployment from broader employment interventions. Direct social policy initiatives, as distinct from Keynesian-style fiscal and monetary interventions, centre on job creation and work location. In the past public works programmes were widely used to generate employment. The public sector has also been used as a means of maintaining or boosting employment. Nordic governments, for instance, have long functioned as employers of last resort. Like other Keynesian-style policies this approach has lost favour in recent years. However, the employment effects of continuing high public service expenditure, especially for women, should not be gainsaid. Nor from a UK perspective should that of recent service expansion.

Governments, national and local, can also intervene to influence employers' decisions over the location of work. This may be for long-term economic development or national security purposes, but it may also counter the socio-economic and political costs of regional or local decline and safeguard particular cultures. The instruments used range from planning regulations, subsidies, infrastructuring and government contracts to the siting or relocation of government agencies. Under EU rules, whilst direct subventions to declining industries are usually forbidden, the regional development and social funds provide other means of supporting areas affected by economic change. The direct management of industrial development remains key to social and economic policy in East Asia. In many other countries, however, it has been scaled back amidst concerns over adverse effects on firms' decision-making. Instead, as with unemployment, there has been a common movement towards supply-side measures.

### Influencing labour supply

Government action to either increase or decrease labour supply again meshes economic with social policy concerns. One major and highly contentious issue relating to labour supply with extensive welfare ramifications concerns policies regarding mobility between countries. National governments may, like post-Second World War Australia, subsidise immigration or, as currently, attempt to control migrant numbers and their skills whilst seeking to support those regarded as genuine asylum seekers.

Countries vary temporally and cross-nationally in their active promotion or discouragement of 'internal' labour supply. One common trend is the progressive exclusion of children and increasing numbers of young adults from the workforce. This is due primarily to state-funded or subsidised education combined in the case of younger children with protective regulation. Nonetheless, the impact of high youth unemployment on this process should not be overlooked. In many countries state-funded or -assisted pensions and, more recently, early retirement schemes have curtailed the supply of older workers.

Many societies have also attempted to limit female employment and prevent that of married women and mothers.

Others are beginning to experiment with newer stratagems. Perhaps the best example is the 'polder system' in the Netherlands, which has encouraged expansion of male as well as female part-time work and cut pay differentials between full-time and part-time workers (Visser and Hemerijck, 1997). Other examples include France's controversial thirty-five hour week and wider regulatory changes to support job-sharing. In part these reflect the impact of 'green' concerns and predictions of a jobless growth resulting from technological advances. They have also led to proposals for supporting 'voluntary' non-employment, placing socially useful activities on a par with paid work and the use of basic income schemes. However, in the face of the cost and disincentive effects and competing accounts of the direction of workplace change, radical proposals for less productionist policies (Gorz, 1982; Offe, 1996) have made little headway. Indeed the current weight of policy advice suggests that far from discouraging or redistributing employment, governments need to maximise it. It is in this context that measures to boost labour supply need to be examined.

### Maximising employment

For governments across the developed world attention has shifted from concerns about the absence of work for all to ones about the likelihood of a deficient supply of labour in the face of demographic change (an ageing population and a falling birth rate). This theme is explored in chapter 12, noting the way in which policy proposals are based on relatively firm demographic data but a lack of clear evidence on the way in which the demand for labour will evolve.

In many countries worries are being expressed about the sustainability of early retirement and low economic activity rates, particularly amongst older men. Having engineered this as a means of tackling unemployment, governments now face the trilemmas of retention, re-recruiting early retirees and moving the large numbers on incapacity benefits into employment. It is widely argued that demographic pressures necessitate more than policy reversal. They demand two further developments: maximising labour market participation amongst all those of working age and boosting productivity. Since women constitute the largest pool of partial or non-employment, the challenge here is to do so in ways that also stem falling birth rates. Somewhat paradoxically, expanding female employment also has welfare as well as gender-equality spin-offs in that it is 'one of the most effective' means of combating child poverty and social exclusion (Esping-Andersen, 2002, p. 95).

However, these imperatives link back to, and may be contradicted by, the broader question of sustaining competitiveness in the face of the increasing internationalisation of trade, the spread of complex global supply chains, and the operations of transnational financial and telecommunication markets. The extent to which these and other features of 'globalisation' amount to a new economic order, with distinct welfare effects, is debatable (see chapter 13). Hitherto, heightened competition has been driven more by trade within the developed world than with developing countries. Moreover, growth in global interdependency has been paralleled by that of local markets offering household, recreational and care services that can only be used and therefore produced locally. Nevertheless, the rapid development of China, India, Brazil and other low-wage economies with strong research and science sectors is adding to the competitive pressures on OECD countries.

Looking at these, analysts like Porter (1990) argue that to retain their competitive edge established economies need to move up the value chain and shift from a reliance on high-volume mass production to specialist 'added value' goods and services. This is contingent on a number of factors. Foremost of these is the adoption of high-performance work practices by employers, and their corollary – a skilled creative workforce responsive to shifting purchaser patterns. This thinking has gained widespread currency. It draws on and reaffirms a growing body of opinion that sees high productivity and sustained competitiveness as a function of human resources rather than other factors of production (Becker, 1964; Reich, 1991; Pfeffer, 1998).

*Measures to influence employability*

In the context of the twin concerns about the size of the labour force and high 'value-added' employment, there is extensive attention to issues about the 'quality' of the labour force. Whilst there is widespread agreement on the need for lifelong learning, there are significant variations in approach. They reflect differing views of both the role of employment policy and the nature of lifelong learning.

For its proponents, and the **human capital** theorists on whom they draw, lifelong learning benefits employees, employers and the wider society. Individuals are secured against economic change and gain wider job openings, higher wages and more fulfilling work. Organisations profit from a high-performing workforce and increased productivity as does the economy. Likewise, public services are better placed to meet rising expectations and budgetary constraints.

For individual employers and workers, however, the gains may not be so clear-cut or mutual. From an employer's perspective, the promise of enhanced performance may be offset by higher wage and training costs and the possibility of 'poaching' by competitors who do not provide training. Small organisations may have insufficient resources to support staff development, whilst enterprises trading in low-cost markets may see no need to invest in upskilling despite broader economic needs. To compound matters, employers are only likely to fund or provide organisationally specific training, whereas employees may be seeking rather broader forms of training.

This mix of welfarist, consumer protection and economic concerns underpins policy development in mainland Europe where it has long been held that employee development cannot be left to the market (Rubery and Grimshaw, 2003). Many Southeast Asian countries too found it necessary to adopt a highly statist approach. Though the institutional arrangements vary (Harrison and Kessels, 2004), market deficiencies led governments in both regions to establish:

- national systems of occupational and related qualifications (increasingly competency based);
- national standard-setting and assessment systems;
- state training systems (as in Denmark or Sweden);
- regulation of training providers.

Most have also introduced funding mechanisms to incentivise either employers or employees or both and to maximise opportunities for take-up of training across the workforce or for particular groups (Germany's apprenticeship system) or skills (particularly IT). Some countries, notably France, operate compulsory levies. But to avoid both 'irrelevant' training and the possibility of financing employer and employee outlays that might be made anyway, government subventions generally involve some form of matched contributions, particularly by employers.

Behind these commonalities, however, lie significant differences in governance and policy formation. In much of Southeast Asia, provision is ensconced in national workforce-planning structures, whereas developments in Europe emanate more from tripartite consultative systems, often operating at local and sectoral as well as national levels and involving collective bargaining rights.

Here again we see signs of a difference in regime perspectives. The liberal regimes (particularly the USA and UK) have tended to prefer approaches to vocational training that are essentially voluntaristic, market-based and marked by the absence of coherent national systems and a plethora of unregulated providers. However, there are signs that change is taking place in the UK (bringing us back here to Lodemel and Trickey's characterisation of the UK cited above). It has embarked on an ambitious skills strategy and a campaign to promote high-performance working practices. This involves a more sophisticated skills training strategy and the development of a network of advice services supported by best practice guidance and award schemes akin to those elsewhere in Europe (Bell, Gaj, Hart, Hubler and Schwerdt, 2001; May and Brunsdon, in press). Its approach is heralded as signifying a reformatting of the post-war welfare order into a 'social investment state'. Though conceptualised and operationalised in different ways (Lister, 2004), the term denotes the ways in which governments in many societies are increasingly prioritising enabling asset-building interventions over direct social transfers. Equipping employees to meet the many task and organisational changes they are likely to encounter throughout their working lives constitutes one such 'investment'. Like the coterminous workfare schemes, it promises to meet both welfare and economic needs. It addresses the productivity pressures noted earlier, with the political advantage of a clear return to tax-payers. Moreover, there is argued to be an added benefit in that an accumulation of skilled labour in itself may affect employer behaviour, generating demand for more expertise and levering firms into higher value activities.

These developments are claimed to also bring significant welfare gains, not least in combating social exclusion and widening opportunities. To achieve these, however, means more not less state action. For instance, in championing its 'supply-side agenda for the left' based on 'lifetime access' to education and training (Blair and Schroeder, 1999), the UK government has come under pressure to create new citizen entitlements. Whilst some commentators see lifelong learning as a personal responsibility, a strong current of opinion holds that, as in France, employees should be given a statutory right to paid leave for training and development. Opinion divides over the form of such leave, its focus, whether employees should be compelled to use it and whether it should be funded by the state, employers or both, with employees 'topping up' if they wish. But it is symptomatic of a wider debate about how existing employability arrangements might be strengthened and in ways that reduce inequalities.

## Employment Regulation

The regulation of employer–employee relations was a key element in the post-war welfare settlements in Europe and central to state-managed industrialisation in many East Asian countries. For reasons that can be inferred from the list below, the late twentieth century saw a widespread extension of labour and workplace regulation as governments responded to established and new concerns ranging from health and safety to equalities and other issues arising from the spread of 'atypical' working. Within the EU these pressures were accentuated by the need for a common trading framework. Summarising the options open to governments and the measures taken is a complex task, not eased by the fact that they are subject to judicial decisions and, in many countries, collective bargaining arrangements. Looked at very generally, however, OECD countries have, in differing ways, taken steps to regulate the following:

- recruitment practices;
- termination of employment (dismissal, redundancy, retirement);
- remuneration, i.e. pay (e.g. minimum wages, equal pay requirements) and benefits (pensions, sick pay, redundancy payments);
- working time (e.g. maximum working hours/days/weeks; rest breaks; flexible working requests/family-friendly working);
- holiday and other leave (e.g. maternity, paternity, parental, carer, compassionate leave);
- workplace health and safety;
- prevention of discrimination, promotion of equal opportunities;
- (more variably) provide employees with rights to information and consultation.

These regulations and, on a pro-rata basis, the rights they carry increasingly cover part-time as well as full-time workers and, more variably, those on temporary contracts. Equally fundamentally, employment protection also encompasses trade union membership, recognition and bargaining rights and provisions for worker consultation. The merits of each collective and individual entitlement and regulatory measure are hotly disputed and analysis complicated by the varying policy mixes adopted by different countries. Looked at overall, however, inventories like the one above suggest that on most dimensions the liberal regimes (particularly the USA) are the least regulated, whilst conservative and social-democratic regimes provide the highest levels of employee protection and involvement. In comparative terms, the last named also have the most proactive equality strategies.

Unlike the USA, workplace regulation across much of Europe is framed by consultative systems and a social partnership approach. In many senses employment is 'perceived as a social relation, not simply a contractual issue' (Hyman, 2004, p. 421). With its belated minimum wage and modest application of EU requirements, the UK has followed its own path.

For neo-liberal analysts it is these differences that ultimately make for high levels of employment in the USA and the UK and continuing unemployment in Europe. In their view freely negotiated contracts between employers and employees, and employers' untrammelled ability to deploy labour lie at the heart of free, functioning markets. Such a view is challenged by those who argue the following.

- The predominance of broad comparisons between America and Europe is misleading. It focuses on Germany and France, overlooking developments elsewhere (Bonoli and Sarfati, 2002) and the place of labour regulation in other, particularly East Asian economies. Despite comprehensive 'employee-friendly' measures, unemployment has for instance fallen in Sweden, Denmark and the Netherlands, whilst Korea's post-1997 recovery saw enhanced worker protection and union rights as well as improved benefits (Harasty, 2004).
- These developments and the prevalence of 'top-up' practices amongst large enterprises demonstrate that there is a strong business case for regulation as improving rather than constraining labour market functioning (Deakin, 2001). In economies based on human rather than other assets, job security is a prerequisite for gaining the employee commitment necessary to sustain organisational flexibility and competitiveness (Marsden, 1999; Mitchie and Sheehan-Quinn, 2001). By the same token, employee rights and workplace regulations are essential tools in governmental drives for high-performance working and raising productivity. As such they can be used to foster high-quality rather than the low-paid low-quality work associated with the USA's flexible economy (Coates, 2005).
- Finally, and fundamentally, there is an equally powerful welfare case for protecting workers, the weaker signatories to the employment relationship. At the very least a floor of workplace rights would seem to be an essential co-requisite to supply-side measures designed to maximise employment and centre welfare on paid employment.

Crucially, it also contributes to social equity. Certainly, the USA and the UK, the two least regulated economies, are the most unequal.

## Conclusions

Once again in this chapter regime theory seems, with modifications, to suggest some bases for comparison between societies. One approach to this modification is to recognise (1) the emergence in Europe of new compromises between the liberal approach and a more regulatory approach in Denmark, the Netherlands and the UK and (2) some of the special characteristics of the state-directed productivist regimes of East Asia. This is supported by comparative human resource management studies that point to distinctive 'employment regimes' (Hyman, 2004). These embody different property and business systems, variations in financial and product markets, their governance and policy-making processes, as well as labour market, gender and employment policy. They draw on the literature on 'varieties of capitalism' (see chapter 2, p. 39; also Whitely, 2000; Hall and Soskice, 2001; Perraton and Cliff, 2004; Coates, 2005) and thus link to, but go beyond, Esping-Andersen's classification.

Nonetheless, there are signs of cross-national change propelled in part by the pressure of international bodies like the OECD and EU. Of these the most significant for this chapter are the near-universal importance attached to work as the best form of welfare and the expanding reach of employment policy. For the UK the increasing centrality of employment policy is particularly significant. The question that follows is whether harnessing the two will lead to a subordination of welfare to economic concerns and social to economic goals.

### GUIDE TO FURTHER READING

Research in this area tends to date quickly. If used critically, the best way of keeping up with current developments and ongoing debates over the direction and shape of employment policy is through the OECD's many publications (see www.oecd.org). A different perspective can be gleaned from the studies found on the ILO website (www.ilo.org) through its many links, and from Gough et al.'s (2004) ground-breaking study of the 'informal security and insecurity' regimes characteristic of the many societies where there is little secure formal employment or national action. Walker and Wong (2005) include some good material on these issues in East Asia.

# CHAPTER 6

# HEALTH SERVICES

## Introduction: Identifying the Issues

It was noted in chapter 1 that it is often unsatisfactory to use input measures to compare countries. This is particularly the case with health policy, where it is important to look for relevant output or outcome measures. However, evaluating these is not easy. Good health does not depend solely upon direct medical provision. It also depends on a whole range of social, economic and environmental factors.

There are issues to be addressed about the extent to which the maintenance of good health depends on a combination of the decisions people take for themselves and the protection from risks provided by public policies other than medicine. An extreme version of this position sees medicine as an almost unnecessary intrusion into health maintenance, indeed even as a source of illness ('iatrogenic disease'; see Illich, 1977). A more moderate version stresses the way in which health improvements in societies have depended more on environmental improvements and raised living standards than on medical advances (McKeown, 1980).

Another important question is that alongside issues about the medical treatment of the sick, there is a range of issues about the care of the sick, which have been the concerns of families and communities throughout the ages, regardless of whether any medical intervention is feasible or not. The reason for identifying this here is that there is a danger of confusing 'care' in this sense with 'treatment', the direct application of medical skills and technologies. Medical expertise may be needed to recommend the best kind of care but that expertise is not necessarily required to provide it. Looking at the issue the other way round, the successful application of medical expertise may require that people are cared for in a satisfactory way.

This distinction is being laboured a little here because of a variety of important policy questions that flow from the alternative ways 'care' and 'treatment' may be combined. The hospital has evolved from a long-term caring institution, where social and nursing care were generally more important than medical care, to a site for the practice of high-technology medicine. The modern hospital generally endeavours to confine its provision of inpatient care to very brief episodes in which patients need to be present to be given intensive medical or surgical attention. Accordingly, there are issues about the extent to which the nursing and social care of the sick then occurs largely in patients' homes, with implications for themselves, their families and perhaps social care services as much as for health services. Such a focus on the caring side highlights the fact that (1) doctors themselves need to work in partnership with other carers (both formal and informal) to ensure that poor 'care' does not undermine 'treatment' and (2) that within health services themselves there are other workers, professional and non-professional, whose roles particularly concern the caring side.

These two key issues about health care and health policy are connected. Hence, in this chapter, whilst the focus will be on the way in which health policy has developed as a way of regulating and providing modern scientific medicine (and dentistry), it will be recognised that there is a variety of issues to be considered about:

- the extent to which health status improvements in societies are attributable to medicine;
- tendencies for so-called 'health services' to be primarily 'illness services';
- the importance of care in a wide sense for the well-being of those treated by health services (an issue that has implications for other services as well as for those parts of health-care activity often regarded as the responsibilities of individuals and their families).

The factors outlined above about the need to see health policy in a wider context and to recognise the complex relationship between 'treatment' and 'care' lead on to one other issue that must be mentioned before the discussion moves on to more specific points. Any system of publicly supported health care has to draw boundaries around the services it will provide. These will identify treatments that will not be provided (e.g. cosmetic surgery). They may exclude some treatments because of doubts about their efficacy (e.g. some forms of 'folk medicine'). There may also be, often controversial, attempts to exclude 'heroic' surgical interventions or very expensive medicines where chances of success are low and costs are high (e.g. some transplant surgery). As systems run into difficulties with scarce resources, these boundaries may be redrawn. Thus the issues about what health care can do for people and the issues about what governments will let it do (at least with public money) can become very confused.

The pursuit of good health, the quest for cures for diseases and concern about the care of the sick have been universal preoccupations of human societies. Health policy, implying the involvement of the state in these concerns, is a comparatively modern phenomenon. Its emergence, like all the policy concerns discussed in this book, parallels the development of the active state in general. But it has also been linked with the development of scientific medicine. This has involved the identification of a complex range of activities, which have required regulation. These activities have become costly not merely because the application of modern therapies is expensive but also because the development of those therapies rests on costly education, research and equipment. These have provided a variety of motives for developing ways of socialising the costs of medicine, spreading them so that they do not necessarily fall upon the very sick at the time of their greatest need.

## Alternative Roles for the State in Relation to Health Care

There are a number of roles the state may play in relation to health care: (1) regulator, (2) funder/purchaser and (3) provider/planner. Any specific system is likely to involve a combination of all or most of these roles. While logically there is no reason why the state cannot be involved in planning and providing without funding, in practice the three are likely to be combined, although the state may be only a part funder. This section will look at what these roles may involve, some of the alternative ways these roles may be fulfilled and some of the ways they may be combined.

### The regulator role

Governments have accepted the case for regulation of the activities of doctors, not necessarily performing that regulation themselves but delegating regulatory responsibilities to professional organisations. Similar regulatory issues have also arisen with regard to other health professionals and semi-professionals: dentists, opticians, pharmacists, nurses, midwives, etc. Governments are also likely to be concerned about standards of hygiene, about work conditions and about standards of care in hospitals, clinics and nursing homes.

With the extension of private insurance into health care, some states became concerned about the need to regulate business practices in this area of activity. Customers were vulnerable to exploitation because of their need for help. In some societies the private insurance option was then seen as the way forward for the care of all. This meant that the state moved to require individuals to take on insurance, to require companies to offer policies to all and to lay down certain standards for these arrangements. Such an approach put the state in a position in which it might be hard to resist demands for it to 'underwrite' the protection offered, subsidising bad risks and companies that got into difficulties (note the similar issues in respect of pensions, discussed on pp. 80–1). In many societies efforts to universalise private insurance can be seen to have been a stage down the road towards state-supported 'social' insurance (Immergut, 1993).

### The funder or purchaser role

For the purposes of this discussion the role of the state as a funder of health care has deliberately been separated from consideration of other roles. Just like the regulator role the funder role can be seen as independent of the other roles, notwithstanding the fact that a strong funder role for the state tends to lead to its involvement in provision and planning of services and, at the very least, to the strengthening of the regulator role. Nevertheless, when health care is examined comparatively, it is clear that countries combine these roles in very different ways.

The alternative approaches to state funding involve either taxation (including local taxation) or a state-administered or -regulated insurance system. However, these two may occur in combination; in particular, an insurance system may receive tax subsidies. In certain circumstances the distinction between the two approaches becomes so blurred that an insurance scheme may in practice be described as a 'health tax' scheme (note the questions raised in chapter 3 about whether payers distinguish insurance contributions from taxes). The analysis is then further complicated by the public/private mix in health-care funding. State systems will be found that aim to be as far as possible comprehensive, together with systems where there are substantial areas of activity left to private (but probably insurance supported) provision and systems where it is the public sector rather than the private sector which is the residual one. In practice, five variations on these funding themes are found in OECD member countries:

1 comprehensive tax-funded schemes (UK, Sweden);
2 tax-funded schemes involving elements of earmarked taxation, often called health insurance (Canada, Australia, Hungary);
3 comprehensive insurance schemes (France, Japan, South Korea);
4 partial schemes involving public and private insurance plus elements of tax funding (Germany, Netherlands).
5 residual systems with some injection of tax funds and state-controlled insurance into broadly privately funded systems (USA).

Tax funding is probably the most straightforward way for a state to assume the funder role. Yet even this model is susceptible to many variations. First, states take many forms themselves: they may be federal, they may have highly developed systems of local government and they may have partially autonomous administrative systems. Thus whilst the health service systems of Australia, Canada, Sweden and the UK all fall, in general terms, into the tax-funded category, that of Canada involves delegation to provinces, that of Australia federal funding but state-level providers, that of Sweden delegation to local government and that of the UK a rather complex (and changing) system of partial administrative devolution. These are important issues for the performance of the service in each country, producing inevitable variations in the forms it takes.

Tax funding may involve alternatives: there may simply be funding out of general taxation, there may be specifically earmarked taxation for health (as identified by the use of a separate category for Canada and Australia above) and there may be elements of **cost-sharing** with local taxation. The hybrid forms of sharing between tax and insurance (as in Canada and Australia) highlight the question of whether it might not be more appropriate to call a universal insurance contribution in which the link between payment and entitlement is exceptionally weak a 'tax'. Crucial here is the fact that concerns about health provision for all lead governments to devise ways of extending coverage to (1) the families of insurance contribution payers and (2) to people with incomes too low to pay contributions.

An aspect of this distinction, and perhaps another reason for describing the Australian system as an insurance-based one rather than a tax-funded one (see for example the usage in Palmer and Short, 1994), is the role the patient is allowed to play in making an initial 'purchase' of care. In the Australian case there are options for physicians as to whether to charge the patient and leave him or her to reclaim from the state or whether to bill the state directly. The picture is then further confused by the range of situations in which the provider can offer a private alternative option or charge for supplementary services.

An important and growing form of cost-sharing, even in tax-funded health-care systems, is the expectation that patients will pay some part of the cost of their treatment (see Blank and Burau, 2004, pp. 93–6). Such payments may include charges for prescriptions, fixed charges for consultations, contributions towards dental treatment and charges for the 'hotel' costs of inpatient stays. There may also be situations in which government imposes reimbursement limits for services but allows practitioners to charge more (this has been a controversial aspect of the French system; see Wilsford in Ambler, 1991). In some systems which initially aspired to offer a free service, these charges have increased as a response to government concerns about the growing cost of health care, being seen as ways both to raise money and of trying to curb unreasonable demands on systems. As they have grown, two effects have occurred. One is that some universalistic systems have turned back towards some of the forms of means-testing that were often characteristic of earlier systems in that society. The other is that incentives have increased for a minority of citizens to opt for private health care.

No democratic state that has developed a comprehensive publicly funded health-care system has entirely outlawed private medicine. This leaves a situation in which wealthy citizens may opt for private care. This may be done to get swifter attention, to get care superior to that offered in publicly funded institutions (more luxurious 'hotel' conditions, more privacy, etc.) or to get treatment the state is unprepared to offer. This demand by the well-off, at the margins of the state system, has led to opportunities for insurance companies, in the process spreading private care beyond the ranks of the very rich. This development has been particularly strong in the USA, the Netherlands and France (Blank and Burau, 2004, quoting OECD health data which does not include Switzerland, probably another country where insurance is highly developed). Health insurance is particularly important in the USA, where employers often include health insurance as part of the contractual deal for their employees. In Australia, where the public funding of health care has been so significant an area of controversy between the political parties that comprehensive schemes have in the recent past been set up, then abolished and then imposed again (Palmer and Short, 1994, chapters 1 and 4), private insurance is also strong.

One feature of a mix of public and private medicine in which the former is dominant is that the public sector is likely to subsidise the private one. If doctors are trained in public hospitals but can then practise in private ones, the latter will secure the benefit of their expensive training. Similarly the private sector is likely to benefit from developments in knowledge from research in the public sector. Much the same occurs when doctors move between countries and when research findings are disseminated internationally.

There are other forms of cross-subsidy. If patients have a general entitlement to state health services, then they can choose to confine their private care to situations where the private sector offers special advantages, when waiting lists are long for example. Private hospitals can choose to carry out only those procedures where returns to their investment will be high, for example straightforward surgery making relatively low demands on expensive equipment. They can enjoy the protection that if complications arise the public system cannot morally refuse to take over the case. A justification for this cross-subsidy in tax-funded systems is provided inasmuch as the purchasers of private health care are also tax-payers contributing to the cost of the public sector. The benefits of cross-subsidy have the effect of muting the complaint that private patients should not have to pay for a state sector they do not use. In any society, the more the private sector is able to secure itself wide support amongst the well-off and become a sector offering comprehensive health care, the more vociferous will become the call for a break from a universal tax-funded model for the state. In such a context any weakening of the capacity of the public sector to meet need, particularly lengthening waiting lists for operations the private sector is willing to take on, stimulates private-sector growth. Another way in which a mixed pattern of care may grow, also evident in the history of the UK health service, is if the private sector is allowed to offer extra benefits in partnership with the public sector or to cushion (through private insurance) the impact of the cost-sharing that sector requires of patients.

The insurance approach to the state-funding role in health services, with the state underwriting, subsidising, perhaps managing and certainly regulating contributory insurance, perhaps copes with this public/private tension better than a universal tax-based state health service. However, to present the issue like that is probably to confuse result with cause. It has been the very power of the protectors of the private model, manifested largely in modern times by private insurance, which first confined state intervention to the filling of gaps in private insurance. In attempting to resolve the problems with providing universal health care in this way, many states not unnaturally went on to gradually shift their systems from private insurance domination to state insurance domination (Immergut, 1993).

Where states have sought to develop comprehensive health insurance systems the details can be very complex. That complexity often derives from a gradual evolution away from private insurance. France's compulsory national health insurance covers 99% of the population, but is organised into a complex network of quasi-autonomous funds (Caisses Nationales) together with friendly societies and private insurers.

Germany and the Netherlands provide interesting examples of what have been described above as 'partial schemes', with lower-income people insured compulsorily and many higher-income people voluntary members. Differentiation between types of contributors, based on occupational status or income, together with provisions for opting out of all or part of the scheme with corresponding differences in benefits, may involve explicit provisions for choice by contributors about levels of premiums to pay with corresponding alternative benefits. This is particularly likely where private companies or organisations are partners. In such a situation the state's role may be to regulate in order to secure a minimum standard, and to expect this for those it has to subsidise, but to allow a wide range of possibilities above that minimum.

One issue that arises when there are, as in Germany, alternative insurance schemes which individuals may join is inequities in the costs and/or services available to different socio-economic groups. In Germany, health insurance contributions vary in the percentages they charge, with many schemes at the expensive end of the range containing 'disproportionate numbers of the poor and unhealthy' (Moran in Clasen and Freeman, 1994, p. 97). This has encouraged state moves towards creating greater uniformity. In Korea, the increasing demand for state intervention to reduce such inequities led to the unification of the scheme (Shin, 2003).

The most obvious example of what was described above as a 'residual system' of public funding of health care is that of the USA. There are two key state ingredients.

1 Medicare: a federal insurance programme for persons over 65 years of age that is tax supported but to which individuals are required to pay low premiums and for which there are 'cost-sharing' charges often covered by individuals through supplementary private insurance.

2 Medicaid: a system of health care cost subsidy for low-income people linked to the public welfare (social assistance) system and supported by federal and state taxation.

Whilst variants of either tax funding or insurance funding of health services dominate in modern societies, there are two other ways in which the state subsidises health services. One of these is in situations in which it provides specific services and/or controls over sick individuals in the name of the 'public interest'. If the state insists that people with fevers should be treated in isolated institutions or that mentally ill people should be incarcerated, it is likely to have to pay all or most of the cost of this. Although actions in these two categories are rare today, their importance in the nineteenth century was a major influence on the development of large state-owned institutions. Their modern equivalents are likely to be less draconian measures designed to promote public health, limit the spread of disease and provide responses to natural disasters.

The state may also inject funds into health care because of concern about the health of its own employees, particularly its military. Finally, state investments in medical education and research may provide an element of public funding which also benefits private health-care systems.

This discussion of funding has provided little in the way of figures, on levels of funding or on the nature of the public/private mix in various countries. This is done in a later section.

### The provider and/or planner role for the state

The relationship between the role of the state as funder and the role of the state as provider can logically take any of four forms: funder and provider, neither funder nor provider, funder but not provider, and provider but not funder. However, the state is normally involved in funding to some degree, so the crucial alternatives involve the relationship between the nature of provision and the funding method. The alternatives are set out in table 6.1. A third dimension could be added to this table by making a distinction between institutions and services; this complication will be introduced from time to time. In view of what has already been said about insurance, readers should not be surprised to find that some very complicated mixed forms occur.

The history of health provision in the UK has involved what may generally be seen as an evolution from category 4 in the above

**Table 6.1** Relationship between the nature of provision and the funding method

| Funding | State as provider | |
|---|---|---|
| | Yes | No |
| Tax | 1 | 2 |
| Insurance | 3 | 4 |

taxonomy towards category 1 and then some shift away towards category 2. In the period 1911 to 1948, the main state contribution was social insurance (plus the poor law), the main providers of **primary care** were general practices (operating as private businesses), whilst hospital care was available in voluntary and local authority-owned hospitals. Since 1948 there has been a tax-funded universal health service. Between 1948 and 1990 the state owned all the hospitals providing health service care. General practitioners, whilst allowed to continue as self-employed workers under contract to the health service, lost the right to buy and sell practices. After 1990, hospitals became self-governing 'trusts', still in the state system but with some autonomy and a right to do private work. There was an effort to make the system a quasi-market one in which primary carers bought services from those providing **secondary care**. At the end of the century, the system moved away from any real effort to 'mimic' the market but the notion of a two-tiered system in which the former commissioned services from the latter was continued. Included within this is an option, under certain conditions, for services to be bought by public-sector organisations from private ones.

Saltman and von Otter (1992; see also Saltman 1998) have demonstrated similar complexities in the Swedish system, where local authorities are the key units in the system and recent developments have also involved the evolution of mixed provider systems. Federal systems like those of Australia and Canada have, as already noted, similar characteristics. However, there is a contrast to be made between these two countries inasmuch as in the former the providers are still public bodies (albeit not federal government run) whereas in the latter many private organisations are providers (Deber, 1993). France comes rather more clearly into category 3 as far as hospitals are concerned, whilst the Netherlands is in category 4.

All the cases where funding and provision are not unified require quite complex arrangements to deal with issues such as:

- the making, variation and termination of contracts;
- determination of the amounts and forms of reimbursement for services provided;
- the ways in which public and privately funded activities may be mixed;
- the rights of patients in respect of choice of services and the avenues for the redress of grievances;
- determination of where the benefits or costs of 'externalities' may fall (health prevention, medical education, research, etc.);
- monitoring of standards and the determination of needs for new services.

The various mixtures of provision tend to lead governments to assume a planning role in the absence of overall direct control. The interest in the viability of mixed market or quasi-market models for the provision of health care involved a belief that the 'hidden hand' of the market beloved of the classical economist could replace planning (for discussion of this see Le Grand, 1990; Glennerster, 1992, chapter 10; Hudson, 1994). The examples of the UK, Sweden and Finland studied by Saltman and von Otter suggest three reasons why this is not the case.

First, many ventures in health care, particularly in hospital care, are very big business. Market entry costs are therefore enormous. It would be a rash entrepreneur indeed who engaged in investment in a new hospital without some clear guarantee of 'business'; only some kind of planning process can offer that. In the UK case, an option has been developed in which private capital has been brought into the health services, with the state shouldering the risk. This has been criticised as guaranteeing private profits but leaving the state with long-run cost problems (Pollock, 2004).

Second, there are a variety of situations in health care where 'externalities' are very considerable. Medical education and research have already been identified as creating situations where others are bound to benefit from investment in these activities. These, together with the organisation of efforts to deal with rare diseases and to supply special forms of treatment, call for some degree of regulation and planning, at the very least.

Third, health care is a topic about which everyone, not surprisingly, has strong feelings. Health-care organisation decisions are therefore very much concerns of everyday party politics. Cries to 'keep politics out of health care' are a waste of breath. Hence issues about 'gaps' in services, issues about the closure of services, and so on are kept on the public agenda. If the outcome is not necessarily 'planning' in some ideal sense, it certainly is interference with market forces and efforts to match resources to political rather than economic demands.

## Evaluating Health Services: Inputs

Table 6.2 sets out information on health expenditure in the OECD countries. The countries are listed from the highest spender (as a percentage of GDP) to the lowest one. The second column gives the public sector spend as a percentage of GDP, and the third cites the public spend as a percentage of the total spend.

There are great differences in the levels of expenditure, but in only three nations (USA, Mexico and Korea) does the private spend exceed the public one (though Switzerland and Greece come close). All the countries where over 80 per cent of health expenditure is public are European except for Japan. There does not seem to be a division of nations closely corresponding to Esping-Andersen's regimes. Apart from the USA, all the nations in the 'liberal' group have systems dominated by the public sector, with Canada and Australia featuring as quite high spenders overall. It is impossible to find a clear social democratic–conservative division, but there is some basis for a north–south division in the European group.

This suggestion about a rather different 'regime' pattern for health care is supported by Bambra (2005a,b), who explicitly 'tests' Esping-Andersen's theory by looking at health policy for the dates he used in his work (1980) in terms of three measures:

- private health expenditure as a percentage of GDP;
- private hospital beds as a percentage of total bed stock;
- the percentage of the population covered by the state health system.

She arrives at three 'groups' that have much in common with the suggestions above, inasmuch as the 'liberal' group of nations is split.

There must be some question as to whether the 'liberal' model is an influence on some of the later additions to the OECD group, such as Mexico, though it seems to have had little impact on the former Communist states included in table 6.2. It is instructive to look at the role of the public sector in nations outside the OECD group. World Health Organisation statistics enable this to be done and table 6.3

**Table 6.2** Health expenditures for various OECD countries, 2003

| Country | Total health expenditure as percentage of GDP | Public spend as percentage of total spend |
|---|---|---|
| USA | 15 | 44 |
| Switzerland | 11.5 | 59 |
| Germany | 11.1 | 78 |
| Norway | 10.3 | 84 |
| France | 10.1 | 76 |
| Finland | 10.1 | 77 |
| Canada | 9.9 | 70 |
| Greece | 9.9 | 51 |
| Netherlands | 9.8 | 62 |
| Portugal | 9.6 | 70 |
| Belgium | 9.6 | _[a] |
| Australia | 9.3 | 68 |
| Sweden | 9.2 | 85 |
| Denmark | 9.0 | 83 |
| Italy | 8.4 | 75 |
| New Zealand | 8.1 | 79 |
| Japan | 7.9 | 82 |
| Hungary | 7.8 | 71 |
| Spain | 7.7 | 70 |
| UK | 7.7 | 83 |
| Austria | 7.6 | 70 |
| Czech Republic | 7.5 | 91 |
| Ireland | 7.3 | 75 |
| Mexico | 6.2 | 46 |
| Poland | 6.0 | 72 |
| Slovak Republic | 5.9 | 88 |
| Korea | 5.6 | 49 |

[a] Data not available.

*Source*: data from OECD (2005b). Figures for 2003, except in the cases of Australia, Austria, Hungary, Ireland, Portugal, Korea, Sweden and the UK where it is 2002.

looks at a sample of these. These statistics are for two years earlier than the OECD ones, but they nevertheless bring out some strong contrasts. Nations are again listed from the highest spender to the lowest.

**Table 6.3** Health expenditures for various countries, 2000

| Country | Total health expenditure as percentage of GDP | Public spend as percentage of total spend |
|---|---|---|
| Argentina | 8.9 | 55 |
| South Africa | 8.7 | 42 |
| Brazil | 7.6 | 41 |
| Zimbabwe | 7.4 | 51 |
| Cuba | 7.1 | 86 |
| Iran | 6.4 | 42 |
| Jamaica | 6.2 | 47 |
| Tunisia | 6.2 | 74 |
| Mozambique | 5.7 | 67 |
| Russian Federation | 5.3 | 70 |
| China | 5.3 | 37 |
| India | 5.1 | 18 |
| Saudi Arabia | 4.4 | 74 |
| Ghana | 4.3 | 56 |
| Pakistan | 4.1 | 25 |
| Ukraine | 4.2 | 68 |
| Bangladesh | 3.6 | 45 |
| Indonesia | 2.7 | 24 |

*Source*: data from WHO (2005).

These nations all slot in towards the end of the OECD chart, though it must be pointed out that the figures in the first column are percentages of often very low per-capita GDP levels. Only in two cases does this exceed a purchasing power equivalent of $US10,000 per head (Argentina and Saudi Arabia). Only one nation in the OECD sample (see table 6.4), significantly Mexico, has a per-capita GDP below this figure and most have levels between twice and three times it. We return to this subject below.

However, it is interesting to note the big differences within these nations in the public share of the spend. To what extent may it be assumed that those with a high public proportion have a more egalitarian spread of health expenditure? It would be rash to jump to this conclusion from the spending figures alone; obviously in some cases the relatively well-to-do (particularly public officials and the military) may be the main beneficiaries.

Whilst the focus of this book is on public policy, from the viewpoint of a society as a whole it is the issues about overall health status and correspondingly about total expenditure which are important. A view can be taken that it is only state expenditure that should be a matter for public policy, since what individuals spend their money on is their own concern. Alternatively, it can be regarded as worrying that individuals are spending high proportions of their incomes on their health care, on the grounds that this is an inefficient use of resources. In this discussion the determinants of *both* indices will be considered, whilst recognising that there may be issues about the relationship between the two. Thus an exceptionally high level of private expenditure (as in the USA) may suggest that the state could do a more cost-efficient job than private enterprise. Conversely, a relatively low level of state expenditure that is at the same time a high proportion of total expenditure may offer evidence of a deficient effort by the state, evidence that the state is very good at cost control or evidence for a need to stimulate the private sector. These are alternative interpretations of the situation in the UK. It all depends on what may be taken as an appropriate yardstick for a satisfactory level of expenditure, and that all depends on the determinants of levels of expenditure.

Thus there are a number of factors to be taken into account in evaluating expenditure figures and in comparing data from different countries. First, there is an association between overall economic achievement and expenditure on health. In the comments on the World Health Organisation statistics, attention was given to that issue. Table 6.4 returns to it, with respect to the OECD group of nations. Table 6.4 indicates a distinct tendency for the richer nations to spend not just more but proportionately more than the poor nations. The exceptions to this obviously attract questions. What is it about Greece, Portugal and Hungary that leads them to spend so proportionately highly on health care despite their relative poverty? Contrastingly, why do rich Norway, Ireland and Korea (also to some extent Japan, the UK, Finland and Austria) spend proportionately so much less? Beware rushing into assumptions about these data, particularly ones about relative national hypochondria, bearing in mind the warning at the beginning of this chapter about interpreting input statistics. There may be issues here about the efficiency of services.

In all the relatively low-spending countries other then Korea the public spend is proportionately high. But there are also questions to raise about other differences. It will make a difference whether a nation has a comparatively young population. This is likely to be important in explaining the Korean case. From there we need to go on to other influences on health that lie outside health services, influencing lifestyles

**Table 6.4** Relationship between health expenditure as a percentage of GDP and per-capita GDP

| Country | Total health expenditure as percentage of GDP | GDP per head in $US (using purchasing power parities) |
|---|---|---|
| USA | 15 | 37,600 |
| Switzerland | 11.5 | 30,400 |
| Germany | 11.1 | 26,300 |
| Norway | 10.3 | 36,100 |
| France | 10.1 | 27,800 |
| Finland | 10.1 | 27,400 |
| Canada | 9.9 | 31,000 |
| Greece | 9.9 | 19,500 |
| Netherlands | 9.8 | 29,100 |
| Portugal | 9.6 | 18,400 |
| Belgium | 9.6 | 28,400 |
| Australia | 9.3 | 28,500 |
| Sweden | 9.2 | 28,100 |
| Denmark | 9.0 | 29,800 |
| Italy | 8.4 | 26,100 |
| New Zealand | 8.1 | 22,800 |
| Japan | 7.9 | 28,000 |
| Hungary | 7.8 | 14,600 |
| Spain | 7.7 | 23,200 |
| UK | 7.7 | 29,000 |
| Austria | 7.6 | 28,500 |
| Czech Republic | 7.5 | 16,700 |
| Ireland | 7.3 | 33,200 |
| Mexico | 6.2 | 9,400 |
| Poland | 6.0 | 11,500 |
| Slovak Republic | 5.9 | 13,000 |
| Korea | 5.6 | 20,300 |

*Source*: data carried forward from tables 2.1 and 6.2.

and well-being, particularly the well-being of the poor. It is therefore important to look at outcome measures.

## Health Outcomes

In the case of health care, few measures are available that provide direct evidence on system 'achievements' inasmuch as the objectives of health services are to improve health status in general. What is available is evidence on, in a sense, the failures of the system, namely numbers dying and numbers unwell. Turn this on its head and it may be possible to regard low numbers as evidence of system achievement. Comparisons of data of this kind offer evidence on health status differences between different nations and groups and on trends over time. Mortality and morbidity statistics are in this rather back-to-front sense ultimate *outcome* measures for health services.

Interpretation of mortality and morbidity data is by no means problem-free. Mortality data are obviously important. General mortality rates need to be read carefully, adjusted to take into account the age structure of the population. Demographers calculate age-specific mortality rates. Untimely death may offer particularly telling evidence on the health problems of a society. One death rate that has therefore been given particular attention has been the **infant mortality** rate: deaths of children under one year of age standardised to take into account the overall numbers at risk. Table 6.5 sets out data from the OECD group of countries on this, and on expectation of life for females (who live longer than males in modern societies). The countries are listed from those with the lowest infant mortality rate to those with the highest. The infant mortality data reveal differences much more clearly than the life expectancy data, the nations being bunched remarkably close together in the latter distribution.

Examining the infant mortality data in terms of Esping-Andersen's regimes throws up one issue: the tendency of the 'liberal' group of nations to have poorer records in respect of the prevention of infant mortality. All the nations in the list that have emerged from Soviet domination, except the Czech Republic, have relatively high rates too. The figure for Mexico indicates how infant mortality differences highlight welfare differences between different parts of the world, a point that will be further evident from the WHO figures cited in table 6.6.

The last column of table 6.5 repeats figures from table 6.2 on the percentage of health spend accounted for by the public sector. What this does once again is highlight the exceptional position of the USA. Spending on health in the USA is high overall but the size of the public sector is limited and there are relatively poor records on the crucial infant mortality indicator. However, the fact that the other 'liberal' regimes have relatively poor infant mortality rates despite being relatively high public spenders emphasises the point made in the introduction about the extent to which health outcomes are likely to be influenced by many other things in addition to health expenditures.

**Table 6.5** Infant mortality rates and female life expectancies in OECD countries, 2003

| Country | Infant mortality rate (deaths/1000 live births) | Female life expectancy (years) | Public spend on health as percentage of total spend |
|---|---|---|---|
| Japan | 3.0 | 83 | 82 |
| Finland | 3.1 | 82 | 70 |
| Sweden | 3.1 | 82 | 85 |
| Norway | 3.4 | 82 | 84 |
| France | 3.9 | 83 | 76 |
| Czech Republic | 3.9 | 79 | 91 |
| Spain | 4.1 | 83 | 70 |
| Portugal | 4.1 | 81 | 70 |
| Germany | 4.2 | 81 | 78 |
| Belgium | 4.3 | 81 | _a |
| Switzerland | 4.3 | 83 | 59 |
| Italy | 4.3 | 83 | 75 |
| Denmark | 4.4 | 80 | 83 |
| Austria | 4.5 | 82 | 70 |
| Australia | 4.8 | 83 | 68 |
| Greece | 4.8 | 81 | 51 |
| Netherlands | 4.8 | 81 | 62 |
| Ireland | 5.1 | 80 | 75 |
| UK | 5.3 | 81 | 83 |
| Canada | 5.4 | 82 | 70 |
| New Zealand | 5.6 | 81 | 79 |
| Korea | 6.2 | 80 | 49 |
| USA | 7.0 | 80 | 44 |
| Poland | 7.0 | 79 | 72 |
| Hungary | 7.3 | 77 | 71 |
| Slovak Republic | 7.9 | 78 | 88 |
| Mexico | 20.1 | 77 | 46 |

[a] Data not available.

*Source*: data from OECD (2005b). Data are for 2001 or 2002 in several cases, but changes between years are very slight.

All the countries listed in table 6.6 have higher infant mortality rates than those listed in table 6.5 (excluding Mexico) with the exception of Cuba. Female life expectancies are generally lower, the exceptions being Cuba, Jamaica and Argentina. But what is really significant is

**Table 6.6** Infant mortality rates and female life expectancies for various non-OECD countries, 2000

| Country | Infant mortality rate (deaths/1000 live births) | Female life expectancy (years) | Public spend on health as percentage of total spend |
|---|---|---|---|
| Cuba | 7.1 | 77.5 | 86 |
| Jamaica | 12.5 | 76.6 | 47 |
| Russian Federation | 15.5 | 72.0 | 70 |
| Ukraine | 16.2 | 73.3 | 68 |
| Argentina | 16.8 | 77.8 | 55 |
| Saudi Arabia | 23.9 | 73.5 | 74 |
| Tunisia | 24.0 | 73.4 | 74 |
| China | 30.9 | 73.0 | 37 |
| Iran | 35.9 | 69.9 | 42 |
| Brazil | 37.1 | 71.9 | 41 |
| Indonesia | 39.3 | 69.9 | 24 |
| South Africa | 49.0 | 52.1 | 42 |
| Ghana | 61.6 | 57.9 | 56 |
| Bangladesh | 63.0 | 60.8 | 45 |
| Zimbabwe | 70.7 | 46.0 | 51 |
| India | 76.7 | 62.7 | 18 |
| Pakistan | 86.0 | 60.7 | 25 |
| Mozambique | 145.6 | 39.5 | 67 |

*Source*: data from WHO (2005).

the very wide spread on both indices in this list of countries by comparison with the OECD list. Another feature is a distinction that can be made between the countries with relatively good health records once children get through the first year and those with low overall life expectancies. Crucial here is the incidence of endemic diseases killing in early or middle life, notably AIDS. Only female life expectancy is cited; an examination of male life expectancy would highlight greater differences, and some other countries with poor records, notably the Russian Federation.

Whereas the public sector health expenditure proportions seem to throw some light on differences within the OECD group, this is not the case in table 6.6. This again highlights the importance of influences on health outcomes beyond the performance of the health-care sector.

Rates of death from specific conditions may offer evidence on preventable deaths, where knowledge about the feasibility of treatment may enable further reflection on the effectiveness of health services. A difficulty with condition-specific death rates is that evidence may be crucially dependent upon the classification practices of the doctors who sign the death certificates. These naturally vary over time and from society to society according to the state of knowledge and perhaps medical fashion.

Morbidity statistics are needed to supplement mortality statistics. Populations suffer from many health problems that do not kill them. Yet morbidity statistics are even more difficult to interpret than mortality statistics. There are two alternative sources: medical judgements about the health problems brought to practitioners or self-reported morbidity data (based on surveys of the population). The latter produces much larger numbers than the former method, with obvious variations according to the condition.

All kinds of morbidity statistics have subjective elements. People very often treat themselves or manage to live with conditions without seeking treatment. Statistics derived from patients depend on their assessments of the seriousness of their own problem, whilst those derived from doctors depend (notwithstanding their expertise) also on interpretations of the seriousness of other people's conditions. It is perhaps most useful to combine these two data sources, examining the extent to which the 'gap' between them is influenced by the availability, accessibility and approachability of doctors. Evidence of larger gaps in some places or for some categories of patients (identifiable, for example, by class, race or gender, or the nature of the condition) can lead to questions about the way services are provided.

The discussion in the last paragraph raises issues about much more specific approaches to comparisons between illness incidence rates. These are important for mortality as well as morbidity rates. These differences may raise considerations about the performance of health services. There are some important issues about 'inequalities of health' within nations as well as between nations. Any single national 'rate' may conceal variations, particularly if it is derived from a very large population. Thus an infant mortality rate for a large country like the USA may give a very different picture to a set of rates from different regions, racial groups and socio-economic groups within that nation. For example, in 2000 the infant mortality rate for whites was 5.7 and that for blacks 13.5 deaths per 1000 live births, whilst female life expectancy for whites was 80.0 and that for blacks 74.9 years (US National Center for Health Care Statistics, 2002).

As suggested in the introduction, many improvements in the health of nations are attributable to economic and environmental advances (McKeown, 1980), and many inequalities of health within and between nations are attributable to differences in incomes and environments (both within and outside the home). There is clearly a need to look at such data in relation to evidence on the differential use of health services. However, results are difficult to interpret; there is a package of interlocking factors here, particularly where income and environment deficiencies themselves have a direct impact on access to health services. Particularly important evidence on this suggests that health inequalities are rather more a reflection of overall inequalities than of either health spend or the overall prosperity of the nation (Wilkinson, 1996).

These interactions, however, may raise policy questions for those responsible for the design of health services. To what extent can good health services compensate for other disadvantages? The answer is, probably not very much: this involves concentrating on cure when prevention would have been much more effective. But if this is the case, to what extent can a health service see the elimination of disadvantages as part of a preventative health programme? This is an issue that has clearly been grasped for a long while in relation to adverse environmental factors, with health experts becoming involved in the attack on pollution and other health hazards. It has been less readily grasped in relation to problems of income deficiency, where health specialists have often been reluctant to get involved with the political issues about management of the economy, the incidence of taxation and the availability of income maintenance benefits.

## Cost Control within Health-care Policy

Health cost growth has been a continuing preoccupation across the OECD group of nations. Table 6.7 provides some evidence on the magnitude of that growth. The countries are listed in order of the size of their overall health expenditure growth as a percentage of GDP. Some caution is needed with the use of this index. There is a need to bear in mind the extent to which some of the nations where relative costs have grown least have experienced particularly high economic growth (e.g. Ireland) and have not necessarily been particularly successful at curbing health costs.

It is important not to rush to judgements about table 6.7. Leaving aside for a moment the complexities that arise from demographic change, there are two alternative interpretations of these increases

**Table 6.7** Health cost growth, 1980–2002

| Country[a] | Total health expenditure as percentage of GDP, 1980 | Total health expenditure as percentage of GDP, 2002 | Growth (1980 = 100) | Growth in population over 65 years (1980 = 100) |
|---|---|---|---|---|
| USA | 8.7 | 14.6 | 168 | 109 |
| Portugal | 5.6 | 9.3 | 166 | 147 |
| Switzerland | 7.3 | 11.2 | 153 | 112 |
| New Zealand | 5.9 | 8.5 | 144 | –[b] |
| Greece | 6.6 | 9.5 | 144 | 138 |
| Belgium | 6.4 | 9.1 | 142 | 119 |
| Spain | 5.4 | 7.6 | 140 | 154 |
| UK | 5.6 | 7.7 | 138 | 107 |
| France | 7.1 | 9.7 | 137 | 117 |
| Canada | 7.1 | 9.6 | 135 | 135 |
| Australia | 7.0 | 9.1 | 130 | 132 |
| Norway | 7.0 | 8.7 | 124 | 101 |
| Netherlands | 7.5 | 9.1 | 121 | 119 |
| Japan | 6.5 | 7.8 | 120 | 202 |
| Finland | 6.4 | 7.3 | 114 | 127 |
| Sweden | 9.1 | 9.2 | 101 | 106 |
| Austria | 7.6 | 7.7 | 101 | 101 |
| Denmark | 9.1 | 8.8 | 97 | 103 |
| Ireland | 8.4 | 7.3 | 87 | 104 |

[a] Germany has been excluded because of the complications related to unification.
[b] Data not available.

*Source*: data from OECD (2004b).

(in all but two countries) in proportional levels of expenditure. To put them in what are essentially value-loaded terms:

- it may be that the nation was spending too little in 1980 and that there has therefore been a necessary rise since then (an argument that may be applied above all to Portugal but also perhaps to New Zealand, Greece, Belgium, Spain, UK, Japan and Finland);
- it may be that the nation has difficulties in containing health-care costs (an argument that may be applied particularly to the USA and Switzerland and perhaps to France, Canada and Australia).

That leaves the rest as examples of contained or modest growth. It should be noted that these deductions rest simply on applying arbitrary judgements about the increases shown.

However, there is a need to pay attention to demographic change. Demographic pressures are particularly evident as a source of growth in health-care costs. Countries are experiencing growth not merely in the numbers of the elderly but particularly in the numbers of the very elderly. Incidence of chronic conditions amongst the very elderly is very high and the more medicine can do to prolong life, the more it has to cope with high demands on its services in that extra period it has added to people's lives. Table 6.7 thus has a final column indicating levels of growth in the size of the elderly population in the countries examined. An examination of these indicates the following.

- The case for regarding expenditure growth as necessary in Portugal, Greece, Spain and, above all, Japan is further strengthened.
- Any argument that health expenditure was out of control in Canada and Australia needs to take into account the quite marked demographic change there.
- The relative 'success' of Sweden, Austria, Denmark and Ireland in containing health cost growth needs to take into account the low level of demographic change there, while in the same sense Norway can perhaps be added to the group of nations seen as having unexplained cost growth.

Another source of upward pressure on health-service costs comes about because of advances in medical science and technology (including here advances in drug uses). In areas where very high costs force the rationing of treatment (e.g. transplant surgery or kidney machines), it is very difficult for politicians to deny efforts to bring such services to all who need them. The remorseless upward cost pressure exerted by scientific advance can easily have consequences for other services that are less dramatic in their impact, and less likely to secure media attention. There is an ever-present danger that the indirect 'casualties' of scientific advance will be the sufferers from minor chronic conditions or from mental illness. High-technology medicine requires politicians and other decision-makers to face up to the issues about equity in the provision of health services in society. These will not merely concern the way the state orders its priorities, but also the extent to which market mechanisms are allowed to 'solve' the rationing issues in favour of those with the resources to buy.

Health costs are pushed up by changes to the prices charged by those who supply the medicines and the technology. There are also other critical 'suppliers' of health services whose costs increase. These are the staff, whose wages, salaries and fees have to be paid. Governments will try to resist rises in these, but they may also tackle this particular cost control problem another way, by seeking an efficiency gain in return for a pay rise. Extensive comparative analysis is possible on the various elements within these costs, particularly issues about the numbers and costs of doctors and about how they are used. Similarly, arrangements that affect patient access, the incentives and disincentives operating in relation to referrals between doctors, and the mechanisms which enable the cost implications of treatment choices to be evident before referral affect the way issues about control over access to expensive services can be influenced in various countries. There is a lack of good comparative information on this.

## Conclusions

This chapter has given particular attention to the ways in which the state becomes involved with the provision of health care. Much of the discussion has focused on the implications of the two alternative, yet subtly merging, approaches to state funding: through central funding from taxation and through insurance (often involving an accommodation with private insurance systems).

The examination of differences in health expenditure has suggested that Esping-Andersen's regime theory is of comparatively little help for their analysis. It is impossible to draw clear distinctions between the 'social democratic' and the 'conservative' nations. Within the liberal group, a quite fundamental distinction needs to be made between the USA and the rest. All the liberal regimes seem to have relatively poor records on the key outcome measure of infant mortality, but since several of them are quite high spenders on health care and in all (except the USA) the public sector spends a relatively high proportion of the money, we are surely strongly reminded of the extent to which there are influences on that measure that lie outside the health sector. In short, a high infant mortality rate is a key indicator of inadequate poverty prevention measures.

### GUIDE TO FURTHER READING

Blank and Burau's *Comparative Health Policy* (2004) is an up-to-date textbook on this topic. Bambra (2005a,b) explores the case for the application of regime theory to health policy. A now rather dated book by Ham, Robinson and Benzeval (1990) provides a good accessible comparative introduction to the health-care reform issue, while Ranade's edited volume *Markets and Health Care* (1998) focuses on market or quasi-market developments in a selection of countries. Wilkinson (1996) is a key source on inequalities in health from a comparative perspective.

# CHAPTER 7

# SOCIAL CARE

## Introduction: Identifying the Issues

Social care policies are difficult to compare because they involve mixes of public, private, community and family efforts, and because they interact very significantly with other policies, particularly health, income maintenance and education policies. But these very 'mixed economy' characteristics deserve attention because they throw light upon crucial contemporary debates about the most appropriate ways to mix the various contributions to care. They are also very central to issues about gender divisions of welfare.

Systems for dealing with 'care' issues vary widely between societies, and are attached in various ways to other services. There is a lack of a common pool of ideas, data and concepts, of the kind that facilitate comparison in income maintenance or health policy. There are two reasons for this. One is that there are particularly tough problems about identifying the circumstances in which social care problems emerge from that category of issues regarded as personal or family concerns to become those of the wider society and especially of the state. The other is that the boundaries between social care and the other social policy categories are difficult to identify, and are arranged rather differently in different societies. It is important therefore to start with these two issues and their implications.

In chapter 1 it was recognised that the main options for responses to social problems are for them to be regarded as:

- needing to be solved by the individual (taking into account his or her 'market' position);
- family concerns (in either a narrow or a broad sense of family);
- social but not state concerns (again the options range from narrow neighbourhood and community responses to wider voluntary organisations);
- state (including of course local state) responsibilities.

The problem about the definition of need can be illustrated by the statement that I 'need' someone to do the housework so that I can write books. The best the author in need of help with housework can expect is some concern from the family (though even here there may be issues about the extent that this will be expected to involve some sort of reciprocity, approaching the notion of an economic exchange). Formal organisations, if approached for help, will probably expect a payment which will render any transaction a pure market one or will apply some rules to define need that disqualify this kind of application.

However, then the so-called 'need' may not arise simply because of a personal priority but may be:

1  derived from physical inability to perform domestic tasks;
2  leading to self-neglect;
3  leading to child neglect;
4  involving some combination of (1), (2) and (3).

Where 'need' derives from physical inability to perform domestic tasks, a more sympathetic response is likely all round. However, responses from outside the family may be muted by a view that the family has the main responsibility. These assumptions may be further reinforced by assumptions about caring roles. In particular, the response of the state may be to look first to others, especially family members but also perhaps neighbours and friends. Evers, Pijl and Ungerson (1994, p. 4) explore these issues, talking about the individual as in the middle of a 'welfare diamond' with four corners: state, family, community and market. Actual services then involve combinations of these four.

Potential carers, and particularly formal carers, may well raise issues about the capacity of the person in need of help to pay for that help. Hence there may be a three-part test of need, one part based on the nature of the condition, one based on the availability of informal carers and one based on the availability of resources to buy care (a means-test). Of course, this triple test may be applied in other areas of social policy, but the point here is that it is particularly likely to occur in relation to social care. What makes these situations different is the much greater strength of 'normal' assumptions about how basic domestic caring problems should be solved.

If the need is accepted as something requiring a formal response, then there is a number of options. First, there is a choice to be made between providing a domestic service in the person's own home and providing these sevices in an institution. The latter option has tended until recently to dominate care provision. Second, responses to need may be in the form of direct intervention by the agencies assuming responsibility or involve the commissioning of someone else to take on the task. On the face of it the latter is another version of the purchaser/provider split observed in some health services. However, in the case of something as simple as domestic care the commissioned provider may be a friend or neighbour. The purchaser may then be engaged in monetising a caring relationship, which might develop without this outside intervention. The logical point to follow from this is to ask: if it is acceptable to formalise and monetise that sort of relationship, what about family care?

The third alternative is to provide money directly, either to enable the person in need to pay for care or to subsidise carers. However, the issues about the relationship between cash and care are more complex than this. If the rationing of care involves consideration of whether the person in need is able to pay for it, then issues about the adequacy of incomes interact with issues about the extra costs of care. There are two polar positions in relation to this. On the one hand it may be argued that so long as individuals have adequate incomes, any exceptional needs can be met out of those. On the other hand, there is a view that certain special care needs merit extra subsidy regardless of individual income.

The first 'pole' highlights how questions about social care for elderly people cannot be entirely separated from issues about the adequacy of pensions. It seems somewhat illogical that, for example, there is an extensive debate in Taiwan about the case for care insurance when that country has not yet established a satisfactory pension system. In the same way, issues about the subsidy of pre-school child care in Europe need attention in the context of low wages (particularly for women) and of child benefits in general. The second 'pole' highlights questions that may reasonably be asked about what it is that distinguishes education costs from pre-school care costs or health costs from social care costs in the many societies in which free education and health care are available regardless of income.

So there are difficult questions about the circumstances which make various forms of social care matters of public policy. In other words, take them out of the contexts of *either* the private world of individual and family choice *or* of the private market. But then to complicate this further are the facts that pre-school care is to some extent education and that adequate health care cannot be readily distinguished from social care. Not surprisingly, therefore, comparative studies of social care are complicated by these and other boundary issues. Different national systems draw the boundaries between distinguishable social care concerns and income maintenance (or even employment) or health care or education concerns differently.

This chapter thus has to deal with the implications of these considerations. Whilst some initial attention will be given to the scope for generalisations across the forms of care, the chapter will then divide into two largely distinct topics: (1) the care of adults (principally elderly adults) who have difficulty in caring for themselves, and (2) the care of children.

## Making Comparisons Across the Care Sectors

Anttonen, Baldock and Sipilä (2003), who studied care for both children and elderly people in Finland, Germany, Japan, the UK and the USA, had hoped to apply a version of the regime typology to care but concluded that this was not feasible. They argue:

> Two main complications have arisen, one to do with how social care is consumed, the other to do with how it is produced. First, the manner in which the citizens of any one country use or consume a particular form of care is rarely standardized in some monolithic or dominant manner. The take-up and use of particular social care services is highly varied, even among those with broadly similar care needs . . . Second, on the production side, nations do not exhibit coherent patterns of social care in terms either of the principles that inform them or the ways in which they are delivered. A country may simultaneously provide or support care services that are universal and appear to confer genuine citizenship rights alongside others that are selective and sharply rationed. Equally, there is within each country, and even within the provision for a particular form of care, a considerable variety of delivery mechanisms. In some aspects of a nation's care services, direct public provision may be the rule, in others contracting out to the private or voluntary sectors, the use of tax credits or payments for care may be the dominant method. (ibid., p. 168)

However, Esping-Andersen, in his *Social Foundations of Post-industrial Economies* (1999, see table on p. 71), calculated 'family service spending' as a percentage of GDP, suggesting a distribution of nations in 1992 with the social democratic regimes the highest spenders, followed by the conservative and then the liberal regimes (though there were exceptions in the latter two categories that suggest some problems about drawing a clear contrast between them).

Bettio and Plantenga's (2004) comparison of European care regimes uses a mixture of indices of care strategies to arrive at a categorisation that is more complex than Esping-Andersen's.

- 'Countries that appear to delegate all the management of care to the family' (Italy, Greece and Spain) with two 'outlier' cases: Portugal, where there is high female labour market participation; and Ireland, lying between this group and the next one.
- Countries with high dependence on informal care, but where this is much more salient in respect of child care than of care for elderly people (UK and the Netherlands).
- Countries with 'publicly facilitated, private care' (Austria and Germany).
- Countries with quite well-developed formal care strategies (Belgium and France).
- Countries with moderate to high levels of formal care (Denmark, Finland and Sweden).

Here distinctions between adult care and child care may be noted, and this discussion now moves on to look at the two separately.

## Adult Care

Within adult care, it is care of elderly people that dominates. The numbers of adults below pension age who require intensive social care are very small in all of the richer countries in the world, whilst in the poorer ones formal systems of care are largely absent. In both cases complexities arise because of the extent to which care is a combination of family care, privately purchased care and publicly provided care. To further the discussion we need to try to tease out comparative information, from the limited range of sources, that will throw light upon different patterns of care. Attention here will be largely confined to issues about care for elderly people.

There is an OECD report of a working party that examined the problems of estimating expenditure on what they called the 'long term care' of elderly people, namely care to people who need 'ongoing health and nursing care on a continuing basis' (OECD, 2004g, p. 5). The report acknowledges the difficulties about achieving comparable statistics, particularly in relation to care in the home and to private expenditure. Tables 7.1 and 7.2 report the estimates for several countries, using information from the OECD standard health-care survey,

**Table 7.1** Expenditure on long-term care of elderly people as a percentage of GDP, 2000

| Country | Total spending on long-term care as percentage of GDP | Percentage of spending used by public authorities |
| --- | --- | --- |
| Canada | 1.23 | 80 |
| Germany | 1.14 | 83 |
| Japan | 0.78 | 91 |
| Netherlands | 1.41 | 95 |
| New Zealand | 0.68 | 66 |
| Spain | 0.14 | 86 |
| Sweden | 2.89 | 95 |
| Switzerland | 2.03 | 37 |
| UK | 1.37 | 65 |
| USA | 1.29 | 57 |

*Source*: data from OECD (2004f, pp. 15–16), quoting data from the OECD Health Data Survey and also a special long-term care study.

**Table 7.2** Percentage of expenditure on long-term care spent on institutional care, 2000

| Country | Percentage of total spending on long-term care spent on institutional care |
| --- | --- |
| Canada | 86 |
| Germany | 59 |
| Japan | 97 |
| Netherlands | 57 |
| New Zealand | 82 |
| Spain | Not known, probably most |
| Sweden | 72 |
| Switzerland | 90 |
| UK | 70 |
| USA | 74 |

*Source*: data from OECD (2004b).

supplemented for some countries by information from a special study. Table 7.1 sets out the estimated total spend (as a percentage of GDP) and the share of that spend which is public. Table 7.2 sets out the share of that expenditure spent on institutional care.

From these figures we can identify two contrasting cases where there is high spending, one public (Sweden) and the other private (Switzerland), and note that institutional care is more dominant in the latter than the former. There is then one very low spender, Spain, where most of the spending is public funding of institutional care, but two other countries (Japan and New Zealand) where the pattern is very similar to this (but with a slightly higher spend). In most of the other countries the level of spending is much the same, with relatively high private and non-institutional spends in the USA and the UK and interesting figures for the Netherlands, where there is a high public spending proportion but extensive use of home care.

Given the acknowledgement that these figures do not deal effectively with the issues concerning home care, particularly about private funding of that care (which implicitly includes, inevitably uncosted, family care), it is worthwhile to cast around for other sources of information. One such is European data on the residential locations of very old people. The European Commission, in its annual survey of social conditions (European Commission, 2004), publishes the predicted residential arrangements of older people in the different countries of the Union. Table 7.3 looks at people over 80, a group that may be expected to contain many who have some needs for care. It divides them into four groups: people living alone, people living only with a partner, people living in households in which there are others and people living in institutions. The original data source is a table predicting 2010 figures using a 1995 baseline. Table 7.3 uses this, obviously taking the risk that inappropriate assumptions have been used (particularly about the likelihood of institutional care).

Table 7.3 demonstrates a contrast between countries where co-location with non-spouse family members is likely and where it is unlikely. This is to some extent a south–north division (but with Ireland having 'southern' characteristics). The percentages living alone or only with spouses in Sweden and Denmark, and to a lesser extent in Germany, France and the UK, are very high. In fact very many of these are living entirely alone (around two-thirds in each case).

Evidence on the residence patterns of elderly people clearly does not tell the complete story about European patterns of family care. A great deal of care is given outside the home. Family care may also be provided without co-residence. However, it is much more difficult to assemble good comparative evidence on contributions to care (meals, cleaning, cooking, etc.) outside formal arrangements. A UK study of informal carers reported by the Royal Commission on Long Term Care (1999) suggested that about 9 per cent of the population said they

**Table 7.3** Estimates of residential locations of people aged over 80

| Country | Percentage living alone | Percentage living only with a partner | Percentage in households with others (in addition to spouses where applicable) | Percentage living in institutions |
|---|---|---|---|---|
| Belgium | 51 | 28 | 14 | 8 |
| Denmark | 62 | 26 | 2 | 10 |
| Germany | 52 | 29 | 8 | 10 |
| Greece | 36 | 35 | 16 | 12 |
| Spain | 30 | 34 | 32 | 4 |
| France | 46 | 34 | 10 | 10 |
| Ireland | 39 | 19 | 23 | 19 |
| Italy | 39 | 30 | 17 | 13 |
| Netherlands | 44 | 27 | 5 | 24 |
| Austria | 43 | 29 | 17 | 11 |
| Portugal | 32 | 35 | 30 | 4 |
| Finland | 49 | 23 | 14 | 14 |
| Sweden | 62 | 30 | 3 | 4 |
| UK | 50 | 31 | 11 | 8 |

*Source*: European Commission (2004, p. 180).

had informal care responsibilities, and two-fifths of these were for persons outside the household. But this source is not clear about to whom care was given. In this respect it is important to recognise that alongside care for the old by the young is care by the old for other old people. According to data quoted by the Royal Commission (1999, p. 16), 19 per cent of informal carers are spouses and 20 per cent of carers are over 65.

The size of the undertaking involved in 'looking after' is unclear. The UK Royal Commission commented 'Most carers spend no more than 4 hours a week providing unpaid care, but about 800,000 people provide unpaid care for 50 hours a week or more' (ibid., p. 15). In the context of a shared household, and particularly with spouse care, there may be great difficulty in distinguishing what would be defined as informal care from a taken-for-granted exchange of support activities.

Clearly, statistics on informal caring activities are hard to collect. It has been argued (Finch, 1989; Finch and Mason, 1993, Twigg and Grand, 1998) that family care patterns are very complex, resting on personal and cultural assumptions rather than on legal duties, and therefore taking many different forms in different situations.

**Table 7.4** Data on main carers of dependent elderly people (percentages)

| Country and year of study | Main carer in household | Family carer not in household | Home help is primary carer | Other primary carer |
|---|---|---|---|---|
| Australia 1988 (over-70s) | 73 | –[a] | – | – |
| Denmark 1988 (over-70s) | 28 | 28 | 44 | 0 |
| Finland 1987 | 46 | 19 | 19 | 16 |
| Japan 1984 | 82 | 6 | – | – |
| Sweden 1975 | 46 | 21 | 23 | 10 |
| UK 1976 | 64 | 21 | 13 | 15 |
| USA 1982 | 74 | – | 10 | – |

[a] Data not available.

*Source*: data from OECD (1994a, table 2.6, p. 36).

There is OECD material providing evidence from the late 1970s or 1980s about who are the primary carers of people over 65 in need of help with some services in different countries. Table 7.4 sets out some data from this source. It is impossible to work out from this table what proportion of the carers in the household were spouses. However, this table does reinforce the view that family carers who live outside the home may be very important, and that formal non-kin care is important in the Scandinavian countries. The latter is reinforced by some slightly later evidence set out in table 7.5.

This rather unsatisfactory mixture of sources suggests some basis for making distinctions between:

- countries where family care is clearly very important (Spain, Portugal, Japan);
- countries where heavy use is made of institutional care (Netherlands, Switzerland);
- countries where publicly funded formal home-based care is important (Sweden, Denmark, Australia).

The existence of a group of nations that considers family care to be very important, to which the 'conservative' nations of northern Europe do not belong, provides evidence to support a 'fourth world' with

**Table 7.5** Percentage of people over 65 receiving public home help services in various countries

| Country | Percentage receiving formal help at home |
|---|---|
| Australia | 11.7 |
| Austria | 24 |
| Belgium | 4.5 |
| Denmark | 20.3 |
| Finland | 14 |
| France | 6.1 |
| Germany | 9.6 |
| Ireland | 3.5 |
| Italy | 2.8 |
| Japan | 5 |
| Netherlands | 12 |
| Spain | 1.6 |
| Sweden | 11.2 |
| UK | 5.5 |
| USA | 16 |

*Source*: Casey et al. (2003, p. 59); the date this information was collected is not clear from the source but was earlier than 2001.

respect to regime theory (in southern Europe and perhaps East Asia). There are distinct hints of a stronger emphasis on privatisation within the 'liberal' group of nations. But the variable that seems to be important here, yet will split up the nations in a rather different way (other than the strong family care-oriented ones), seems to be dependence on the use of institutional care. To some extent, perhaps, this is because recognition of the case for care outside institutions has developed rather faster in some countries than others. A factor here may be the extent to which demographic change has advanced in each society, the de-institutionalisation option being grasped first in the countries that experienced ageing first (such as Sweden and the UK).

However, the whole picture is likely to become further confused by recognition of the case for meeting concerns about care through the development of new cash benefits, which distance public support from the issues about provision. A related issue here is the development of care insurance, where Germany and Japan have been the pioneers, but with the difference that in the German case it gives choice of care (including family care) to the recipient, whereas in the Japanese case disbursement is firmly linked to formal services (either domiciliary or institutional).

Comparison between nations in respect of care of elderly people inevitably focuses attention first on who pays and second on the form the care takes, but there is another issue: who provides? There is a substantial literature, particularly in the UK, about the extent to which there is a separation between payment for care and the provision of care. The link between the state as payer and the arrangements for provision may be complex. Various efforts have been made to specify the options. For example, a complicated matrix to delineate purchaser–provider relationships in the UK reported in Wistow, Knapp, Hardy and Allen (1994, figure 3.1, p. 37) identifies, on one dimension, the public, voluntary and private sectors and, on the other, the following:

- coerced collective demand;
- voluntary collective demand;
- corporate demand;
- uncompensated individual consumption;
- compensated individual consumption;
- individual donation.

On the provider side the main options, other than direct provision by the state, are the private sector, the voluntary sector and informal care (meaning in most cases the extended family). There are three questions here about possible differences between states in respect of:

- propensities to use the private sector;
- willingness to subsidise families;
- propensities to use the voluntary sector.

It was noted in chapter 3 that the logic of the Esping-Andersen model suggests that where the public sector does fund care, interest in drawing in the private sector might be expected to be strongest in the 'liberal' regimes and weakest in the 'social democratic' ones. However, as far as can be judged (in the absence of discovery of a systematic study), interest in enabling the private sector to become providers seems to have been as widespread in Scandinavia as in the UK and the USA. It was suggested in chapter 3 that there are grounds for expecting voluntary sector providers to exist where there has been a strong cultural commitment to the delegation of care tasks to local organisations. However, many different societies have strong voluntary organisation traditions.

Issues about the subsidy of families are complicated by the diversity of ways in which this may occur. This has been given more comparative attention than the issue of levels of subsidy per se. A European study by Pacolet, Bouten, Lanoye and Versieck (1999) notes a whole range of variations in ways in which the presence of other family members may be taken into account:

> In Belgium, the presence of a social network is taken into account when providing district nursing and home help. The availability of other social services for elderly persons living in the community does not differ according to the presence of a social network or spouse. In Denmark, when allocating home help, meals-on-wheels and the installation of an emergency alarm, the local authority considers the ability of the spouse. In Germany, home nursing aid can partly be provided in cash instead of in kind when a social network is available. In Finland the package of services is reduced when informal care can take over some duties. In France, one of the eligibility conditions for receiving home help is that the spouse must be incapable of providing informal care for his or her partner. In Spain, access to health and social services is in general dependent upon family circumstances. In Ireland, the presence of a spouse reduces the likelihood of some public services, particularly home help services. In Italy, no home help is provided when a social network is available. The spouse has an important task in taking care of the disabled. (ibid., p. 102)

A particular concern of analyses of the role of women in welfare has been with the implications of alternative ways of providing state support for care (chapter 10 will return to this subject). There are important differences between providing services and providing subsidies. In relation to subsidies there are alternatives. Paying the cared-for leaves them choices about where to purchase care, including of course the possibility of using the money within the family, whilst paying the carer tends to involve a more prescriptive stance on who is to do the caring. But this topic is more complicated than that. Ungerson (1995) and Daly (2002) have identified that subsidy to carers may come in a variety of ways: cash payments, opportunities to secure subsidised leave from work, credits for social security, and relief from taxation.

However, it is important to return here to the overall warning at the beginning of the chapter about how different countries identify social care issues rather differently. Some attention has been given here to the income, and income maintenance, aspect of this, but it is important not to forget the issues about the overlap between health care and social care. If people are ill they may need some combination of care in a simple physical sense – someone to provide food, do household tasks, perhaps to wash and feed them – and care in a strictly medical sense. These two overlap in quite complex ways. In addition, a health condition may be such that people also need advice, counselling, social and emotional support and even, exceptionally, control to prevent them damaging themselves and others. These interactions are particularly evident in situations in which mental illness is involved or physical illness has behavioural or emotional consequences.

Clearly, it is logically possible to conceive of a health service system that deals with all the implications of these issues itself. However, it will be a health service that draws on a variety of skills and has to cope with *within-system* boundary problems: the transition from hospital to home care, the construction of the relative responsibilities of doctors, nurses, social workers, domestic care workers, etc. It is much more likely, in practice, that many of these will be *between-system* boundary matters, with issues about who is responsible for what, and particularly who pays for what, a source of tension between health and social care systems. This issue has been given extensive attention in many societies because of efforts to control health costs. One particular focus has been the high cost of hospital care, leading to efforts to reduce the length of hospitals stays, which inevitably shift costs from health care to social care systems.

## Child Care

As a prelude to looking at contemporary child care policy, it is appropriate to identify separate policy issues that are intricately intertwined in practice. Child care policy may be seen as about:

- provision of care that will supplement the care provided by parents, simply as something that reduces stresses and pressures particularly in the early years of a child's life;
- activities for children, particularly pre-school children, that will supplement the normal education system;
- care to facilitate labour market participation on the part of the parents;
- child protection as a regulatory activity, a special (generally social work-based) system concerned with dealing with problems of child neglect, child abuse and child delinquency.

This discussion will not concern itself with this last-named issue. Comparative work on this topic is largely descriptive; it is hard to develop any systematic approach to this specialised topic, which is handled in a variety of different ways across the world.

In each of the first three cases, such activities may or may not be the concern of the state. They may alternatively be seen as supplements to family life that may be purchased or provided through reciprocal community and extended family networks. But then there are rather different arguments for each and rather different rationales for public subsidy.

In the first category, simple supplementary care, the case for state provision is likely to be seen as linked to the need for child protection (concerned with supporting orphans, abandoned children and children at risk of abuse). Such care may reduce family stress and it may be appropriate to develop it where this is particularly likely or where others (e.g. families or neighbours) cannot provide it. The justification for public subsidy will be much the same as that for other parts of the child protection system. In comparative studies, spending on this aspect of child care is likely to figure as a very small item within social policy as a whole (and therefore as a very low percentage of GDP).

The second category, child care as a form of supplementary education, arises particularly with regard to provision for pre-school children (but may also apply to after-school and holiday activities). Justification for such activities in general would seem to be based on a view that what is provided by the regular education system is not sufficient or does not start soon enough. If the regular education system is provided free by the state, is there a case for this education to be free too? An argument against this view will be that it is an inessential extra, in which sense it may be regarded as much like post-school education. In practice we find an official view often being taken which stands somewhere between these two positions: that it is an extra that some may purchase but that the resulting inequality requires subsidy on behalf of low-income families. This argument is of course particularly relevant where this additional education is seen as 'compensatory', providing extra for those who may otherwise not take full advantage of the regular education system. The problem with identifying this as a 'care' expenditure is that it is actually education expenditure (a topic explored in the next chapter).

The issues involving the third category are closely intertwined with views about the desirability of labour market participation. The central issue is of course labour market participation by women. Closely connected with this is the issue about such participation by single parents, most of whom are women. Those who regard this as unnecessary, or simply a matter of private choice, will equally see child care provision as a private matter. If, on the contrary, it is seen as every parent's right, then there will be a case for state provision of child care. But even here it may be regarded as a matter for attention by employers rather than the state. Again, there is a middle position, which sees a need to subsidise child care to facilitate employment where the rewards from work are low. We have then, as far as comparative studies are concerned, another example of a cost that may alternatively be absorbed by employers, employees or the state. Where the latter is involved there is an alternative to direct provision, namely the subsidy of one or both of the other parties. Where families are subsidised, the expenditure may be classified as a social security expenditure or even as tax relief.

So we have here a topic where the interactions between issues about employment and issues about education will be complex and where data sources giving it explicit attention as a care item will be limited. For example, table 7.6 distinguishes variations between countries in pre-school education, but obviously gives no sense of the extent to which either care needs or parental employment influence the different participation rates.

Another complication concerns who is to pay. It may be assumed from the expenditure data in table 7.6 that any country that is a low spender on this item is expecting significant parental contributions. Hence Australia stands out as a society where the public contribution

**Table 7.6** Pre-primary education in various OECD countries

| Country | Public expenditure on pre-primary education as percentage of GDP | Enrolment rates of 4-year-olds in pre-primary education (percentage of age group) |
|---|---|---|
| Australia | 0.03 | 41.1 |
| Czech Republic | 0.45 | 81.9 |
| Denmark | 0.86 | 90.9 |
| Finland | 0.40 | 40.0 |
| Italy | 0.42 | 100 |
| Netherlands | 0.36 | 98.0 |
| Portugal | 0.52 | 68.0 |
| Sweden | 0.59 | 69.2 |
| UK | 0.42 | 94.6 |
| USA | 0.36 | 59.6 |

*Source*: data from OECD (2001, p. 188).

is minimal. It may perhaps also be deduced that in any country where a high proportion of 4 year olds are enrolled in pre-primary education but where the public expenditure figure is relatively low, child care costs are likely to be falling (to some degree) on some or all parents. The UK and the Netherlands can then again be identified as places where the public contribution is relatively low. Daly and Rake's (2003) exploration of this issue produces rather similar divisions, with a slightly different sample of European countries:

> when the spotlight is turned on the provision of child care services
> . . . France, Germany and Sweden are the highest providers, and Ireland and the UK the lowest. Italy and the Netherlands are similar in favouring private provision for younger children but public provision once children reach the age of three. (ibid., p. 52)

The issues about payment for care are complicated further by the relationships between this aspect of child care and those other aspects, of which cash support is salient, discussed in chapter 4.

It is difficult to unpick the issues about social care for children much further than this. As a mainstream policy area (as opposed to the care of the minority of seriously neglected and ill-treated children) it is, as noted, one on which employment and education issues are salient. It is also an issue of great importance for gender divisions of welfare. As such chapter 10 will return to it.

## Conclusions

Social care concerns arise in a variety of ways, and link fundamentally with many other social policy issues. It has been suggested that in ideal terms it may be possible to see social care as fundamental to all social policy, treating people, families and communities as 'wholes'. Hence comprehensive approaches to income maintenance policy, health policy, education policy (and so on) may recognise the spillovers from specific concerns to general ones. Yet, societies expect adult individuals to be responsible for their own lives and to use their incomes to meet their needs, and they expect families to be the main caring institutions for children and often also for adults unable to be responsible for their own care. These considerations render social care services in a residual position, to be there when the other institutions fail. This is an observation on what occurs in practice, not a value judgement.

The exploration of social care as a specific policy area raises, more strongly than with other policy areas, issues about the 'mixed economy of welfare' (see chapter 3) inasmuch as care issues are, to a considerable extent, seen either as family concerns or as issues where individuals can make private arrangements. Public provision is not comprehensive, rather it is conceived as only essential in special circumstances where the scope for family care is limited. Social care services are emergency services, deployed to help those both unable to help themselves and unable to secure the help of close kin.

This has two consequences that have been explored in this chapter. One is that they are typically services for the poor and isolated; means-tests and family obligation assumptions keep other customers at bay. The other is that they frequently contain a 'control' element, inasmuch as they are imposed on people regarded, rightly or wrongly, as unable to help themselves or use other services in the 'normal' way. They are seen, to greater or lesser degrees, as supplementary to private arrangements.

Only in the most developed of the welfare states, in Scandinavia, are ideas about rights to care on the agenda, and even there they are fragile growths. The exception to this arises in respect of child care, but here the dominant policy developments come either from concerns to extend pre-school education or to facilitate female labour market participation.

## GUIDE TO FURTHER READING

There is a lack of comparative material on this topic, a consequence probably of the difficulties in developing cross-national generalisations. Castles (2004) dips into this subject using OECD data but Anttonen et al. (2003) offer a much fuller but largely qualitative analysis in respect of a limited sample of nations. Pacolet et al. (1999) explore adult care issues in Europe. An article by Bettio and Plantenga (2004) explores comparatively some of the issues about child care in Europe, as do some of the books that particularly focus on gender divisions (discussed in chapter 10), notably Daly and Rake (2003).

# CHAPTER 8

# EDUCATION

## Introduction: Identifying the Issues

The decision to include education in this book means that an area of
policy is included which is not defined as social policy in the OECD
statistical compilations. It also means that this chapter will discuss a
topic on which there is a substantial specialised comparative literature
within which connections to the social policy literature are almost
totally absent. Educationalists make a case for comparison in similar
terms to that for comparison in social policy, recognising both the
intellectual and practical reasons for comparing systems (Alexander,
Broadfoot and Phillips, 1999, part one). Within the literature there is a
large body of small-scale comparisons and also an increasing interest
in assembling international databases. The OECD indeed shows a great
deal of interest in education, and both assembles comparative statistics
and commissions studies.

In the face of all this material, I had a difficult decision to make
about how to proceed. In the education field there is no overarching
comparative approach like Esping-Andersen's regime theory, although
the OECD material could be used for such an approach. In practice
there is much controversy over the validity of the large quantitative
comparative studies and a great proportion of the material is qualitative.
What I decided was to take the risk of focusing on broad comparisons,
exploring the extent to which issues about comparing education
systems can be handled in the same way as the other comparisons in
this book. This implies looking at the material assembled by the OECD
in particular and by other quantitative studies. In doing so, I have left
out most issues about higher and further education (except inasmuch
as statements about overall system characteristics and aggregate
expenditure figures include them).

However, in order to approach education policy in a way that enables it to be examined side by side with other social policy, it is also necessary to focus rather specifically on national 'policies' and to give limited attention to some of the quite specific questions about how schools are run and subjects are taught. This is a difficult distinction to make in practice and contradicts my general view, highlighted in chapter 3, that to understand policy attention needs to be given to how it is put into practice. This is a pragmatic decision in relation to a complex subject where much of the crucial international comparative work faces enormous methodological problems and is only just beginning (for a good discussion of this in relation to the important topic of school effectiveness, see chapter 8 of Teddlie and Reynolds, 2000). In practice the chapters on health and social care involved a similar skating over the surface of topics where policy delivery is complex and hard to compare.

This chapter will accordingly start with some general observations about the role of education in society. It will then move on to an exploration of inputs into the education system, how they are organised and how they relate to the public–private divide in this policy area. It then concludes by exploring a limited range of issues about education outputs, recognising that this is where comparison gets into many difficulties.

## Education and Society

The state's role in education in all industrialised societies is obvious and colossal, but it is important to see it in the context of the variety of ways in which the family, the market and the 'community' are involved.

Whilst there is a great deal of formal and institutionalised activity in the field of education, it is also the case that in many respects individuals educate themselves. There are parallels here with health. It is not unknown for children to teach themselves to read. Once they have that capacity, many children secure a great deal of knowledge for themselves. Before the coming of universal formal education, in numerous societies many people were self-educated and colloquially people still refer to the knowledge and wisdom acquired through participation in everyday life. Whether education is acquired within or outside formal institutions, the success of individuals is likely to depend a great deal upon the support of families and friends. With such support a great deal can be achieved with a minimum of formal provision Without it, substantial formal inputs may be of little use.

It is important also to consider issues about the role of the private sector in relation to education. Clearly education is something that may be purchased, and the discussion below will look at some issues about the place of privately purchased education systems in societies. However, it is important to recognise that there is a range of ways in which publicly provided education systems are supported by private expenditures. The costs of education extend beyond the costs of providing teachers and buildings to, for example, books, writing materials and technology (computers, laboratory equipment, etc.). There are many situations in which all or part of these costs are met by parents or students. Some of the more impoverished education systems depend heavily on these additional private inputs, but even in the best-funded systems there is scope for private expenditure by individuals to enhance the resources available to them. This kind of private supplementation of a public system depends heavily on the commitments of individuals and families and accordingly influences educational inequalities.

The cost issues may extend further. There may be costs involved in travel to schools and colleges. Once there, pupils may have to meet maintenance costs for food and accommodation that are additional to the living costs incurred by families. Finally, there are what are called 'opportunity costs', namely participation in education may be at the expense of other activities. Those other activities may include work, so families have to forgo the earnings of children and young people to enable them to secure education. So the key introductory point here is that whilst public education systems are very important in industrialised and urbanised societies, there will be many ways in which their use both requires the support of families and imposes costs upon them.

The point above about 'opportunity costs' also draws attention to the fact that the motivation of individuals and families in respect of education may be influenced by the extent to which it facilitates entry into an occupation. The same issue can be looked at from the point of view of an economic enterprise that may want to recruit educated employees. Enterprises may train and, by the same token, educate (no attempt will be made to draw a distinction between the two here), but they are likely to prefer to recruit people who cost little to train for their specific needs.

Finally, before moving on to the role of the state itself, what about other social institutions between the family and state? A particularly salient institution in the development of education in many societies has been organised religion. Religious bodies have an interest in education as a means to inculcate a set of beliefs. Organised religion has often been a rival to the state for control over education systems.

The development of nation states in Europe and conflicts over religion went hand in hand as part of the same story. The identification with, or protection of, particular religious beliefs played a key part in state formation. Later, attempts to separate religious controversy from nationalism (in divided states like the Netherlands or in new states created from a mixed body of immigrants as in the USA) made it important for states to try to reach arrangements about the provision of education that prevented religion being a divisive force. Direct state provision of education, with religious teaching banned or carefully controlled, or the disbursement of subsidies to religious bodies in ways designed to accommodate different interests emerged as alternative ways to deal with this issue (Holmes, 1985).

Two separate, and sometimes conflicting, themes dominate explanations of the emergence of public educational provision: one of these concerns what will be called 'citizenship', whilst the other concerns economic interests. These will be examined separately and then brought together (this discussion draws partly upon the work of Archer, 1979 and Green, 1990).

It has already been established that individuals have an interest in securing education. It gives them access to a range of ideas, symbols, beliefs, etc. that may be loosely described as 'culture'. It therefore opens up possibilities of religious and political participation. In this sense education may be seen as being transformed over the ages from the preserve of an elite (kings, nobles and priests) to something more widely shared. Opening the system up in this way was therefore amongst the demands of democratising movements. To what extent did democratisation bring demands for mass education and to what extent did demands for democracy follow upon the expansion of education? The answer is that there was a complex interaction.

However, it is possible to identify reasons why elites and states promoted education before democratisation. The special interest of religion has already been identified. Furthermore, where a state's claim to rule over a territory was based on assertion that there was a single religious community, it was in the state's interest to promote that religion and ensure its dominance. But the establishment of nation states depended on other aspects of culture as well as religion. Language in particular was important. Also important were things like the acceptance of a common currency, common ways of measuring, and common conventional and legal practices to deal with matters of dispute. Education could play an important part in achieving a measure of unity, particularly if it began to impose a common language. Green's (1990) exploration of the role of education in state formation looks at these issues, particularly in relation to Germany in the eighteenth and nineteenth centuries. In some studies of the role of education in colonial societies, and other countries where there is external domination, it has been suggested that education may play a key role in 'cultural domination' (Welch, 1993).

Green's analysis goes on to show how, as the activities of states increased in complexity, the state's educational needs increased. The development of an army, a civil service and a legal system required moving from dependence on a narrow educated elite to inclusion of a wider range of citizens. Moreover, even the education of an elite is something that states find it risky or inefficient to leave entirely in private hands. The tendency was inevitably for states to want to control elite education. Then, as has been suggested with regard to health policy, aspirations to control tends to suck states into subsidy or direct provision.

There are obviously very different concerns embedded in narrow arguments that people should be educated to read and write a common language and to participate in basic political and legal institutions and in wider arguments related to the education, socialisation and selection of governing elites. However, the two are connected by democratisation. One key demand of democratic and radical movements has been for state intervention to open up elite education to social groups. Another has been that the education of citizens should be a common process, in which elite and mass share, as far as possible, common educational experiences (Dewey, 1976).

The issue of competition for scarce opportunities touches on the second theme of this section, the 'economic' arguments for education and their influence on the state. It is not a passion for democratic participation that motivates most pressure for more state support of education, but a recognition that education provides a 'meal ticket'. This point is deliberately put in that colloquial way. This is because there is a major fallacy embedded in many discussions of education in economic terms, namely that it provides economically necessary qualifications (see Wolf, 2002). This may be the case. However, the demands of employers for specific or general qualifications and their selection of employees on the basis of educational qualifications should not be regarded as sufficient evidence in itself that the educational efforts that produced those qualifications are essential to the needs of the economy. The discussion below will return to this point, with particular reference to 'human capital theory'. However, the key point is that educational achievement, whether intrinsically necessary or not, is often important for individuals in competition for economically advantageous positions in industrial society. This is what generates intense concern about education in democratic political systems, stimulating demands for state provisions and expenditure and fuelling the pressure for equality of opportunity in education.

Employers are also interested in getting the state to shoulder the main burden of education. Their interest in the issues links with the citizenship and culture issues outlined above inasmuch as economic activity requires the use of shared linguistic and mathematical skills and the capacity to participate in a common economic community. Nevertheless, it implies an approach to education that is much more pragmatic than concerns about the sharing of a complex common culture embodied in traditional approaches to elite education. It may also embody views about topics the education system should *not* cover, perhaps including those encouraging and enhancing aspirations about citizenship rights. Some analyses of educational policy have stressed the strongly 'capitalist'-determined model of education deriving from that perspective. It is argued that employers do not want education to create participating citizens. They want a disciplined and conformist labour force, cheerfully accepting the inequalities of rewards and power implicit in the labour market contract. Radical analyses suggest how the demands of capitalism have created a narrow model for state education (Bowles and Gintis, 1976, p. 48).

Marxist theory about the need for the state to socialise some of the costs of capital is amplified in various ways with the notion that the state has economic needs of its own. In the field of education this has taken its strongest form in emphases on the need for substantial educational investments in developing societies. There is a substantial body of comparative work that has sought to explore the relationship between education and economic growth, stimulated by the concerns of bodies like UNESCO and the World Bank about the impact of assistance with the development of public education programmes (see Kogan, 1979; Hurst, 1981). This emphasis in aid programmes seems to be very influenced by a belief in the importance of educational opportunity in generating an open and efficient capitalist society.

In developed societies, the equivalent to the development concern involves a preoccupation with competition with other nations and a fear that a nation may lose its competitive edge. Weaknesses in the education system are then seen as not producing enough engineers or not doing enough to encourage scientific innovation or undermining the entrepreneurial spirit. This concern has had an important influence on comparative work on education systems, encouraging a 'league table' view of education systems in which questions are raised about

whether the poor economic attainments of particular nations is attributable to aspects of their education system. This is discussed further
later in the chapter.

A theoretical perspective that has contributed to and channelled
some of these debates is human capital theory (Blaug, 1970). This
focuses directly upon the economic value of education, and can be
conceptualised in both individual and collective terms. The individual
version sees education as making a distinct contribution to the earning
power of a person. This is fairly uncontroversial in itself; the problems
lie in its application to societies. As suggested above, the reasons why
individuals may enhance their earning power through education are
multiple, and may owe as much to social conventions about selection
as to real increases in their value to society. Herein lies one problem
about human capital theory: the real effects of investing in people
(i.e. allegedly enhancing human capital) may be illusory when viewed
from a society-wide perspective (Wolf, 2002), however much social
processes make it obviously beneficial to the individuals concerned.
Another is that its preoccupation is solely with the needs of the formal
economy and not with the worth of such investments to society in a
wider sense.

The mechanisms by which investment in education is transferred
into economic growth is complex and indirect. Many other factors
come into play. Effects that may be detectable are likely to be very
specific, concerning educational inputs which are probably better
conceived as training (enhancing specific job-related skills) and results
which are industry or even enterprise specific. The arguments about
undervaluing technology, original scientific research or the entrepreneurial spirit involve complex connections, in which many other
social factors may be relevant (Hüfner, Meyer and Naumann in Dierkes,
Weiler and Antal, 1987).

The importance of human capital theory for the discussion of
education policy, like many popular social theories, lies not so much
in its accuracy as in the influence it has on policy and practice. Bodies
like the OECD and the World Bank play a role in disseminating the
use of this narrow perspective. Human capital theory offers a widely
accepted argument for public educational investment.

## Comparing National Expenditure on Education

The above discussion sets out some of the factors to take into account
in evaluating expenditure on education, and the role of the state in

**Table 8.1** Education expenditure for various OECD countries, 2000

| Country | Total education expenditure as percentage of GDP | Public-sector education expenditure as percentage of GDP | Public spend as percentage of total spend |
|---|---|---|---|
| Korea | 7.1 | 4.3 | 61 |
| USA | 7.0 | 4.8 | 69 |
| Denmark | 6.7 | 6.5 | 97 |
| Sweden | 6.5 | 6.3 | 97 |
| Canada | 6.4 | 5.2 | 81 |
| Australia | 6.2 | 4.6 | 74 |
| France | 6.1 | 5.7 | 93 |
| Norway | 5.9 | 5.8 | 98 |
| New Zealand | 5.8 | 5.8 | 100 |
| Austria | 5.7 | 5.4 | 95 |
| Portugal | 5.7 | 5.6 | 98 |
| Switzerland | 5.7 | 5.3 | 93 |
| Finland | 5.6 | 5.5 | 98 |
| Belgium | 5.5 | 5.1 | 93 |
| Mexico | 5.5 | 4.7 | 85 |
| Germany | 5.3 | 4.3 | 81 |
| UK | 5.3 | 4.5 | 85 |
| Poland | 5.2 | 5.2 | 100 |
| Hungary | 5.1 | 4.4 | 86 |
| Italy | 4.9 | 4.5 | 92 |
| Spain | 4.9 | 4.3 | 88 |
| Japan | 4.7 | 3.5 | 74 |
| Netherlands | 4.7 | 4.3 | 91 |
| Czech Republic | 4.6 | 4.2 | 91 |
| Ireland | 4.6 | 4.1 | 89 |
| Slovak Republic | 4.2 | 4.0 | 95 |
| Greece | 4.0 | 3.7 | 93 |

*Source*: data from OECD (2004c, pp. 66–7).

relation to that expenditure. Table 8.1 follows the pattern used in table 6.2, setting out the basic information on education expenditure in OECD countries, listing them from the highest to the lowest in terms of overall expenditure and then identifying the amount spent by the public sector and the relationship between private and public spending.

It is interesting to compare the pattern here with that for health expenditure. There are some interesting similarities and revealing

**Table 8.2** Nations compared in terms of levels of spending and the public component of that spending

| | Expenditure over 6% of GDP | Expenditure 5–5.9% of GDP | Expenditure under 5% of GDP |
|---|---|---|---|
| Public sector above 90% | Denmark, Sweden, France | Norway, New Zealand, Austria, Portugal, Switzerland, Finland, Belgium, Poland | Italy, Netherlands, Czech Republic, Slovak Republic, Greece |
| Public sector below 90% | Korea, USA, Canada, Australia | Mexico, Germany, UK | Spain, Japan, Ireland |

differences. The overall expenditure on health is a higher proportion of GDP, except in Korea. However, several of the developing welfare states (e.g. Mexico, Poland and the Slovak Republic) spend nearly as much on education as on health. In all cases the proportion of the education spend drawn from the public purse is higher than that from the private one, whereas in relation to health the USA has a higher private than public spend and several other nations have private spends close to half (Korea, Switzerland and Greece). Overall, public spending on education is much higher than private spending, with two nations where there is effectively no private sector (New Zealand and Poland) and many more where it is very small. Whereas in the health case the big public spenders are all European nations, in the education case New Zealand figures as a big public spender alongside the European nations.

A rough classification of nations is set out in table 8.2 but it is difficult to see more than a rudimentary basis for a typology. The 'social democratic' nations are up there amongst the big public spenders, but so are most other European nations and New Zealand. All of Esping-Andersen's 'liberal' group of nations, apart from New Zealand, do feature as lower relative public spenders (but only in relation to the very high cut-off of 90%).

## How Does the State Involve Itself in the Education System

Chapter 6 identified a number of roles the state may play in relation to health care. Education policy may be presented in the same way. These roles are (1) regulator, (2) funder/purchaser and (3) provider/ planner. This discussion will be divided into, first, a fairly brief section on the issue of regulation of the private sector, then a discussion of administrative divisions within the public sector and finally a section on issues about public partnerships with private or voluntary sectors.

## *Regulation of the private sector*

The rationale for state concern about the private sector in education tends to be, as with some regulatory concerns in social care, derived from the fact that children are minors. In such circumstances the state may deem it appropriate that it should not leave decisions about education solely to parents, notwithstanding their capacity to make private purchases. In many cases this concern follows logically from legislation that determined that education up to a certain age should be compulsory. Once the state had determined that it should try to reach certain standards in the provision of education, it logically had to concern itself with the standards offered outside its remit. However, issues about the regulation of private education may not only concern the core educational product but may also extend to standards of accommodation, issues of child health and welfare, and matters of discipline.

## *Administrative divisions within the public sector*

In federal systems the provision of school systems, and sometimes higher education systems (e.g. in Switzerland), is the responsibility of the lower tier of government. Yet many states have seen federal governments seeking justification for intervention in the lower tier in many areas of social policy, notwithstanding apparent constitutional prohibitions. In the USA, federal interventions have been justified in terms of two provisions within the constitution. The interventions that have received the most international attention have been those based on equal rights clauses in the constitution, which were used to justify federal moves against segregated education in the southern states (Crain, 1968). These may be seen as regulatory interventions. More important for the day-to-day business of education has been the clause in the constitution which gives Congress the power to 'provide for the common defense and general welfare of the United States' (Article 1, section 8). Under this clause the federal government provides cash to support educational activities within the states, justified in terms of a concern about the overall strength of the nation.

Similarly, in Australia the constitution does not identify education as a responsibility of the federal government and it is therefore the preserve of the states. However, in the constitution the federal government can make grants to the states on 'such terms and conditions as' the federal parliament deems fit. This has led to a situation in which much of the funding for government schools, and nearly all funding for universities, comes from the federal government.

Once there is a situation in which a federal government is pouring substantial funds into an activity at the state level, it has a lever it can use to influence the form that activity takes. Outside federal systems, responsibility for schools (but generally not for higher education) is very often delegated to local government. In the relationship between central and local government, as in federal systems, a great deal of central power will stem from funding arrangements. Local government systems often involve local taxation, but these generally do not raise enough money for its costs to be carried entirely in this way.

However, it is inappropriate in the case of central–local relations in respect of education to explain central control entirely by reference to funding arrangements. Education legislation in non-federal states (and in the lower-tier units in federal ones) is characteristically heavily prescriptive on matters of school systems, arrangements for the employment of teachers, curricula and assessment systems. There are likely to be inspection systems to reinforce these concerns.

In various societies some part of the education system is directly administered by central government. This is particularly true of higher education systems. Clearly there is a sense in which, in all systems, the educational institutions themselves represent another administrative tier. The very nature of a school is such that a great deal of crucial day-to-day decision-making will be carried out at that level, and will exert a strong influence on its educational outputs. Variations in educational performance that are neither determined by the system as a whole nor attributable to the social characteristics of the pupils have been the subject of study in various countries, in a search to identify and explain 'the school effect' (Creemers and Scheerens, 1989; Teddlie and Reynolds, 2000).

In various countries the need for decentralised management of schools has led to administrative arrangements designed to give schools or groups of schools a measure of autonomy, perhaps accompanied by democratic or quasi-democratic arrangements for parent or community representation separate from other aspects of local government.

*Public partnerships with private and voluntary sectors*

Most of the governments in the OECD group of nations spend most of their money in the public sector. There are two striking exceptions to this: the Netherlands, where only around 20 per cent is spent on direct support of the public sector, and Belgium where the figure is a little less than half (OECD, 2004a). The only other nations where expenditure levels fall far below 100 per cent are Australia, Denmark, New Zealand, Sweden and the UK, where around 70–80 per cent of public education funds are spent on the support of public providers.

Hence, to return to the question about the evidence for 'regimes', posed in the discussion about table 8.2 above, the introduction of a variable identifying publicly supported private systems would do little more than highlight the special characteristics of the Low Countries. The OECD statistics do not enable observations to be made about the characteristics of these 'non-public' providers. These providers are rarely 'private profit-making' bodies in this context, but rather under the control of a voluntary body. The main source of this sector has been the aspirations of religious groups, many of whom were, as noted above, pioneers of education. In the Netherlands the phenomenon of 'pillarisation' (Lijphart, 1975), under which divisions between Protestants and Catholics in that country were handled through the acceptance of separate institutions, seems likely to have been important. In the UK and France, the terms under which religious groups run schools involve such a strong measure of state management that they are scarcely thought of as 'private' at all.

The New Right have argued for a more distinctive shift towards privatisation by way of the provision of education vouchers (Maynard, 1975; Coons and Sugarman, 1978). There have been voucher experiments in the USA (see Raywid, 1985). Vouchers would enable parents to buy a basic education package at any school of their choice whether publicly or privately owned, but they would have to contribute any extra costs, likely at most of the better examples of the latter (called in the UK, for quaint historical reasons, 'public schools').

# The Characteristics of Education Systems

There is a series of important policy issues in education that deal with rather different structural considerations, including when education starts and finishes (and what the related limits are for compulsory education), how education systems are divided along age lines and,

**Table 8.3** Number of years during which 90% of a nation's
population is enrolled in education

| | |
|---|---|
| 15 years | Belgium, France |
| 14 years | Japan, Spain |
| 13 years | Czech Republic, Italy, Netherlands, Sweden |
| 12 years | Australia, Austria, Denmark, Finland, Germany, Hungary, Ireland, Korea, New Zealand, Norway, Poland, UK |
| 11 years | Greece, Slovak Republic, Switzerland |
| 10 years | USA, Portugal |
| 7 years | Mexico |

*Source*: data from OECD (2004a, table C1.2).

often closely related to the last point, the ways in which they offer
forms of specialisation or stratify by ability as well as age. This discussion will confine itself to some observations about school (but not
higher or further education) systems that seem to have some implications for educational inequality.

Systems vary considerably in the ways in which schools are divided
up in respect of the age of the child. These variations will not be
examined here. Perhaps more significant are variations in the length
of education, a function of a combination of starting ages and finishing
ages complicated by the extent to which, in practice, education is either
started before or finished after the compulsory ages. Hence statistics
are available on the number of years during which 90% of the population is enrolled. These are summarised in table 8.3.

Table 8.3 offers an indirect indicator of education inequality in some
of the countries listed. Another way to look at this topic is by examining the proportion of 15–19 year olds in education. Table 8.4 does this,
listing countries from those with the highest percentage to those
with the lowest. This brings out rather better the way in which many
students are dropping out of education quite early in various relatively
high-spending countries: Austria, the UK, the USA, New Zealand and
Italy may be identified thus.

An important division in education policy concerns the extent to
which attempts are made to give children a common schooling regardless of ability or performance. Generally, countries adopt unitary
(comprehensive) systems for children up to the age of 11, unless
exceptional handicaps require special attention. Even at this early
stage, performance differences affect progress between grades in some
societies (Switzerland, France, Japan): children do not automatically

**Table 8.4** Percentage of 15–19-year-olds in education

| | |
|---|---|
| Belgium | 92 |
| Germany | 89 |
| Czech Republic | 88 |
| France | 87 |
| Germany | 87 |
| Netherlands | 87 |
| Poland | 87 |
| Sweden | 86 |
| Finland | 85 |
| Norway | 85 |
| Australia | 83 |
| Greece | 83 |
| Switzerland | 83 |
| Denmark | 82 |
| Ireland | 82 |
| Hungary | 81 |
| Spain | 80 |
| Korea | 80 |
| Austria | 77 |
| Slovak Republic | 77 |
| UK | 77 |
| Italy | 76 |
| USA | 75 |
| New Zealand | 72 |
| Portugal | 71 |
| Mexico | 42 |

*Source*: data from OECD (2004a, table C1.2); data missing for Canada and Japan.

move up with their age group. After the age of 11, systems move at various speeds towards some degree of educational segregation. The rationale for this is seen to be different educational needs based on future occupational expectations.

Chisholm (in Bailey, 1992) suggests education systems can be analysed in terms of the relationship between selection and participation. In this respect he makes a comparison between Denmark, Germany and the UK. Denmark has a late selection system accompanied by high rates of educational participation. Although the German system selects relatively early, becoming clearly a divided one during the middle teenage years, great efforts are made to ensure that all get an education package of some kind (shifting from full-time to part-time in some cases) until 17 or 18 (see also Clasen and Freeman, 1994, chapter 6). It can be described as an 'early selection/high participation' system. In the UK, by contrast, early exit from education has been a characteristic of under-achievers. Whilst the development of comprehensive education has contributed to moving it in the direction of late selection, this has not produced a consequence for participation comparable to that of Denmark.

## Education Outputs

As with health policy, comparative data on inputs into the education system provide little basis for arguments about the quality of systems. They may also reflect variation between nations in efficiency or in salary levels and other costs. What is needed is output data. However, it is not easy to compare crude data on this either. Variations in numbers in the system cannot be meaningfully compared except outside the compulsory school years, and even then the crucial questions will not be about numbers participating but about the benefits they are acquiring from participation.

Clearly, the most fundamental and basic comparative index of education performance is the elimination of illiteracy. There are comparative statistics on this. Most of the OECD nations do not figure in these data; this is not necessarily an index of the virtual elimination of illiteracy but it certainly suggests that the issue is no longer on the agenda. Table 8.5 provides data on adult illiteracy (the percentage of over-15s who effectively cannot read or write) for those OECD nations where data are available and for a cross-section of other nations.

Going beyond simply comparing literacy rates, scholars have endeavoured to develop standardised ways of measuring educational performance that can facilitate comparisons between countries or over time. Recent OECD reports provide findings from comparative tests on a range of subjects. Table 8.6 provides data from maths and reading tests given to 15 year olds.

The trouble with using a mean to compare countries is that it tells little about the range of performance, and particularly about the percentages in each country doing badly in these tests. There are limits to the extent to which it is appropriate to reproduce statistics here. However, it may be noted that the following countries had particularly wide dispersions around the means for mathematics (listed in order of magnitude): USA, Greece, Poland, Japan, Switzerland, Portugal and Hungary. Of these, it should be noted that the Japanese and Swiss

**Table 8.5** Adult illiteracy rates

| | Percentage of males over 15 | Percentage of females over 15 |
|---|---|---|
| *OECD countries for which data are available* | | |
| Greece | 1 | 4 |
| Hungary | 1 | 1 |
| Italy | 1 | 2 |
| Korea | 1 | 4 |
| Mexico | 7 | 10 |
| Portugal | 5 | 10 |
| Spain | 1 | 3 |
| Turkey | 7 | 23 |
| | | |
| *Other countries* | | |
| Argentina | 3 | 3 |
| Bangladesh | 48 | 70 |
| Brazil | 15 | 15 |
| China | 8 | 24 |
| Cuba | 3 | 3 |
| Ghana | 20 | 37 |
| India | 32 | 55 |
| Indonesia | 8 | 16 |
| Iran | 17 | 31 |
| Jamaica | 17 | 9 |
| Mozambique | 40 | 71 |
| Pakistan | 43 | 72 |
| Russian Federation | 0 | 1 |
| Saudi Arabia | 17 | 33 |
| South Africa | 14 | 15 |
| Tunisia | 19 | 39 |
| Ukraine | 0 | 1 |
| Zimbabwe | 7 | 15 |

*Source*: data from World Bank (2002).

means are well above the overall mean. With regard to literacy, wide dispersions around the means were found in the USA, Greece, Poland, Portugal, Switzerland and Hungary (again listed in order of magnitude). All these countries had mean scores below the overall mean. In each case the USA stands out as a country with both poor overall performance levels and a wide dispersion of performances, despite being a very high spender on education.

**Table 8.6** Mean scores on maths and reading tests

|  | Mean maths score | Mean reading score |
|---|---|---|
| Australia | 533 | 528 |
| Austria | 515 | 507 |
| Belgium | 520 | 507 |
| Canada | 533 | 534 |
| Czech Republic | 498 | 492 |
| Denmark | 514 | 497 |
| Finland | 536 | 546 |
| France | 517 | 505 |
| Germany | 490 | 484 |
| Greece | 447 | 474 |
| Hungary | 488 | 480 |
| Ireland | 503 | 527 |
| Italy | 457 | 487 |
| Japan | 557 | 522 |
| Korea | 547 | 525 |
| Mexico | 387 | 422 |
| New Zealand | 537 | 529 |
| Norway | 499 | 505 |
| Poland | 470 | 479 |
| Portugal | 454 | 470 |
| Spain | 476 | 493 |
| Sweden | 510 | 516 |
| Switzerland | 529 | 494 |
| UK | 529 | 523 |
| USA | 493 | 504 |

*Source*: data from OECD (2004a, tables A7.1 and A6.2).

Data of this kind attract a kind of 'league table' approach to national comparisons. It was suggested above that they need viewing with a high degree of scepticism, since there are grave difficulties about developing measurement techniques that are robust in precisely the same way in different countries with different education systems and different cultures. The data reported above come from the second wave of international studies, conducted for the OECD by the Programme for International Student Assessment (PISA), a three-yearly survey of the knowledge and skills of 15 year olds in the principal industrialised countries. There has been considerable controversy about earlier studies of this kind. Methodological criticisms have focused on the limitations of small sample studies with results quite close together and wide dispersions around national means. Even in mathematics, standardisation of tests is difficult when students learn in different ways in different countries, let alone in a topic like reading where for example some languages may be harder to learn than others.

There are difficult questions to be answered about how differences may be explained. Reynolds, an advocate of the development of comparative studies of school effectiveness, is candid about the complex range of possible variables that need to be related to each other. For example, in a discussion of the apparent educational 'success' of Pacific Rim countries (particularly Japan, Korea and Taiwan) relative to others (particularly the UK) he identifies the following factors.

- Cultural factors: the high status of teachers, Confucian belief systems, high aspirations of parents, the high quality of teachers, high commitment by children.
- Systemic factors: the length of the school day and school year, the focus on raising the levels of achievement of all children, concentration on a small number of attainable goals.
- School factors: mixed ability classes, use of specialist teachers, high levels of collaboration between teachers, frequent testing.
- Classroom factors: whole-class instruction, heavy use of textbooks as opposed to worksheets, a well-ordered rhythm to the school day (Reynolds in Teddlie and Reynolds, 2000, pp. 250–2).

This of course gets us into topics about schools that the introduction to this chapter said we would avoid, but it is used here to illustrate the complexity of the subject and therefore to warn against simplistic policy borrowing. Particularly interesting is the way in which Reynolds recognises overriding cultural factors as well as system issues at all levels.

To return to the 'league table' issue, however, it is clearly problematical that there has been a search for a causal connection between educational systems and economic performance. Within the UK there has been a long tradition of blaming poor economic performance on the education systems in varying ways: how children are taught, how schools are organised, the alleged malign influence of egalitarianism, the overly 'academic' nature of education, and so on. Politicians and journalists are only too eager to seize upon examples of apparent success in other countries as embodying lessons for policy. In practice any systematic quantitative evidence of a connection between education and economic success is hard to find (see Robinson, 1999).

In fact it may equally be argued that far from there being any causal link between education performance and economic performance, the causal connection may run the other way: that there is higher educational success in economically successful nations. In any case, as Reynolds' listing of cultural issues above suggests, apparent correlations may in fact be reflections of wider national cultural characteristics.

## Educational Inequality

Comparative studies in education, like comparative studies in health, may mask substantial inequalities within countries. Moreover, inasmuch as these studies are working towards making a practical contribution to concerns about levels of performance in individual countries, one consideration – alongside the perhaps dominant 'human capital' enhancement one – is the extent to which education makes a contribution to either the diminution of social inequalities or at least to ensuring that inequalities are not needlessly inherited. In this context, the issue about whether it is education or some other social factor that determines outcome is obviously important.

There are several competing models against which an education system's performance on this issue may be evaluated.

1 One ideal may be that education should not sort individuals for different occupational opportunities at all. In this sense education would be a process of socialisation for citizenship in an egalitarian society. It will be apparent that this is an educational ideal, nowhere translated into practical policies. It does serve as a 'lodestar' for many educationalists, has influenced some educational developments and may be put into practice in some parts of the curriculum.

2 An alternative egalitarian ideal is to see education as contributing to equality of opportunity in a society, and particularly as ensuring that its outcomes (which ideally lead to job opportunities) are not determined by criteria other than innate ability. There are difficulties in determining what this last expression really means given the extensive nature–nurture debate about the determination of performance in education and particularly in tests. Nevertheless, a great deal of attention has been given to efforts to arrive at educational systems that do not discriminate in terms of race, gender and social class.

3 The third alternative involves the rejection of the other two. It has two alternative but closely related forms. One of these is embodied

in the preoccupation with the economic function of education. It suggests that the concern about inequality gets in the way of education doing an efficient job in equipping people for the labour market. The object should be to ensure that the system is efficient for each strata in society, educating them (or perhaps 'training' is the better word here) to become effective employees. The other form of this perspective is rather more content to see education as socialising individuals for their, largely predetermined, stations in life.

As suggested above, the key issues in relation to these perspectives concern the role education plays in relation to social stratification. However, there is an absence of good comparative data on these important issues, hence the brevity of the above discussion.

## Conclusions

This chapter has shown that it is probably harder to analyse differences in education systems than differences in social security, health care or social care. Some countries have sought to spend high amounts on education as they developed. We therefore see Korea, not one of the very rich nations, at the head of the table of expenditure as a percentage of GDP. The funding of the system is dominated by government, both central and local, even where the providers are diverse. The ongoing issues about control over the education system are ones that comparative data cannot bring out very clearly.

Education policy is a curious and difficult phenomenon to analyse because there is very broad support for it in general terms – nationalist, economic and democratic arguments all come together on this – but considerable controversy about its content. The very fact that obtaining an education involves a combination of institutional and individual and family inputs means that everyone is to some extent an 'expert' on the subject. The professional expertise of teachers is very much more readily exposed to challenge by the public than is the expertise of doctors.

The debate about the content of education is also very confused by the extent to which actual educational needs are masked by the uses made of evidence on educational achievement in the job selection process. Here, the whole picture is influenced by the characteristics of elite education. This puts educationalists, particularly those of an egalitarian disposition, in a considerable difficulty. Elite education embodies fundamental cultural values: those parts of historical, literary, philosophical heritages that should be passed down from generation to generation. Herein lies the justifications for education for its own sake, not for economic growth or social peace or individual advancement. A utilitarian perspective may involve rejection of this whole educational model: elites and the masses should all share an education oriented towards the needs of the economy. What occurs in practice (especially in the nations particularly concerned about their cultural heritages, e.g. France and the UK, as opposed to the USA and Australia, though the contrast should not be over-drawn) is that the utilitarian model tends to dominate in 'mass' education whilst the cultural heritage one survives in elite education. It is the latter that may be crucial for elite job opportunities, and hence democratic demands for it to be open to all.

The suggestion is then that this tension lies at the heart of contemporary educational controversy. Public expenditure crises together with rising economic difficulties and attendant unemployment lead many to cry for education expenditure (meaning of course expenditure on education of the masses) to be concentrated on subjects of clear economic relevance.

Those who argue for a distinctive egalitarian but not utilitarian approach face a dilemma. Egalitarianism in education has often involved a hostility to traditional education because it transmits a conservative set of cultural values. In this sense there can be some identification with the quest for greater relevance in education. The problem is then how to draw a distinction between the narrowly economic concept of relevance and the wider ideal that egalitarians have in mind (see Ball, 1990, chapter 1, for a good discussion of this issue). They are apt to be ground between the social capital school and the traditionalists. Their adherence to the 'comprehensive' ideal of a shared education for democracy is under assault from those seeking to strengthen the old divided agenda, which separates the issues about a relevant 'mass' education and a traditional elite one.

## GUIDE TO FURTHER READING

The absence of a comparative literature with a quantitative and policy-focused approach comparable to that used for other topics in this book was explained at the beginning of this chapter. The annual OECD survey *Education at a Glance* provides the best source of this sort of information. The survey by Alexander et al. (1999) provides a good overall picture of the comparative education literature. For an exploration of some of the qualitative differences within the European context, Green's (1990) book is recommended.

# PART THREE

# SOCIAL POLICY ISSUES

# CHAPTER 9

# SOCIAL DIVISIONS

## Introduction: Identifying the Issues

One problem that has already been identified about much of the comparative literature on social policy is that it tends to use 'input' data, comparing countries in terms of what they spend. The comparative material is much stronger on this than on how they spend it, whilst 'output' and 'outcome' data are patchy. It also deals with nations as a whole, inevitably paying little attention to divisions within nations whether geographical or social. Taking these two problems together, it has to be acknowledged that nations may have been identified as high performers in respect of social policy when in fact their high expenditure is entirely concentrated on meeting the needs of a select portion of the total population. This is a problem that Esping-Andersen's regime theory attempts to deal with, but the available data limits what he can do. Some of his critics have made similar efforts to deal with this matter, notably Mitchell (1991) and Korpi and Palme (1998). With regard to the OECD data much used in this book, almost the only aspect that throws light on this topic is the distinction that can sometimes be made between private and public expenditure. There are often grounds for assuming that the existence of a distinct private sector is an indicator of the presence of a two-tier system in a society. The private system may be the superior one (as in the case of health care in the USA) but it may sometime be the case that people have to use the private sector because of difficulties in gaining access to the public sector (where the latter concentrates its benefits on public employees or urban dwellers, for example). This latter scenario will be found in some of the states where public systems are rudimentary. It may also be the case that the private sector is the lower status one, as in the case of the university systems of Japan and Korea. However, even here social divisions may emerge inasmuch as the relatively well-off but not the poor can buy education.

Nevertheless, the possibility of social **divisions of welfare** within national welfare systems merits further discussion, even if there are difficulties in exploring this topic comparatively. This chapter looks at this issue in general terms, and particularly focuses on issues about socio-economic divisions. The following two chapters consider gender and ethnic divisions.

## Social Policy and Social Stratification

Social policies occur in societies that are divided or stratified in various respects. Salient divisions occur in relation to socio-economic status or class, gender and ethnicity. Social policies are bound to be affected by these divisions and perhaps influence them. Much of the rhetoric of social policy suggests that it ought to have an impact on those divisions, contributing to the advancement of equality (see Le Grand, 1982, chapter 1). The 'welfare state' has been portrayed in these terms by both its defenders and its critics. A more modest aspiration for social policy is that it may play a role in alleviating or mitigating the worst effects of capitalism. However, there are altern-ative possibilities. Social policies may have no significant effect on divisions but merely reflect them. It is also possible that far from redu-cing divisions in society, social polices may reinforce or increase them. Overall, social policy may itself be a creative influence on stratifica-tion, producing divisions of its own.

With particular reference to social security, Walker (2005) notes that even when social policies involve redistribution, it is important not to confuse aims with consequences, and that redistribution can take various forms. He goes on to note that vertical redistribution is not necessarily always from rich to poor, and that there may be two other forms of redistribution: horizontal ('transfers to people that may have high demands on their budgets irrespective of their incomes', ibid., p. 32; note the child support issue here); and life-course ('facilitating people transferring surplus incomes from period of their lives when they are comparatively prosperous to times of relative shortage', ibid., p. 34).

To examine how the operation of social policy interacts with, and has an impact on, social structures it is necessary to explore some of the basic elements in social structures, and then to look at the extent to which social policies can be seen to be divided along similar lines.

This can then lead to consideration of some of the more dynamic aspects of the relationship between social policy and society.

The approach to comparative analysis adopted by Esping-Andersen is rooted in the notion that some social policy systems may reflect and contribute to social solidarity. The concept of 'decommodification' is used to suggest that some policy systems achieve universalism, which treats all sections of society alike. The decommodified systems of Scandinavia are contrasted with corporatist and liberal systems that more clearly reflect labour market divisions and market ideologies. This is an attempt to classify national systems as a whole, in which the Scandinavian systems are seen as more inclusive than the others. This does not mean they are without divisions. Decommodification is a relative concept.

This discussion will emphasise divisions within systems, eventually coming back to address comparative questions about the extent to which some systems are more divided, or divided in different ways to others. It will be carried out primarily in terms of social class (with, as noted above, the similar and related issues about gender and ethnicity left until later chapters). Since this book is about social policy and not about social stratification, it cannot therefore explore all the complex issues involved in analysis of the latter. At the same time, as suggested above, it cannot ignore stratification. It is, for analytical purposes, necessary to deal with each aspect of stratification separately. The order in which they are considered should not be taken to indicate a view of their relative importance. Feminists, for example, have justifiably criticised the primacy given to class analysis whilst other sources of inequality are ignored or are assumed to emerge from class divisions. Yet the way in which much argument about stratification has been shaped around class analysis makes it appropriate to look at that first.

## Social Class: Concepts and Theory

Social class concepts are used in a variety of ways, both in everyday discourse and in sociological analysis. It is easy to arrive at a situation in which people are talking past each other because of their different usages. In the context of this book it is necessary to pause and dwell on a little basic sociology in order to establish the parameters of the discussion to follow. In doing so, elements from an elaborate debate will be set out as succinctly as possible.

Perhaps the most common popular usage of class sees it in subjective terms, with cultural overtones about who people identify with, feel comfortable with and are able to talk to (sometimes quite literally in the last case, given differences in language usage). This approach ignores the income, occupation and power differences in society that these subjective and cultural phenomena reflect and often reinforce. It makes the achievement of a classless society a matter of breaking down these cultural barriers, a comfortable 'egalitarian' objective for those who do not want to sacrifice more material privileges.

There is an alternative approach to defining class in subjective terms that offers a direct challenge to this. The most strident formulation occurs in Marxist theory, which defines class in terms of the relationship to the means of production. If stripped of its tendency to work with a simple class division into ownership and non-ownership, its link with a prediction of increased polarisation and its association with a direct attack on capitalism, this approach has the following merits:

1 it focuses on the very concrete and evident differences between people in terms of income, wealth and power;
2 it recognises that these differences are relational (if a cake is divided unequally, some have less because others have more).

These basic points need to be confronted before going on to any arguments about justifications. People may want to argue that differential participation in the creation of the cake justifies unequal shares; the point here is merely to establish that measurable differences, with consequences for other activities, arise out of the sharing process and that this process involves a relationship.

Most modern usages of class in these terms have moved a long way from Marx's capitalist/proletariat distinction. They owe a great deal to the German sociologist Max Weber and to more recent developments of his work (see Dahrendorf, 1959; Bendix and Lipset, 1967; Giddens, 1973; Giddens and Held, 1982). The characteristics of these usages are as follows. It is recognised that labour market relationships are important but cannot be simply dichotomised into ones involving either buyers or sellers of labour. Most labour market participants are sellers of labour but selling involves very different levels of skill in very varied situations. At the most advantaged end are, for example, people with skills that are much in demand, people who have secured managerial roles within capitalist enterprises, professionals who have secured state monopolies, and bureaucrats who acquire rights to their jobs so strong that they may almost be regarded as property. At the disadvantaged end are the traditional proletariat who have nothing to sell but their labour power, who (in the event of competition for work) may be further divided amongst themselves in terms of other differences. Between these two extremes are various gradations of 'market situation', very dependent on education and skill but also on the success of specific social groups in securing legal status and/or trade union protection for themselves.

In trying to add the wide range of considerations into the analysis, factors that facilitate entry to advantaged positions and factors that protect individuals once in those positions have been mixed together. A further feature of a class structure is that individuals endeavour not merely to protect themselves but to pass advantages on to others, notably their children.

In capitalist societies, differential advantage in the labour market leads to differential rewards. The main way advantages are passed to the next generation is through the effective use of those monetary rewards within the family. The comparative openness of the labour market in many industrial societies, inasmuch as posts are not inherited or passed on through patronage but are the subject of competition, makes family economic advantage only one of the factors that influences the life chances of children. In other words, the class structure is an open one in which family members may rise and fall between generations. This fact, when also associated with a lack of cultural divisions between the classes, is also referred to by those who argue that their societies are classless. Conversely, social mobility studies indicate that a parent's position in the class structure is still a very strong predictor of his or her children's likely future position (Goldthorpe, 1980). However, it is important not to confuse very real divisions at any one point in time with the possibilities of change over time and between generations in the context of a changing society.

The relatively abstract theory set out above is translated into operationalised social class concepts. A limited number of socio-economic groups are identified. These are classified by occupation but with the recognition that a 'high' position in this classification normally implies a high income and vice versa (taking a long view not a short one, and noting also issues about stability and the opportunities to increase income over time without an occupational change). Non-manual and professional jobs tend to dominate the top end of any such classification, manual ones (particularly low-skilled ones) the bottom end. In the middle, the manual/non-manual distinction, once comparatively clear in such systems, is today very blurred. There are some groups that are hard to classify. The self-employed (Marx's bourgeoisie) range from very minor business people with poverty-level incomes to major magnates. There are obvious problems about classifying someone without a labour market attachment (a very relevant point for women in many countries). Past employment or the nature of the employment sought by those out of work may also be an unsatisfactory basis for classification.

Socio-economic 'class' indices are used in the examination of the performance of social policy systems, notably in relation to health and education, where there are distinct links between final outcomes (likelihood of survival of birth, likelihood of success in the education system, etc.) and socio-economic status. There will be various explanations for these differences and they cannot, without consideration of other factors, be used to *judge* the outputs of social policy systems.

## Social Divisions of Welfare

Social policies, particularly income maintenance, employment and education policies, may have an important part to play in relation to the dynamics of a class structure. It has been suggested that there are 'social divisions' in social welfare systems that reflect, and may reinforce, social divisions in society. As was noted in chapter 3 on this theme, Titmuss (1958) and Sinfield (1978) drew attention to the way tax reliefs and untaxed fringe benefits may convey privileges to some, largely better-off, workers so that their incomes in adversity (particularly when they are sick or retired) are state subsidised or state protected in ways not available to other, largely worse-off, workers. These two forms of welfare, subsidised by the state but often not identified in the 'welfare package', are described as 'fiscal' and 'occupational' welfare.

A related vein of British work has shown that better-off families may secure considerably more state-subsidised services than worse-off families (Le Grand, 1982; Townsend, 1979). Two crucial ingredients in these findings are that the better-off are likely to make much more use of the most expensive elements in the education system (particularly higher education) and that they are likely to make more effective demands on a state health-care system. However, the thrust of this work is a little different to that in Titmuss's and Sinfield's essays. It points to underuse, by poorer people, of universally available services as opposed to subsidies for private privileges. These are rather different issues, calling for very different remedies by those who are unhappy with the inequalities demonstrated.

Nevertheless, it is worth considering to what extent the implications of both approaches to differential experience of social policy can be generalised to model the association between class inequalities *before* and *after* social policy inputs. This relationship could be traced in simple terms of a comparison between the welfare expectations of two broad 'classes' distinguished by work, an upper non-manual class and a lower manual one. This sort of approach was dominant in discussions of the topic around the time Titmuss wrote his essay on the 'social divisions of welfare' in 1958. It is not so applicable today largely because of the increasing merging in the middle already referred to. It is perhaps more appropriate now to work with a three-'class' model that recognises the following:

1 market situations and tax situations of the very well-off have improved in various societies (notably the USA and the UK; see Hutton, 1995, 2002);
2 policy developments in favour of the traditional working class have, wherever employment can be maintained, contributed to a merging of that group and the lower earners amongst non-manual workers;
3 falling opportunities for unskilled manual work and the related high unemployment have separated this group from the rest of the old working class.

One way of dealing with the last of these three developments has been to characterise the resultant disadvantaged group as an '**underclass**' (Myrdal, 1962; Wilson, 1981, 1987; Field, 1989). However, this usage has been linked with arguments about the behavioural characteristics of the disadvantaged, emphasising not social but psychological processes (Murray, 1984, 1990). Mann (1994, p. 94) condemns the attempt to identify the economic and social forces that create this division as 'sloppy' sociology, encouraging a popular media usage that, in treating the underprivileged as being 'outside' of society, blames the victims and derives harsh policy prescriptions from its focus on behaviour. Rank (1994) offers powerful evidence in support of Mann's view from his study of 'welfare' recipients in the USA, showing that they share the dominant values (even to the extent of stigmatising their fellow benefit recipients!). The underclass concept implies, at best, the absence of a relationship to other classes and, at worst, a deliberate opting out of society. In the latter sense it is used with stigmatising intent. It is therefore not used here.

Moore (in Coenen and Leisink, 1993) similarly argues that the pejorative connotations of the term 'underclass' create problems for a realistic analysis of the issues. He directs attention to the extent to which the situation of this group might be analysed in terms of the concept of 'citizenship', where the absence of work opportunities leads to exclusion from full social participation. This notion of citizenship is important for the connections between social class analysis and social divisions analysis. Marshall's (1963) influential analysis of the development of citizens' rights portrays rights to social benefits that provide economic security as crucial, alongside legal and political rights, for the establishment of full citizenship. The politics of the growth of the welfare state is often interpreted in terms of the struggle for social benefits as a crucial stage in the battle for full citizenship. The model set out in the next section therefore highlights the role of social policy for citizenship.

## A Social Divisions Model

A connection between the divisions in society and the 'social divisions of welfare' may be made by tracing the nature of the latter. In the discussion below three 'groups' will be identified in terms of their likely experience of social policy. The expression 'groups' rather than classes is used in order to try to avoid confusion with the sociological analysis of class. The groups identified will be called simply 1, 2 and 3. There are obviously strong connections between these and 'class' stratification, but the purpose of the exercise is to identify how social policy works. Where it seems likely that this is a reflection of the more general stratification system that will be identified, the usage of the rather non-specific concept of 'group' is designed to try to avoid eliding policy effects and wider social factors. The initial treatment will leave the issues relating to gender to be followed up in the next chapter. Furthermore, no attempt will be made to suggest what influence ethnicity will have on who gets into which group, as this too is to come (in chapter 11).

Before proceeding to this analysis there is a need to interpose one qualification. One of the difficulties about the analysis of stratification concerns the relationship between a description of a situation at a specific point in time, which tends to be static, and the fact that the object is to explain an essentially dynamic aspect of social life. This is evidently a problem inasmuch as labour market attachment is of central importance. The third of the groups discussed below is defined largely in terms of failure to secure an adequate labour market attachment. How then can those at the beginning of an actual (or potential) working life be described? An important modern phenomenon is the temporary difficulty that most young people have in securing work, which is then followed by market entry. It may make comparatively little sense to describe those who by virtue of family and educational advantages are likely to be only temporarily workless as members of a disadvantaged and vulnerable group. On the other hand, some of them will fail to benefit from their initial advantages. There is a need to recognise their probable temporary dependency, seeing their situation as relying on the capacity of their family of origin to offer support whilst they are in this position. It is, of course, in this context that the difficulties the children of those without effective labour market attachments themselves also face in securing employment assumes particular policy significance.

Employed people in 'group' 1 are unlikely to experience breaks in their working lives before retirement. If they are temporarily sick, their employers will make up their pay. They may thus be practically unaware of entitlements to state benefits when sick or unemployed. Once retired, private pension schemes are likely to determine their income; they will probably have state insurance pensions too but in some societies these will be dwarfed by private scheme entitlements. Additionally, the privileged situations of state employees in many countries was noted in chapter 4. These are forms of 'occupational welfare' often subsidised by tax relief (fiscal welfare). If they live in a society with a good state health system, they make use of it but readily turn to private schemes if it lets them down. They may use the state education system for their children (differences in the coverage of the state system were noted in chapter 8) though if they do so they will be very fussy about school standards and may make efforts to ensure access to the 'best' schools in the public system. Their children's educational achievement is in any case heavily influenced by additional inputs from home. Employers and systems of tax relief may subsidise private health or education expenses. They are very unlikely to occupy subsidised rented housing; in many societies they are likely to be owner-occupiers and may perhaps benefit from tax subsidies to that sector. Public employment services are irrelevant to them. Social care services are largely inaccessible to them because of means-tests.

'Group' 2 are the main beneficiaries of the mainstream welfare systems. State benefit systems are important in reducing the impact of temporary absences from work and in providing support in retirement (chapter 4 noted some important differences in the extent to which different countries have public schemes that provide high levels of income replacement). Tax- or insurance-funded health schemes are very important in preventing severe difficulties in the event of serious illness. Children are sent to the nearest available state schools. This is only regarded as a problem if there are many poorer (or ethnically different) people in the catchment area. Housing choices may minimise this 'problem'. Depending on the country they are either the owner-occupiers of modest, mainly modern, houses or the tenants of the better-quality property available from a social landlord. In either event they are likely to have taken some care to avoid stigmatised areas. Public employment services may be used, particularly early in the career in countries where labour market training has been given attention. This group are also low users of social care services.

'Group' 3 can now largely be defined by contrast with group 2. Low wages and low levels of job security tend to undermine social insurance entitlements, and means-tests very often determine their incomes. Housing is likely to be poorer-quality social housing (with initial desperate need and then limited income minimising choice), though they may be in very poor-quality old private rented or owner-occupied housing. School and health-care choices are minimal, and they will not be particularly effective at making demands on professional staff. The employment service is an important but also a very controlling element in their lives (as highlighted in the discussion of measures to combat unemployment in chapter 5). They are likely to be able to gain access to social care services, but this may bring social controls with it too.

The situations of those in group 3 feature as a key ingredient in the debate about the 'underclass' (see above). The pattern of disadvantage to which that label has been applied is much more salient in high-unemployment and low-wage economies, particularly where certain areas of the manual labour market have collapsed and opportunities have been low for a long while. It follows from what is being said here about the way social policies work – how limited labour market participation undermines insurance rights, how low income limits housing choices and how this implies limited location choices and thus limited choices about other services – that the downward spiral involved reinforces the problems encountered.

## Using the Model Comparatively

The three-group model outlined here is an attempt to generalise across industrial societies. In devising the model I was inevitably influenced by my own country, the UK, where the advance of the 'welfare state' accompanied, and contributed to, the erosion of the old non-manual/manual divide. This movement towards classlessness was undermined however by two things: (1) a massive advance in economic insecurity and (2) the widening of the income gap through increased rewards and reduced taxation at the top of the income distribution during the 1980s (Commission on Social Justice, 1994). This was accompanied by deterioration of the more universal public services (health and education), increasing the incentives for group 1 to use private services. Since 1997 the first of these processes has been slightly checked (Piachaud and Sutherland, 2001).

The availability of secure employment is particularly important for preventing the growth of a large group 3. Many European countries, other than the UK, have comparatively small numbers in this group, because of a combination of minimum wage laws, measures to combat part-time and insecure employment, and policies to try to avoid concentrating the burden of unemployment. In the USA, on the other hand, the phenomenon of the 'dual labour market', with a significant group undertaking very poorly paid and insecure work, has been recognised for a long time (Wachtel, 1972; Rank, 1994).

The model seeks to explicate the relationship between economic arrangements and social policies. Social policies, as suggested at the beginning of this chapter, may reinforce or counteract stratification. The notion of 'solidarity' in income maintenance schemes is important. A great deal turns upon how social insurance has developed. Alongside any analysis of the 'dual labour market' in the USA for example, there needs to be some consideration of the dual character of social policy. Weir, Orloff and Skocpol (1988) argue:

> The critical feature of New Deal social policy that would continue to shape public intervention for the next half century was the bifurcation of policy into two tiers: a top tier of increasingly generous, politically legitimated social insurance programs and a bottom layer of politically vulnerable programs aimed at the poor. Once established, this pattern of policy channelled the development of federal government capacities along particular lines and affected possibilities for alliances of social interests. (ibid., p. 287)

In other countries great efforts were made to make social insurance a scheme for all, with pension arrangements sufficiently good to ensure participation at the top end of the income distribution, and the 'insurance' element muted to prevent people with weak labour market attachments from falling out of the scheme. In such circumstances it plays an integrating role, minimising social divisions. This is the case in Norway and Sweden. Yet it is difficult to separate the success of these countries' programmes to keep people in the labour market from their inclusive approach to income maintenance; the two policies reinforce each other (Furniss and Tilton, 1979).

The other important role social policies play in reducing the divisions outlined above is in the provision of services which are regarded as universal across the groups. This applies to education and health in a number of countries.

## Universalism

It is appropriate to dwell a little on the principle of universalism in social policy. In this context it involves the provision of a single, relatively uniform service for all citizens regardless of income or class. Can this universalism play a role in countering divisive features within a social structure? There is a muddle in some discussions of this issue between the case for universalism within a service, on the grounds that this is desirable in itself, and the case for universalism because it advances equality in society.

The fundamental problem, as Le Grand's (1982) analysis shows, is that in an unequal society people 'bring' their inequalities into a universalistic welfare system. People with higher incomes, higher-status jobs and better education can more easily take time off to visit the doctor, relate to the doctor more comfortably, know the right questions to ask and how to argue for what they want. The range of ways in which such people can assist their children to take the best advantage of state education are even more evident. In any case, as far as 'final outcome' is concerned, health status or educational achievement is a result of a combination of use of the services and the presence or absence of other social and economic advantages (ibid.).

The issues about universalism in income maintenance are more complex, since benefit systems explicitly redistribute. Simple egalitarianism would demand unequal contributions and equal benefits. The problem with this, as universalist advocates like Titmuss (1958) recognised, is that it generates a situation in which the better-off have very strong incentives for avoiding participation or for adding private systems that enhance their prospects of warding off adversity or a severe fall in income in old age. A compromise position then involves recognising the need to modify an absolute redistributive approach by one which accepts that higher contributors will be able to take more out, in the interests of universal participation. This is an argument particularly effectively deployed in Korpi and Palme's comparative work, where they explain a 'paradox of redistribution':

We find that by providing high-income earners with earnings-related benefits, encompassing social insurance institutions can reduce inequality and poverty more efficiently than can flat-rate or targeted benefits . . . The traditional arguments favouring low-income targeting and flat-rate benefits have focused on the distribution of money actually transferred and overlooked three basic circumstances. (1) The size of redistributive budgets is not necessarily fixed but tends to depend on the type of welfare state institutions that exist in a country. (2) There tends to be a trade-off between the extent of low-income targeting and the size of redistributive budgets. (3) And because large categories of citizens cannot or are not willing to acquire private earnings-related insurance and because of the socioeconomic selection processes operating, the outcomes of market-dominated distribution tend to be more unequal than the distribution found in earnings-related social insurance programs. Recognition of these factors helps us understand what we call the paradox of redistribution: The more we target benefits at the poor only and the more concerned we are with creating equality via equal public transfers to all, the less likely we are to reduce poverty and inequality. (Korpi and Palme, 1998, pp. 174–5)

The arguments for universalism within social policies are as follows.

- There are some quite explicit ways in which good services for the poor may contribute to social mobility. These are of course explicit in education, inasmuch as a state education system can make a contribution to social mobility. Somewhat similar if weaker arguments apply to the health advances to be achieved as a result of a good health-care system. Conversely, it may be argued that a system that concentrated subsidy on schools and health services for the poor would do this better. This leads on to the other arguments.
- It is suggested that a fragmented system, in which different schools or different health services or separate pension schemes are provided for different socio-economic groups, involves a very explicit state endorsement of inequalities in society.
- Such a clear acknowledgement of inequalities can itself contribute to widening them. The second-class service will tend to be inferior, operating close to a minimal level of acceptability and attracting relatively less qualified staff. A related point is that the strong demands of better-off people for quality services, expressed both through direct demands on service providers and through the political system, will contribute to rising standards for all (see Goodin and Le Grand, 1987).
- Finally, certainly as far as health services and income maintenance are concerned (and this could apply to social care services), there

are arguments for universality that have nothing to do with social divisions per se. There is a case for public intervention to ensure that exceptional problems do not disadvantage people relative to their socio-economic equivalents. A universally available health service ensures that the rich as well as the poor do not experience devastating health bills. In these circumstances the poor get treatment they might otherwise have to reject and the rich avoid a sharp reduction in their income and wealth. In this respect social policy may prevent downward mobility even if it cannot assist upward mobility. There are also issues about children as a concern of the whole society, and thus appropriate charges on the state, and not just their parents (see Pedersen, 1993 for an account of arguments on this in the UK and France).

## Comparative Evidence on Social Divisions

Although it has been argued that countries may be contrasted in terms of the extent to which there are social divisions within them, little concrete evidence of this has been produced so far. It is much easier to pursue this analysis with one country in mind than to compare countries in this respect. However, two outcome variables that are given extensive comparative attention are poverty reduction and the extent of inequalities in health. These are considered here in two separate sections.

### Inequality and poverty reduction

The evidence, explored by writers like Korpi and Palme (1998), about the extent to which social policies reduce poverty obviously focuses on social security benefits rather than services (free health care, social care and education will make contributions but they are harder to measure comparatively). The supposition is that high poverty reduction figures (or increased equality) after the impact of taxes and benefits suggest some tendency for the gap to be reduced between groups 2 and 3 in the theoretical model set out above.

These two concepts of **poverty** and inequality are closely linked. In many respects poverty may be defined as unacceptable inequality. Clearly, social policy contributions can be measured in terms of their impact on overall inequality or on poverty. There have been many attempts to identify a way of defining poverty that highlights the problems at the bottom end of the distribution. There are difficulties in arriving at a definition of poverty in terms of an absolute minimum necessary for survival in the context of societies with a high average standard of living. In such societies people rarely starve to death, yet there are differences in life expectancy and the physical quality of life that do suggest that the term 'poverty' should not merely be seen as a way of stressing 'inequality' (Townsend, 1970, 1979, 1993). The difficulties with such an emphasis come about because of problems with establishing where the cut-off point should occur, below which people are defined as 'in poverty'.

These difficulties lead some authorities to prefer to define poverty in comparatively arbitrary relative terms as a fixed percentage of a national average (Deleek, Van Den Bosch and De Lathouver, 1990; Smeeding, O'Higgins and Rainwater, 1990; Department of Social Security, 1993). As far as income maintenance is concerned, it will often be the relation between low-income groups and the average that will be of concern politically. This approach is also easily used in comparative research, which would otherwise face some severe problems of developing a common yardstick for use in several rather different cultures.

Table 9.1 contains indices of poverty and inequality for most of the OECD members and a sample of other countries. The poverty figure uses the yardstick mentioned above, looking at the percentage within a country with incomes (subject to adaptations to take into account family incomes) below 50 per cent of the median income. The other column features the 'Gini coefficient', an index developed by an Italian statistician that provides an index of inequality, where 0 represents absolute equality and 100 absolute inequality.

At this stage, readers will find that the figures for a lot of countries correspond with what might be expected from the profiles of social policy expenditure provided. The Scandinavian countries, with the partial exception of Denmark, all have low rates of poverty and inequality. The 'liberal' nations of Esping-Andersen's classification are amongst the OECD countries with relatively high rates of poverty and inequality, not surprisingly particularly the USA. But there are some surprises, especially the low poverty and inequality rates of the new EU member countries from the former Soviet bloc and the combination of relatively high poverty and low inequality in Japan. It needs to be recognised that a comparatively crude poverty yardstick has been used, one that although indicating how many are below the poverty line gives us no information on how far below that line they are.

Ultimate income depends on market-determined income *minus* taxes and within-family transfers *plus* social transfers and within-family

**Table 9.1** Poverty and inequality indicators

| Country | Percentage of population living below 50% of median income | Gini coefficient |
|---|---|---|
| *OECD* | | |
| Australia | 14.3 | 35.2 |
| Austria | 8.0 | 30.0 |
| Belgium | 8.0 | 25.0 |
| Canada | 12.8 | 33.1 |
| Czech Republic | 4.9 | 25.4 |
| Denmark | 9.2 | 24.7 |
| Finland | 5.4 | 26.9 |
| France | 8.0 | 32.7 |
| Germany | 8.3 | 28.3 |
| Greece | | 35.4 |
| Hungary | 6.7 | 24.4 |
| Ireland | 12.3 | 35.9 |
| Italy | 12.7 | 36.0 |
| Japan | 11.8 | 24.9 |
| Netherlands | 7.3 | 32.6 |
| Norway | 6.4 | 25.8 |
| Poland | 8.6 | 31.6 |
| Slovak Republic | 7.0 | 25.8 |
| Spain | 10.1 | 32.5 |
| Sweden | 6.5 | 25.0 |
| Switzerland | 9.3 | 33.1 |
| UK | 12.5 | 36.0 |
| USA | 17.0 | 40.8 |
| | | |
| *Others* | | |
| Argentina | 52.2 | |
| China | 44.7 | |
| India | 32.5 | |
| Indonesia | 34.3 | |
| Iran | 43.0 | |
| Jamaica | 37.9 | |
| Mozambique | 39.6 | |
| Russian Federation | 45.6 | 18.8 |
| South Africa | 59.3 | |
| Ukraine | 29.0 | |

*Source*: data from UNDP (2004).

transfers. Hence in evaluating social policy there is a need to give consideration to the ways in which these ingredients may be determined. In principle (and this was noted as one part of Castles and Mitchell's objection to the classification of Australasia by Esping-Andersen, see pp. 30–1), even market-determined income will be to some extent influenced by policy interventions (minimum wage laws, protected collective bargaining, measures to combat unemployment, etc.). However, the impact of these is hard to measure and compare. Rather in the comparative study of social policy, attention focuses on the other sources of income adjustment and particularly the impact of state transfer policy.

The achievements of income maintenance schemes may be seen in terms of the alleviation of poverty, in terms of the reduction of overall inequalities in income distribution in societies, and in terms of the balancing out of income variations in the lives of individuals. Modern data on incomes, benefits and taxes enable these issues to be studied. However, if a sensible overall assessment of income maintenance policy is to be made, any effect detected must be related back to the original distribution.

Table 9.2 sets out some data from the EU (before its 2004 enlargement) that looks at the role of social security in relation to the alleviation of poverty, defined in terms of low incomes relative to the median. Looking at these European countries in terms of achieved 'poverty' rates (i.e. in terms of the after-transfers column in table 9.2), we find an ordering of nations that bears some correspondence to Esping-Andersen's regimes, the three social democratic regimes (Denmark, Finland and Sweden) having the best results and the two liberal regimes (UK and Ireland) with poor but not the poorest results. The poorest results are found in the nations identified as belonging to the 'southern' family, highlighted when Esping-Andersen's conservative regime is split. A study based on a more international dataset, the Luxembourg Income Study (LIS), by Mahler and Jesuit (2004, table 1, p. 30) places three liberal regimes (Australia, Canada and the USA) as the least efficient redistributors. However, there is no clear distinction visible in their dataset between the nations in the other two regime groupings. Mahler and Jesuit's study does not include any of the southern European nations.

An alternative way of looking at the figures in table 9.2 is in terms of the scale of the transfers relative to the initial size of the problem. Here the two liberal regimes, Ireland and the UK, which are high users of means-tests, come out rather better than their after-transfer figures suggest. This provides some support to the categorisation of

**Table 9.2** Poverty rates[a] before and after income transfers, 1998

| Country[b] | Poverty rate before transfers | Poverty rate after transfers | Reduction as percentage of poverty before transfers |
|---|---|---|---|
| Netherlands | 21 | 12 | 43 |
| Italy | 23 | 20 | 13 |
| Greece | 23 | 22 | 4 |
| Germany | 24 | 16 | 33 |
| Spain | 25 | 19 | 24 |
| Austria | 25 | 13 | 48 |
| Denmark | 26 | 9 | 65 |
| Finland | 27 | 8 | 70 |
| Portugal | 27 | 20 | 26 |
| France | 28 | 18 | 36 |
| Belgium | 28 | 16 | 43 |
| Sweden | 30 | 10 | 67 |
| Ireland | 33 | 17 | 48 |
| UK | 33 | 21 | 36 |
| EU 15 | 26 | 18 | 31 |

[a] The poverty line is defined as 60 per cent of median equivalised income.
[b] Listed from lowest poverty rate before transfers upwards.

*Source*: data from European Commission (2003, annex 2, table 6).

these as 'radical' regimes. On the other hand, the data in the third column for Italy, Greece, Spain and Portugal reinforce the 'fourth world' view of these countries.

The European figures used in the above discussion of the impact of social security systems on the relief of poverty employ a definition of the numbers of poor people 'at risk of poverty', which is relative to each country. This is the percentage of the population with an equivalised (i.e. after correction of the data to take into account differences in family situations) income below 60 per cent of the national median. In this case the EU 15 median is €7263 purchasing power units, ranging from €12,532 in Luxembourg and €9414 in Denmark to €4753 in Greece and €4400 in Portugal. Without getting into the arguments outlined above about the validity of a relative approach to poverty based on the comparatively easily measured national income data, it is appropriate to comment that in a sense the poorer the poor,

**Table 9.3** Percentage poverty reduction by household type

| Country | Elderly couples | Couples with children | Single parents |
| --- | --- | --- | --- |
| Australia | 68.4 | 33.5 | 18.3 |
| Belgium | 87.1 | 61.5 | 73.9 |
| Canada | 92.4 | 37.5 | 23.3 |
| Denmark | 95.5 | 71.8 | 85.0 |
| Finland | 92.2 | 76.5 | 79.4 |
| Germany | 81.3 | −4.3 | 15.1 |
| Italy | 92.3 | −39.0 | 0 |
| Netherlands | 88.4 | 23.1 | 62.3 |
| Norway | 97.4 | 57.1 | 74.3 |
| Spain | 72.0 | −20.0 | 8.6 |
| Sweden | 99.1 | 72.1 | 91.9 |
| UK | 55.4 | 12.1 | 34.1 |
| USA | 69.7 | 10.7 | 11.5 |

*Source*: derived from Bradshaw and Chen (1997, table 4, p. 15).

the more important effective redistribution is. The reality of social transfer systems is that, broadly speaking, in respect of this EU group, the richer the nation, the more effective its transfer systems are.

An early sample for the LIS has been analysed by Bradshaw and Chen (1997) in an attempt to offer a more complex analysis of the extent of poverty reduction for different groups in the population. Although this study is rather dated (the samples are from the early 1990s), this ambitious analysis has not been repeated with more up-to-date data. Hence table 9.3 reproduces some of their results. The interesting finding is the almost universality of redistributive measures for the elderly (except in the UK, but these may be dated since there has been a strong focus on measures for the elderly poor in recent times). The big differences are in relation to child poverty (in table 9.3, a minus figure in the second column means that the effect of tax is not offset by any social security transfers). The Nordic pro-welfare orientation is very evident, particularly concern about the single-parent family. However, there is little evidence of a clear difference between the 'conservative' and the 'liberal' regimes, while the 'southern' fourth-world countries stand out as states unconcerned with child welfare (the family stands alone).

*Health inequalities*

Evidence on the extent of health inequalities offers another potential measure of the degree to which there are social welfare divisions within a society. However, this is an index much harder to use than poverty. Much of the key raw material simply enables us to observe (as reported and noted in chapter 6) significant differences between nations. We need to look inside each nation to develop an index of comparative inequality. Even when we can do that we cannot necessarily distinguish the different influences on the pattern observed. There is not the scope offered by income surveys for distinguishing health inequalities before and after interventions. We may infer, especially when we have evidence about how its health services work, that a particular pattern of inequality reflects, at least in part, inequality in access to health services (as in the case of the USA). Some data of this kind was reported on p. 135; significantly the inequalities identified were between racial groups not socio-economic ones (though these are in this context more or less synonymous).

Studies in various countries have similarly demonstrated the extent of mortality and morbidity variations between social classes (or socio-economic groups) (see Townsend, Davidson and Whitehead, 1988). In the UK, the death rate in 1990 for children between one month and one year was 2.0 per 1000 live births for children whose parents were in the top two social classes in the Registrar General's five-point scale and 4.0 per 1000 live births for those whose parents were in the bottom two classes (ibid., p. 268). Similar findings are reported for France, with infant mortality rates for the children of labourers double those for children in the professional classes (ibid., p. 90).

Clearly some powerful comparisons between survival chances can be made if between-nation contrasts and within-nation contrasts are brought together. Leon, Vägerö and Olausson (1992) have done this for infant mortality data from the UK and Sweden:

> The authors calculate that if all Swedish infants had the same level of mortality as the non-manual classes in Sweden, then 10 per cent of neonatal and 29 per cent of post-neonatal deaths would be avoided. If English and Welsh babies had the same level of mortality as the Swedish non-manual classes, then 40 per cent of neonatal deaths and 63 per cent of post-neonatal deaths would be avoided. (Whitehead in Townsend et al., 1988, p. 310)

However, there are other possibilities for the exploration of the impact of policy interventions on health inequalities. Van Doorselaer et al.

(2004) have carried out a study of inequity in doctor use in a sample of OECD countries. They find low levels of inequity in respect of inpatient care utilisation, nearly universal inequity in access to dentistry, and also the following rather more mixed patterns:

> *With respect to physician utilisation*, need is more concentrated among the worse off, but after 'standardizing out' these need differences, significant horizontal inequity favouring the better off is found in about half of the countries, both for the probability and the total number of visits. The degree of pro-rich inequity in doctor use is highest in the US, followed by Mexico, Finland, Portugal and Sweden.
>
> The picture is very different with respect to *consultations of a medical specialist*. In all countries, controlling for need differences, the rich are significantly more likely to see a specialist than the poor, and in most countries also more frequently. Pro-rich inequity is especially large in Portugal, Finland and Ireland. (ibid., p. 6)

Whilst this must be seen as an 'output' rather than an outcome study, it points in an interesting direction for the development of comparative studies, and highlights the overall point of this chapter that social divisions of welfare may be found in places that are not highlighted by aggregate national comparisons, particularly those using input data.

## A Global Dimension

The overall suggestion in this chapter is that:

- social policy systems are stratified in ways which have a close correspondence to wider social stratification in each society, but that they may influence the latter in various respects;
- countries differ in the ways in which their social policy systems are stratified, and it is this that is important for the differences between systems highlighted by Esping-Andersen and by Korpi and Palme (see also Goodin, Headey, Muffels and Dirven, 1999).

It follows from these two points that it may seem to be difficult to further suggest that the countries of the world may be identified as themselves within a larger stratification system, whilst at the same time being careful to say that we are talking about policy systems not overall stratification. However, if nations differ in the extent of their internal divisions, it is quite logical to suggest that there is an international division which mirrors these. This would run along the following lines:

1  nations where privatisation is widespread, without serious implications for the welfare of quite a broad prosperous section of society;
2  nations where public policies offer a broad measure of protection to
   quite a large cross-section in society;
3  nations (what Gough and Wood, 2004, and their associates describe
   as 'informal' and 'insecurity' regimes) where there is very little protection offered by either market or state.

However, the next point that follows is a suggestion that the distinction between the first and second of these categories follows from
a measure of political choice (cogently illustrated by the fact that despite
the position of the USA as both a rich nation and the archetypical
example of the first category, it is not the case that the nations in
category 1 can be identified as having per-capita GDP levels higher
than those in category 2). On the other hand, what is evident about the
nations in category 3 is the extent to which their policy options, and
indeed welfare in general, are strongly influenced by the nations in
the first two categories. Relevant here are not just the efforts of the
powerful nations to impose policies upon them but also the roles played
by multinational private companies and public agencies in influencing
welfare. On top of this, stratification relationships are only too apparent
in terms of the flow of migrants to the wealthier countries and the
role that contributions from these migrants play in family welfare in
the countries they have left behind.

Furthermore, the argument developed earlier in the chapter – that
a dynamic as important as within-nation stratification systems change
is the role universal benefit systems play in offering protection to the
middle groups in society – is interestingly echoed in the evidence that
those successfully developing nations that have insisted on expanding
state institutions alongside market ones have had a significant measure
of success in containing the growth of inequality and poverty (the key
examples quoted in some of the tables above are the ex-Soviet nations
now in the EU; to them can be added two other nations for which data
was not supplied, South Korea and Taiwan).

## Conclusions

This chapter has developed a theoretical approach to the examination
of social divisions in welfare and explored its implications in relation
to social class. The next two chapters will explore its application to
gender and ethnicity. I have suggested that it may be appropriate to

use a three-group model. I have also argued that policies may partly mitigate divisions in society but may also reinforce them. In addition, I have suggested that the crucial issues here concern the nature of what has been called 'group' 2, the people in this group being seen as the main beneficiaries of direct public social policy provisions. Their security is maintained so long as their attachment to the labour market is maintained.

Although the key dynamic involves the relationship between the mainstream social policy protection accorded to 'group' 2 and the disadvantaged 'group' 3, the role of 'group' 1 in this dynamic should not be forgotten. Those who make the rules for the social protection system are likely to be in this group. The more they perceive the comparatively universal benefits provided for 'group' 2 (social insurance and state-provided or -supported health-care and education systems) as extravagant and in need of better targeting, the more they accelerate the processes under which economically weaker individuals drop into 'group' 3. Devices that impose means-tests or relegate various kinds of help to the needy and diminish incentives to participate in insurance schemes tend to sort the occupants of 'group' 2 into those who can make the strenuous efforts necessary to join the privately protected in 'group' 1 and those who drop down into 'group' 3. Echoes of the conflicts embodied in choices between these options are also reflected in the international order.

The propensity to adopt policies that have the effect described in the last paragraph depends on the extent to which the elites themselves, and those most likely to offer them crucial electoral support, benefit from state services. As already noted, a general benefit that flows from a universal health-care, education or pension system is likely to have effective political support.

Social policy can play a role in relation to such a dynamic. Robust inclusive protection schemes mitigate the factors that lead to the growth of 'group' 3. Conversely, it has been suggested that an outright attack on universalist social policies will polarise a social structure much more profoundly. The gender and ethnic inequalities in social policy to be discussed in the next two chapters may reinforce polarisation along these dimensions.

The argument discussed here tends to answer the questions posed at the beginning of the chapter (on the impact of social policy) in a fairly negative way. The influence of social policy is secondary to the influence of market forces and (as we will see) discriminatory practices, and its character is largely determined by these. Undoubtedly, political activists have sometimes turned to social policy in the hope that it can do more than that. Income maintenance policies have been seen as instruments for the pursuit of a much more equal distribution of ultimate incomes. Education policies have been seen as contributing to equality through social mobility and/or the sharing of a common culture. Universal health and social care have been seen as eliminating fundamental life chance inequalities and reminding us of our common humanity. The achievements of these egalitarian aspirations have however been relatively limited.

## GUIDE TO FURTHER READING

This is another chapter for which the core literature on regime theory is relevant, and the book by Goodin et al. (1999) applies it to some of the key questions explored here. Specific articles looking at poverty comparatively are Bradshaw and Chen (1997) and Mahler and Jesuit (2004). The classic essays on social divisions are Titmuss (1958) and Sinfield (1978). The issues about the underclass and citizenship are well explored in Mann (1992, 1994) and Moore (in Coenen and Leisink, 1998).

# CHAPTER 10

# GENDER DIVISIONS

## Introduction: Identifying the Issues

This chapter will show that just as socio-economic divisions are reflected in and affected by social policy, the same is true of gender divisions in societies. Indeed a substantial amount of recent comparative research in social policy has been concerned with gender divisions, arguing that there is a need to recognise that male and female 'welfare states' may differ and also that comparative analyses need to give attention to the distinction between 'male-breadwinner' and individual rights systems. What also makes this topic very important is the extent to which, as has been mentioned in many places in this book, the family plays an important role in welfare; this needs to be analysed alongside discussions of the role of the state and the market. It is very often the case that family care means care by women.

Before moving on to substantive issues about the treatment and roles of women in social policy, this chapter will (1) revisit the approach to stratification analysis used in the last chapter and bring in issues about gender and (2) look at some of the alternatives to regime theory advanced by analysts of gender and social policy.

## Gender, Social Stratification and Social Policy

The classic sociological literature on social stratification was almost silent on the issue of gender until challenged by the feminist movement in the 1970s. The definition of class in terms of market position was occasionally challenged with the question 'How do you define the class position of women if they are not labour market participants?' The stock answer was 'in terms of the class position of their husbands or fathers' (Goldthorpe, 1983; see Crompton, 1993 for a critique).

The feminist challenge was obviously directed at the assumptions about the dependent and subordinate position of women embodied in this approach. But the approach was also bad sociology. It led to all sorts of muddles about the interpretation of the situation of women who were labour market participants. It led to a lack of attention to the social stratification issues concerning women who lost this implied male 'protection'. Furthermore, it led to the disregard of issues about the way resources may be shared within the family.

The feminist challenge to the invisibility of women in social stratification theory took various forms. The three main forms are often labelled 'liberal feminism', 'socialist feminism' and 'radical feminism' (see Dale and Foster, 1986 or Williams, 1989 for a discussion of them and their application to social policy). It is perhaps unfortunate that these ideas are clothed in ideological language, and seen to be in some senses in opposition to each other, as each has something important to say about the way the relationships between the genders occur in society.

Liberal feminism concentrates on the barriers to equal competition between men and women in society. It is the perspective that has made most inroads into conventional male-dominated policy debates. It offers a critique of many forms of discrimination: in the workplace, in education, and so on. It seems to suggest that the key issue is the removal of the barriers to equal labour market participation. Then women will assume places of *their own* in a gender-blind stratification system. This approach gives some attention to female labour market disadvantages consequent upon roles as mothers, and as carers for other relatives, but sees the solution to these problems as lying in laws that take these things into account (in relation to job security, promotion and pension rights) together with improved provisions for child care.

Socialist feminism (Hartmann, 1979; Barrett, 1980; Eisenstein, 1984) builds on this analysis to see the difficulties women face in achieving equal labour market participation in a context of unequal and exploitative relationships. Women's disadvantages in getting less from the education system, in getting less support in advancement into the world of work, and in needing to withdraw from labour market participation at times to assume nurturing and caring roles are seen as creating divisions in the labour force. They enable women to be relegated to the lower strata in a stratified or dual labour market, to be treated as part of the 'reserve army of labour'. The remedies that stem from this perspective are very like those which stem from the liberal feminist critique, with however the additional emphasis that the whole structure of exploitation needs attention if fundamental progress is to be made.

Neither the liberal nor the socialist perspective entirely opens up the issues about the role of the family. Of course, they both stress the need for egalitarian relationships within the family. If women are to be full labour market participants, their partners need to make adjustments, and ageing parents cannot make assumptions about their availability to undertake caring tasks. It is however the radical feminists who have really concentrated attention on the nature of male power, exercised both inside and outside the family (Millet, 1970; Brownmiller, 1975; Delphy, 1984). They have pointed out that there is another 'market' relationship, implicit if not explicit, within the family in which such resources, care and protection women obtain are 'bought' through the performance of sexual, caring and household duties. This is, at heart, a forced exchange, secured through a combination of direct power and indirect cultural dominance. This perspective, naturally, emphasises a concern about male violence in relation to this. It sees a male-dominated society and state as condoning the use of physical force in family relationships. The radical perspective sometimes involves the rejection of the family as an institution. Concern here is with its contribution to sociological analysis. It suggests a need to examine the reality of the power and exchange relations occurring within the family. It challenges the view of exchanges within the family as voluntary, private and rooted in shared commitments. The difficulties about these assumptions are very clearly exposed when marriages and other 'romantic' partnerships collapse, or when force is used within them.

Overall these approaches for examining the feminist struggle involve a quest for full and equal citizenship for women, through political enfranchisement and the provisions of legal guarantees of equal access to employment and social benefits and the elimination of laws giving men command over the persons and property of wives and daughters.

## The Implications of Gender for the Social Divisions Model

This discussion of the way issues about gender divisions in societies has been put on the modern sociological, and of course philosophical, agenda suggests a range of important considerations for social policy. Daly and Rake (2003) have analysed the issues about gender and social policy in ways that have much in common with the discussion of social policy as an influence on social stratification developed in the last chapter. They write:

The welfare state needs to be seen as a set of processes that have their own agency as well as operating in concert or conflict with other forces. In effect, agency and change need to be to the fore. There are a number of approaches here also. One emphasizes the welfare state as a site of struggle, with economic, cultural and other forms of power relations ongoing in welfare. Understanding the welfare state as a site of struggle means that one should not expect policy to be logical and coherent. This leads to, second, a view of the welfare state as a political and politicized domain. In other words, the welfare state is both an arena of political relations and has itself a political agency. This view of the welfare state sheds light on the relations of power between women and men and the gender-based norms that shape such relations. (ibid, p. 165)

Hence it is appropriate to explore gender issues in relation to the three-group model discussed in the last chapter (see pp. 188–90). The issue about looking inside the family assumes particular importance in relation to the advantages possessed by group 1, when those for women are derived from a 'dependent' position in relation to a male. It is clearly possible that, when the distribution of resources within the family is unpacked, women may be found to be not only in a vulnerable position but actually deprived of opportunities to benefit from the privileges and wealth of the family unit (Pahl in Walker and Parker, 1988).

However, this is of course not only an issue about resources. There are issues about power within the family and about occupational and other choices to be taken into account too. The allegedly 'privileged' position of women defined by dependency as belonging to group 1 may be founded on acceptance of a 'private' caring role. There is an important feminist agenda here about the need to make caring tasks 'public', recognising them as contributions to society not merely private acts.

Parents are less likely to buy expensive education for their daughters than for their sons. Within this education, teachers are likely to make unjustifiable assumptions about the differences between the sexes with regard to abilities and capacity for some kind of future employment (Spender and Sarah, 1980; Kelly, 1981). The key professions providing the services purchased by group 1 are often male dominated and male practitioners may make sexist assumptions about the experiences and needs of women (e.g. in health care; see Roberts, 1981; Stacey, 1988).

Clearly, widowhood and divorce are particularly likely to expose weaknesses in a model of private provision that is very linked to employment in a male-dominated labour market. Widowhood, and particularly divorce, are likely to terminate access to private pensions, employer help with health and education expenses, and so on if these are benefits derive from a husband's employment. Such events are likely to 'relegate' women from group 1 to group 2 or even 3. They do not have a corresponding impact on males.

Women can undoubtedly access some of the benefits described above through their own employment. However, many of the most advantaged occupations are ones which women have found it difficult to enter. Moreover, even when they do secure such employment, their chances of reaping the full career benefits may be affected by the absence of satisfactory provisions to cope with absences on account of parenthood (see Bryson, 1992, chapter 8).

Many of the things that have been said about women in group 1 also apply to those in group 2. Here the heavy dependence on the mainstream state services (education, health and income maintenance) makes for particular problems if male dominance is embedded within them. If unequal treatment of women is to be avoided, great attention needs to be paid to unrecognised assumptions. A 'gender-blind' approach is also questionable when female needs are distinctly different from male needs, as in some areas of health care (by definition in obstetrics and gynaecology but also in some other specialisms).

With income maintenance the issues are rather different for those in group 2. The key concern is the link made between labour market participation and social insurance. A pattern of female labour market participation that is less complete than the norm for adequate insurance protection means that women will be disadvantaged when sick, unemployed or retired. The problems here are a combination of an unavoidable fact of nature, that women bear children, and a variety of social assumptions (which of course the women involved may choose to accept) about women's roles in relation to the care of those children. To these may be added social assumptions about other caring roles. All these things are then compounded by male expectations, as both husbands and employers, about who should make the adjustments to work patterns when caring tasks arise. It is possible to devise income maintenance systems that give due weight to the implications of these reasons for withdrawal from the labour force, and this is an important feature of the evolution of some social insurance systems away from rigid insurance assumptions (Sainsbury, 1993). On top of these issues about care, there are likely to be assumptions about which gender has priority in situations of job scarcity or in relation to new job opportunities, assumptions which even the weakest versions of the belief in gender equality will want to challenge but which are very deeply embedded in many societies.

Many of the early social insurance systems, designed in a more patriarchal age and one where female labour market participation was much lower, dealt with the issues discussed above by regarding married women as the dependants of their husbands. There should not be a need to spell out the objection to this at this stage in the argument. However, as a system of social protection that linked female fortunes to those of male breadwinners, this approach did have the merit of protecting the widows of men in group 2 so that loss of the breadwinner through death had no more serious economic consequences than that likely to occur if he became unemployed. Indeed, if the man was mean about handing over money, his death might be less financially damaging for the woman than his unemployment!

But these relatively cheerful assumptions about 'dependency' under social insurance only applied to widowhood. Moreover, even in the case of widowhood, the relative longevity of working-class women relative to men, once the dangers of childbirth were past, was likely to result in exceptionally long periods of benefit dependency for women (Groves, 1992). More seriously, insurance provision for widows in these traditional schemes did not extend to separated and divorced women or to women whose dependant status was in a partnership rather than a formal marriage.

For female non-participants in the labour market, the consequence of relationship breakdown, other than death of a husband, is likely to be relegation into group 3, with income dependent on means-tests and a variety of other service choices severely curtailed. Furthermore, even when such women are labour market participants, they will often be (given the family and employment assumptions outlined above) in casual, part-time, temporary and/or low-paid employment. In such cases, the termination of a relationship will have much the same consequences as if they had no work at all.

In many modern societies where women are likely to be labour market participants they are expected to be insurance contributors in their own right. However, this can lead to anomalies if the older provisions for women as dependants remain. There will tend to be a problem of double counting, where married women secure pensions in their own right but in the process lose the benefits that would have been provided by their husband's contributions (as in the UK and USA).

This discussion of women in terms of the three-group classification has concentrated on female disadvantages in situations in which their male partners or 'equivalents' would likely be in groups 1 and 2. There is not much more then to say about group 3 except that the discussion has demonstrated the wide range of situations in which the combination of disadvantages and discrimination in the labour market and the weaknesses of social protection schemes will tend to mean that many women who are 'unprotected' financially by relation-ships with men, particularly those who lose that protection, are likely to be in group 3.

## Regime Theory and the Position of Women in Relation to Social Policy

Chapter 2 noted the critique of Esping-Andersen's regime theory that attacks its relative disregard of issues about families and its relatively narrow focus on some aspects of income. A collection of essays edited by Sainsbury (1994) examines ways of fusing Esping-Andersen's work with this critique. It is acknowledged that the concept of decom-modification aims to identify system types in terms of 'the degree to which individuals, or families, can uphold a socially acceptable stand-ard of living independently of market participation' (Esping-Andersen, 1990, p. 37). However, it is argued 'it is crucial for the position of women, whether they are entitled to benefits as individuals or whether rights are tied to families, of which men are normally considered the head' (Borschorst in Sainsbury, 1994, p. 28).

This critique points out the paradox that whilst the social demo-cratic regimes are comparatively 'woman-friendly' welfare systems, it is in these societies that women are to a great extent labour market participants. In other words, women have been 'commodified' in these comparatively decommodified systems, and decommodified in the conservative nations in group 2 where their welfare still depends largely on their family position (ibid., p. 43). The Netherlands is given particular attention in this analysis, as a high-spending nation which Esping-Andersen recognises as a rather marginal case. Bussemaker and van Kersbergen (in Sainsbury, 1994, p. 23) suggest that the Netherlands is a high spender because of a concern that the male breadwinner is a family provider, in the context of its conservative view of the roles of women.

These analyses emphasise the need to examine dominant attitudes to the family in the 'conservative' group of nations, particularly Catholic social theory and the doctrine of 'subsidiarity' that sees the state's role as limited to situations in which there is family and community failure. The analyses also suggest that an application of Esping-Andersen's approach to this issue needs to look at differences in expenditure by

**Table 10.1** Dimensions of variation of the male-breadwinner and the individual models of social policy

| Dimension | Male-breadwinner model | Individual model |
| --- | --- | --- |
| Familial ideology | Celebration of marriage | No preferred family form |
| | Strict division of labour: | Shared roles: |
| | Husband = earner | Father = earner/carer |
| | Wife = carer | Mother = earner/carer |
| Entitlement | Differentiated among spouses | Uniform |
| Basis of entitlement | Breadwinner | Citizenship or residence |
| Recipient of benefits | Head of household | Individual |
| Unit of benefit | Household or family | Individual |
| Unit of contributions | Household | Individual |
| Taxation | Joint taxation | Separate taxation |
| | Deductions for dependants | Equal tax relief |
| Employment and wage policies | Priority to men | Aimed at both sexes |
| Sphere of care | Primarily private | Strong state involvement |
| Caring work | Unpaid | Paid component |

*Source*: Sainsbury (1996, p. 42).

the state on child care (Gustafsson in Sainsbury, 1994, chapter 4) and on 'solo-mothers' (Hobson in Sainsbury, 1994, chapter 11).

Sainsbury (1996, p. 42) explores these variations in terms of two models of social policy, the individual model and the male-breadwinner model, as shown in table 10.1.

One of the contributors to Sainsbury's edited collection goes on to suggest a way of developing Esping-Andersen's typology to add in 'family welfare orientation' (based on the strength of family support policies) and 'female work desirability' (based on the extent of female access to work opportunities comparable to those for men) (Siaroff in Sainsbury, 1994, chapter 6). Also taken into account in this approach is the extent to which family benefits are paid to women. This leads to a classification of nations as follows:

• protestant social democratic welfare states (Denmark, Finland, Norway and Sweden);

- protestant liberal welfare states (Australia, Canada, New Zealand, UK, USA);
- advanced Christian Democratic (often but not necessarily Catholic) welfare states (Austria, Belgium, France, Germany, Netherlands);
- late female mobilisation welfare states (Greece, Ireland, Italy, Japan, Portugal, Spain, Switzerland).

In order to arrive at this classification (particularly the last group), Siaroff takes into account, alongside female labour market participation, female political participation and the religious orientation in the society.

Daly and Rake (2003) extend this analysis with a substantial empirical comparative discussion of gender and the welfare state. Later sections of this chapter will draw on some of their findings. These authors make a direct connection with the concerns highlighted in the discussion of social stratification, about the way in which welfare institutions both reflect and reinforce social divisions:

> First, one cannot acquire a comprehensive understanding of the welfare state without recognizing that norms and values concerning gender relations are a part of all welfare policies and practices. Second, gender relations are, in part anyway, products of public arrangements for welfare. Third, welfare states directly or indirectly affect gender relations by virtue of how they impact on the nature and distribution of resources, social roles and power relations. (ibid., p. 2)

Daly and Rake are critical of regime theory and reluctant to typologise (ibid., pp. 166–7). In this book, however, the preferred perspective is to see this as yet another topic amongst the many discussed where regime theory partly fits.

## Comparative Evidence on Gender Divisions

In the last chapter it was indicated that there is a comparative lack of evidence to enable countries to be contrasted in terms of the extent to which there are social divisions within them. This is not the case as far as gender divisions are concerned. Comparative evidence has been assembled about differences between men and women in respect of:

- poverty levels;
- the way social security systems treat them;

- labour market inequalities (which have social policy implications);
- assumptions about roles embodied in systems of support for parent-hood and in care arrangements for adults.

These are discussed in separate sections below.

### Gender and poverty

Although the OECD statistical sources are not much help for the ex-ploration of gender differences in the incidence of poverty, the EU does report some appropriate data. Table 10.2 sets out some basic statistics on the numbers of men and women at risk of poverty in the pre-2004 EU member states.

Table 10.2 shows that in the EU females are more likely to be in poverty than men and that this applies to every country except Finland and Denmark. It highlights a particularly unfavourable situation in

**Table 10.2** Risk of poverty[a] amongst men and women in the European Union, 1998

| Country | Poverty risk for men | Poverty risk for women | Amount female rate exceeds the male rate |
|---|---|---|---|
| Austria | 11 | 15 | 4 |
| Belgium | 14 | 17 | 3 |
| Denmark | 7 | 10 | 3 |
| Finland | 8 | 8 | 0 |
| France | 18 | 17 | 1 |
| Germany | 15 | 16 | 1 |
| Greece | 21 | 22 | 1 |
| Ireland | 16 | 19 | 3 |
| Italy | 19 | 20 | 1 |
| Netherlands | 11 | 12 | 1 |
| Portugal | 19 | 22 | 3 |
| Spain | 18 | 17 | 1 |
| Sweden | 10 | 10 | 0 |
| UK | 19 | 24 | 5 |

[a] Poverty defined as the percentage with income below 60 per cent of the equivalised median income (see the discussion of definitions of poverty on pp. 194–5).

*Source*: data from European Commission (2004, p. 188).

the UK, which has both a high poverty rate and a very high female poverty rate. It suggests that in a number of countries where poverty is high the male/female differential is quite low (Greece, Italy and Spain). However, this raises a question about the extent to which female poverty is hidden within the family. The trouble with simple poverty statistics like these is that issues about within-family income distributions and transfers are masked by the fact that they are derived from family data and simply apportioned to individuals. It is also the case that the statistics throw no light on the direct impact of social policies, unlike those on pre- and post-tax and income transfer poverty.

The EU data also include indices of poverty amongst adults living alone by gender (many of whom will be old) and amongst single parents with dependent children (nearly all of whom will be female). Table 10.3 reports these statistics. A comparison of the poverty rates for single men and women certainly throws light on the issue of the masking (or is it protective?) impact of the family as far as Greece,

**Table 10.3** Risk of poverty[a] amongst single persons and single parents in the European Union, 1998

| Country | Poverty risk for single men | Poverty risk for single women | Poverty risk for single-parent families |
|---|---|---|---|
| Austria | 12 | 30 | 32 |
| Belgium | 13 | 24 | 25 |
| Denmark | 18 | 36 | 15 |
| Finland | 20 | 19 | 9 |
| France | 22 | 22 | 38 |
| Germany | 22 | 24 | 47 |
| Greece | 19 | 36 | 13 |
| Ireland | 33 | 57 | 48 |
| Italy | 15 | 24 | 18 |
| Netherlands | 16 | 14 | 43 |
| Portugal | 36 | 48 | 40 |
| Spain | 10 | 12 | 38 |
| Sweden | 19 | 20 | 19 |
| UK | 27 | 48 | 45 |

[a] Poverty defined as the percentage with income below 60 per cent of the equivalised median income.

*Source*: data from European Commission (2004, p. 188).

Italy and Portugal are concerned (also perhaps Ireland). We also see differences in the circumstances of single-parent families highlighted, with the Scandinavian countries (plus oddly Greece) standing out as nations where the poverty risk is comparatively low.

The Luxembourg Income Study includes countries from outside the EU. Christopher, England, McLanahan, Ross and Smeeding (in Vlemininckx and Smeeding, 2001, p. 208) show that the female/male poverty differential is even higher in the USA and Australia than in the UK, and is nearly as high in Canada. They also confirm the high poverty rates for single-parent families in Germany and the UK but show that those for Canada and, most dramatically, the USA exceed these whilst that for Australia comes close. These data are rather earlier than the EU data, from the early 1990s.

The data on single parents gets us closer to the examination of social policy impact, although the issues about the differences between pre- and post-transfer incomes may be very significant. The data from Bradshaw and Chen's work in the previous chapter (see table 9.3) highlighted some of the differences between countries in the social security treatment of this group. So does some data from the study by Christopher et al. This looks at the overall impact of transfers on the gender poverty differential, showing it to have a significant impact in the Netherlands and Sweden but little impact in the USA, Australia, Canada, France or the UK (Christopher et al., 2001, p. 209).

Particularly hidden in all this data is the impact of labour market participation. A later section will explore this in more detail, but it is perhaps useful here to relate poverty figures to female labour market participation. Table 10.4 compares the national poverty risk figures for females in the EU countries in three categories (10 or less, 11–19, 20+) and relates them to employment rates (taken from table 10.5 and

**Table 10.4** Relationship between female poverty and labour market participation (LMP)

|  | Poverty risk low (≤ 10) | Poverty risk medium (11–19) | Poverty risk high (≥ 20) |
|---|---|---|---|
| LMP low (< 50%) |  | Ireland, Spain | Greece, Italy |
| LMP medium (50–59%) |  | Austria, Belgium, France, Germany |  |
| LMP high (≥ 60%) | Denmark, Finland, Sweden | Netherlands | Portugal, UK |

classified as under 50%, 50–59% or 60% or more) for women aged 15–64. This suggests a tendency for high levels of employment and low poverty risks to go together, but with a broad spread in the middle and with two significant deviant cases: Portugal and the UK.

All of the poverty data suggest that there are significant differences between countries, to some extent following the four regime altern-ative to the Esping-Andersen model suggested by Siaroff (see pp. 212–13). However, this only allows us a limited exploration of a complex web of factors about how social security systems operate and about how labour markets operate. The next section looks at this in rather more detail.

### Treatment of women by social security systems

The key analytical concept for the examination of the way women are treated by social security systems is Sainsbury's male-breadwinner/individual model dichotomy set out in table 10.1. The important issues here are (1) how benefit entitlement is determined, (2) how contribu-tions are determined and (3) who gets the benefit.

As a rough generalisation it may be said that means-tested systems are more likely to use the male-breadwinner model and that con-tributory benefit systems are more likely to work with an individual model but this only operates to the benefit of females when there is high labour market participation. However, it needs to be added that there has been a tendency, in the face of increased recognition of equal rights issues, for systems to have been modified in the recent past in ways which mitigate (but generally do not eliminate) female dis-advantages, in particular:

- the recognition of either adult member as the applicant whilst retaining the nuclear family as the benefit and assessment unit in the determination of entitlement to means-tested benefit;
- the recognition within contributory benefit systems of the need to compensate for periods outside the labour force on account of family responsibilities.

These dimensions cannot be analysed statistically, although there have been efforts to develop typologies based on the dichotomy outlined by Sainsbury (Langan and Ostner, 1991; Lewis and Ostner, 1994).

Inasmuch as the generalisation above about the distinction between means-testing and contributory benefits holds, it may be suggested that so long as mean-tests use a household basis for the assessment of entitlement (which all seem to do; see Eardley et al., 1996, pp. 63–4) there will always be a 'breadwinner model' bias in such systems. In other words, women cannot apply for benefits without having the resources of their partner taken into account (or of course vice versa, though that is a less common situation). The interesting variations between countries involve the extent to which systems look beyond the household to the extended family and the extent to which the concern when looking within the household is with the just the nuclear family or with everyone. The latter pattern may have implications for women inasmuch as they are located (more than men) in households in which there are other adults. There is also a complex issue here, where it is difficult to interpret where disadvantage may lie, about the definition of the nuclear family in terms of whether or not it only embodies a heterosexual definition of that entity. But all this adds up to no more than a reinforcement of a distinction (discussed in chapter 4 on pp. 84–7) around the salience of means-testing, which tends to separate the 'liberal' regimes from the rest.

On the contributory benefits side, the problem is to sort out, on the one hand, rules that explicitly see women as 'dependants' of male claimants (a central but now waning feature of the UK's national insurance scheme) and, on the other, individual contribution schemes that disadvantage women because the relationship between what is paid in and what is taken out is strict (thus favouring males with their greater likelihood of lifelong employment, full-time work and higher rates of pay).

Daly and Rake (2003) suggest a need to distinguish between three different state agendas: one that recognises high female labour market participation as an overriding principle, one that continues to stress women's roles as mothers and a third which they call a 'productivist agenda in which the employment of women especially has become a quasi-public good' (ibid., p. 174). This muddies any attempt to draw the male breadwinner/individual distinction in any clear-cut way since the productivist nations are impelled to reduce social policy-based disincentives to female labour market participation.

### Inequalities in labour market participation

In chapter 9, universalism was evaluated as a response within social policy regarded as mitigating divisions. What is the similar remedy as far as the inequalities between the genders are concerned? The most obvious answer is 'equal opportunities policy'. The discussion of the respective kinds of feminism partly examined this, since it is the main 'liberal' remedy. What the other forms of feminism indicate is that equal opportunities policy on its own does not tackle the structured forms of inequality associated with the treatment of women as a key element in the 'reserve army of labour' (socialist feminism) and with male power exercised both in society and within the family (radical feminism). Simply requiring policies to be operated in ways that maximise female participation in economic institutions and minimise dependency assumptions (in income maintenance, for example) may disadvantage rather than advantage women if all many can achieve is inferior and poorly paid work from which they return in the evening to partners who expect disproportionate contributions to domestic and caring tasks. This seems to be the underlying threat of the 'productivist' regimes identified by Daly and Rake.

A group of statistics that throw some light on these issues are EU figures on differences in employment rates, rates of part-time or full-time employment, and differences in wage rates. These are set out in table 10.5. While some care is needed in using statistics of this kind,

**Table 10.5** Some indices of female employment in the European Union

| Country | Female employment rate 2000 | Female rate as percentage of male rate | Percentage of the female workforce who are part-time 2000 | Full-time female pay as percentage of male pay 1999 |
|---|---|---|---|---|
| Austria | 60.1 | 78 | 28.3 | 79 |
| Belgium | 50.3 | 74 | 40.5 | 89 |
| Denmark | 72.0 | 90 | 43.1 | 86 |
| Finland | 65.4 | 92 | 17.0 | 81 |
| France | 56.1 | 80 | 30.8 | 88 |
| Germany | 58.8 | 81 | 37.9 | 86 |
| Greece | 40.9 | 58 | 7.8 | 87 |
| Ireland | 55.0 | 72 | 30.1 | 78 |
| Italy | 41.1 | 60 | 16.5 | 91 |
| Netherlands | 65.2 | 79 | 70.4 | 79 |
| Portugal | 61.1 | 79 | 16.3 | 95 |
| Spain | 41.9 | 59 | 16.9 | 86 |
| Sweden | 70.4 | 96 | 36.0 | 83 |
| UK | 65.1 | 83 | 44.6 | 78 |

*Source*: data from European Commission (2003, 2004).

because of the problems of definition involved (see Hantrais, 2004, pp. 74–91), they do show that throughout the EU women are less likely than men to be employed, and when they are employed they are likely to earn less. They also demonstrate significant differences between nations as a whole, though these do not fall into the neat categories required of any effort to develop a typology. The three Scandinavian nations all have high female employment rates relative to males (over 90%), but only Finland also has low rates of female part-time work. The middle group (as far as employment rates are concerned, with relative rates in the 80s or 70s) similarly has high part-time rates (very high in the case of the Netherlands), with one interesting exception, Portugal, where part-time work is less common. Significantly, Portugal is also different from the other southern countries, all ones in which female labour market participation is relatively low. The pay gap figures are hard to interpret: it is not (as might be expected) the case that it is less in the Scandinavian countries. It is noteworthy that two countries where female employment is largely full-time have low pay gaps (Italy and Portugal).

However, it is difficult to work out what these figures tell us about social policies. They may:

- reflect the incidence of direct discrimination (lower pay for similar work, employment opportunities closed to women and other forms of occupational segregation);
- reflect forms of indirect discrimination (differential access to education and training, seniority rules that disadvantage people who have taken time out from employment);
- follow directly from efforts to combine work and caring roles;
- reflect lifestyle choices (though of course that gets us into complicated questions about the extent these may be forced choices, reflecting deep-seated cultural norms instilled through socialisation and other social processes).

Given these variations, there are then questions about the extent to which these differences are (or should be) the subject of policy interventions and the different forms these may take. Are they matters to be largely tackled by regulatory policies (laws aiming to influence contracts of employment, etc.) or by more direct interventions (providing compensatory benefits or services that support labour market participation)?

There are some important questions about the extent to which limited labour market participation has consequences for social benefits.

Ironically, where labour market participation is low, systems of benefit that do *not* link entitlements to insurance contributions or previous earnings may give women a better deal than where they do. Or of course they may split women rather fundamentally on the basis of differences in levels of participation. This applies not only to pensions but also to unemployment and sickness benefits, particularly when the rates paid depend on previous incomes. Another issue here is the extent to which there are provisions that reinforce low income. Here the development of negative income tax and tax credits may bring with it social benefits that will effectively reduce the gender income gap. In terms of Esping-Andersen's regimes, the adherence to stricter insurance conditions plus perhaps a familist stance that limits female labour market participation in his 'conservative' regime type means that it is there that women come off worst. However, it has been suggested in many places in this book that rather too many different countries appear in this category, that changes are occurring quite rapidly in some of the nations within it, and that it particularly obscures north–south differences within Europe.

### Support for parenthood

Two crucial indices of national differences in state support for parent-hood worth examining are parental leave provisions and support for child care. However, assembling comparative statistics on these is dif-ficult. In the case of parental leave, there are several crucial conditions that need to apply if they are to minimise gendered disadvantages:

1 It needs to be paid for, i.e. either state supported or backed-up by provisions that require employers to continue wages in full or in part, not simply protected by rules that require employers to grant leave.
2 It needs to be available to men and women. More than that, there need to be requirements or incentives for men to take a significant share. The Swedish government found that their parental leave benefits were taken much more by women than men, and added provisions forcing men to take a proportion.
3 It needs to meet parental support needs not just over the period immediately after the birth of a child, but also when older children are unwell and unable to attend day care or school. In the case of child care there are issues not just about its availability but also about its cost, and whether it is subsidised directly or through benefits (see Bradshaw et al., 1993; Bradshaw and Finch, 2002).

*Care of adults*

Many of the key points about women as carers have already been mentioned. Not only are there likely to be assumptions within societies and within families that women should assume caring roles with regard to children but there will also often be assumptions about similar responsibilities towards adults with disabilities and health problems. This has been described as 'compulsory altruism' (Land and Rose, 1985), an expectation that unpaid caring for elderly parents (in particular) but also for other relatives will be undertaken by females without financial rewards and perhaps at the cost of abandoning opportunities to participate in the paid labour force (see also Finch and Groves, 1983). Inasmuch as governments regard social care as family care, reducing demands on public funds, this means female care. The availability of female relatives may be a specific criteria for the denial of social care services. Men are of course often found in caring roles, but this is predominantly in situations in which they are caring for their spouses.

Somewhat similar assumptions may be applied in relation to voluntary caring activities and even to state provision of care: that such tasks may be expected to be performed by women for little or no reward. In the case of paid work these assumptions about female altruism may reinforce labour market disadvantages (see Evers et al., 1994). It has been pointed out that much of the growth in female labour market participation has occurred in 'welfare state employment', i.e. caring roles which have 'gone public' (Hernes, 1987). Whilst this is a welcome development from the perspective of female disadvantage, it carries with it the problem that these tasks may be regarded, because they have emerged from the family, as lower status, deserving of lower rewards and dispensable when there is a lack of public resources (some of these issues were explored in chapter 7).

## Conclusions

The starting point for this chapter has been ways in which the gender-blind literature on social stratification has been challenged. Alternative approaches to social policy evaluation that give explicit attention to gender divisions have been examined. It has been shown that female disadvantage remains widespread. It has been suggested that the comparative examination of this has been developed out of regime theory by writers who have suggested that there are problems with the use of Esping-Andersen's concept of decommodification in relation to the situation of women. In the countries where decommodification is argued to be highest, it is the participation of women in the labour force that has particularly contributed to their social welfare. Defamilisation needs to be considered alongside decommodification. Sainsbury's distinction between the male-breadwinner model and the individual model in the determination of social policy best encapsulates this.

In looking at the actual data on female disadvantage, there is a need to see what can be divined from statistics that generally illustrate but do not explain the phenomenon. Daly and Rake's distinction between the recognition of female labour market participation as an overriding principle, stressing women's roles as mothers, and what they call a 'productivist agenda' is a useful approach to the analysis of this issue. Let us call their three alternatives (simplifying them to enable them to be used as labels) the 'equal rights', 'motherhood' and 'productivist' options. The equal rights option calls for the removal of all barriers to female labour market participation on terms indistinguishable from men's participation. The motherhood option is concerned to see that female caring roles, at least in respect of their children, are protected, accepting that this implies more limited labour market participation. The productivist option sees female labour market participation as necessary but is relatively indifferent to the terms under which this occurs. However, Daly and Rake have been cited earlier as critical of simple typologisation and they explicitly make the point that it is difficult to place individual countries unambiguously within typologies. In fact we are talking here about what is very much contested territory. This is an issue that comes out very clearly in the tension between concerns about falling birth rates and concerns about numbers of productive workers (see the specific discussion of the latter in relation to ageing in chapter 12). There is an important question here (particularly pertinent to Japan, South Korea and Taiwan, where demographic changes are occurring very fast) about the feasibility of family-friendly policies that can protect women's rights, promote family life and facilitate female labour market participation. My view is that this is possible, but only under two conditions. One of these is radical changes to male behaviour in respect of family roles. The other is substantial state support of the family through policies like the provision of subsidised child care and parental leave.

## GUIDE TO FURTHER READING

Bryson's *Welfare and the State* (1992) provides a good introductory discussion of the ways in which women experience welfare systems differently to men.

The references in chapter 2 to feminist critiques of Esping-Andersen are also relevant for this chapter, as well as the work of O'Connor (1996) and Sainsbury's edited book (1994) and her sole authored one (1996). Daly and Rake's *Gender and the Welfare State* (2003) is also a key source on this issue. Issues about women's roles in relation to care are covered in general terms in Ungerson (2000) and more comparatively in an article by Daly (2002).

# CHAPTER 11

# ETHNIC DIVISIONS

## Introduction: Identifying the Issues

This chapter explores the relationship between ethnic divisions and social policy in the same way as the previous chapters on socio-economic divisions and gender divisions. However, it is not as easy to develop comparative analysis with this topic as it was with the last two. Ethnic divisions are many and varied and often closely related to socio-economic divisions. There is little work that has tried to analyse them comparatively, let alone to relate them to social policy issues.

Any discussion of racial or ethnic divisions in society starts with a definitional problem which stems from the fact that those divisions are socially and culturally determined. They may be linked with physical differences, but those differences are often exaggerated, difficult to detect at the margin and have none of the connections to abilities and attributes that earlier biological theories of racial differences suggested. Furthermore, divisions within societies may be discovered for which there are no biological cues at all but where patterns of discrimination have been developed and social barriers to contact have been set up of a very similar kind to those found in other societies where divisions are based on physical racial characteristics. Examples are societies where language or religion are the key criteria used by individuals to act in a discriminatory way. In many divided societies these criteria are linked to doctrines of nationalism rather than racism.

This diversity of phenomena makes it difficult to develop a satisfactory terminology. To speak of race relations runs the risk of appearing to subscribe to the theories that have been used to justify racism. It is obviously not very appropriate terminology for many national, religious or linguistic divisions. Some writers cope with this difficulty by using 'race' in inverted commas (see, for example, Williams, 1989, p. ix). Others have turned to the concept of 'ethnicity' (Glazer and

Moynihan, 1975), and this will be used in this discussion as a short-hand term for this group of social divisions.

## The Diversity and Complexity of Ethnic Divisions

The expression 'ethnic divisions', and therefore the discussion in this section, covers a wide range of divisions in societies.

- Divisions whose origins lie deep in the processes by which nation states were formed, as in the case of Belgium, Northern Ireland and the Balkans.
- Patterns of domination that arose from the conquest of territories, as with the indigenous minorities in Australia, New Zealand, USA and Canada and the majority black population of South Africa.
- Patterns deriving from the importation of people to perform menial tasks in societies, i.e. slavery and the introduction of indentured workers.
- Situations arising from movements of people in search of work, ranging from the massive migrations into the USA, the movements of people from colonies and former colonies to Europe to the much more local movements of workers (e.g. between the countries of Europe) some of whom may be regarded as temporary, itself a source of problems for those treated as 'guest workers' regardless of their needs or aspirations.
- Migrations of refugees and asylum seekers.

Clearly this list covers divisions in societies that have been associated with the formation of modern nation states ('the extension of state power over ever-larger areas, and the incorporation of hitherto distinct ethnic groups', Castles and Miller, 1993, p. 37) and others that have arisen from the involuntary and voluntary movement of peoples. The latter phenomena are of fundamental importance in recent times, yet the earlier state developments 'help to determine the conditions for the implantation of new immigrant groups' (ibid.). However, listing the sources of divisions in this way perhaps give insufficient emphasis to cultural divisions, which may be found both embedded in the historical evolution of nation states and affected by contemporary population movements. Particularly salient here are the divisions between the Judeo-Christian world and Islam, with manifestations in the long-standing conflicts in Eastern Europe, efforts to establish nation states in Europe and Asia today, relationship in the countries emergent from European imperialism, economic migration today and issues about the absorption of refugees.

Related to the different ways in which ethnic divisions arise, but also to other aspects of the cultural and ideological milieu in which they occurred, are differences in the intensity of conflict and discrimination. At one extreme are patterns of blatant and outright discrimination, sometimes linked with segregation and the enforcement of a separate legal status, as in the past in South Africa and the southern states of the USA. At the other are distinctions and divisions of a much more subtle kind. Moreover, any divisive system, and particularly a powerful one like the institution of slavery or apartheid, leaves a legacy of division that is very hard to eradicate. The beneficiaries of such divisions, however much they ascribe to egalitarian principles, will not readily relinquish those benefits. The victims of the divisions continue to suffer, and pass on to future generations, disadvantages that stem from the weak position from which they started.

There are, in particular, strong links between ethnic divisions and class divisions in many societies (a source of political and theoretical argument about how these respective phenomena should be interpreted). For Marxist theory, ethnicity, inasmuch as it is acknowledged, is a phenomenon that divides the proletariat, weakening its capacity to struggle against the bourgeoisie. This perspective begs the 'chicken and egg' question: which came first, the economic divisions or the social divisions. There are very good reasons, given the comparatively recent emergence of capitalist economic institutions and the ways in which their emergence occurred in a period of intense nationalist activity, for regarding ethnic divisions as often prior to, or at least linked with, economic divisions. Patterns of colonial domination and slavery obviously involved economic exploitation, but they were not necessarily a product of the struggle between the classes in the Marxist sense (for a discussion of sociological approaches to this aspect of stratification see Rex, 1986).

What is obviously important for contemporary analysis is the ways in which ethnic and economic divisions interact and often reinforce each other. If one can imagine a society that suddenly became 'race blind', it would still have within its social stratification reflections of earlier patterns of racial discrimination, because of the extent to which earlier racism had disadvantaged its victims. Since the reality is only at best a slow evolution towards that liberal ideal, the ethnic and socio-economic divisions are mixed together in a complex way.

## Counting Minorities

At this stage in the discussion it is appropriate to include some statistics on minority groups within nation states. It is relatively easy to identify inflows of people from other countries, the numbers of people who do not have formal 'citizen' status in the country in which they live and the number of people born in other countries. However, as has already been indicated, some ethnic divisions have much deeper roots. In some cases minorities lived in the country before the modern dominated groups arrived, in others they came to the country far back in its history and in other cases the presence of ethnic divisions arises as much from arbitrary decisions or compromises arrived at when the nation state was formed. In these cases individual countries have developed ways of trying to measure divisions (some of them controversial) in population censuses: colour of skin, subjective ethnic identity, birthplaces of parents and grandparents, language spoken, religious affiliation, etc. There is obviously no means of running these together to generate indices of the extent to which societies are divided, let alone measure in any comparative way differences in social advantage. There is a very clear contrast here to the identification of gendered divisions across societies.

Nevertheless, it is worthwhile to look at statistics on inflows of migrants and their countries of origin since quite a lot of the critical issues about differences in the experience of social policy are, for reasons that will be explored more in later sections, particularly related to these. Table 11.1 shows inflows of foreign nationals into OECD countries for which statistics are available for 2000, separating other immigrants from asylum seekers (a distinction that may not be easy to make, and on which national statistics may vary).

These figures need to be treated with some caution (see Lemaitre, 2005 for a discussion about the comparability problems with these data and those in table 11.2). Inflows of people are more likely to be counted accurately than outflows. The statistics for three countries (Australia, Canada and the USA) separate temporary and permanent inflows, with the former dwarfing the latter in Australia and the USA. Given the free movement of people within much of the EU, it may be expected that temporary movers are seriously underestimated in those countries. Of course the impact of incomers has to be interpreted in relation to population size and the flow figures in any one year may be misleading. Table 11.2 provides a better impression of the impact of immigration on the OECD countries.

**Table 11.1** Immigrants and asylum seekers (thousands), 2000

| Country | New immigrants (not including asylum seekers) | Asylum seekers |
|---|---|---|
| Australia | 278.2 | 11.9 |
| Austria | 66.0 | 18.3 |
| Belgium | 68.6 | 42.7 |
| Canada | 313.4 | 35.7 |
| Czech Republic | 4.2 | 8.8 |
| Denmark | 20.3 | 10.3 |
| Finland | 9.1 | 3.2 |
| France | 119.3 | 38.7 |
| Germany | 648.8 | 78.6 |
| Hungary | 15.0 | 7.8 |
| Ireland | 24.1 | 10.9 |
| Italy | 271.5 | 24.5 |
| Japan | 345.8 | 0.2 |
| New Zealand | 38.8 | 1.4 |
| Norway | 27.8 | 10.8 |
| Portugal | 15.9 | 0.2 |
| Sweden | 33.8 | 16.3 |
| Switzerland | 87.4 | 17.6 |
| UK | 288.8 | 98.9 |
| USA | 3590.4 | 57.0 |

*Source*: data from OECD (2002). Note that in the cases of Denmark and Hungary the immigration figures are for 1999. Some countries, notably Germany and Norway, include many asylum seekers in the immigration count.

Asylum seekers have been distinguished as a special group of immigrants because of the extent to which the media focus on them despite the fact that they are a minority of migrants. Economic migration, much of it explicitly encouraged by the receiving country, remains much more significant for immigration to these wealthy countries, as table 11.1 shows. This table suggests that asylum seekers will be particularly evident in countries where other migrants are few: Czech Republic, Denmark, Finland, Hungary, Norway and Sweden. However, the movement of people across borders as refugees seeking asylum is a much bigger issue for the countries really close to the world's most troubled countries than it is for most of the OECD group of nations. In

**Table 11.2** Foreign populations of OECD countries, 2002

| Country | Foreign population as percentage of total population |
|---------|:---:|
| Australia | 27.1 |
| Austria | 8.8 |
| Belgium | 8.2 |
| Canada | 18.2 |
| Czech Republic | 2.3 |
| Denmark | 4.9 |
| Finland | 2.0 |
| France | 5.6 |
| Germany | 8.9 |
| Greece | 7.0 |
| Hungary | 1.1 |
| Ireland | 5.6 |
| Italy | 2.6 |
| Japan | 1.5 |
| Korea | 0.5 |
| Mexico | 0.5 |
| Netherlands | 4.3 |
| New Zealand | 19.5 |
| Norway | 4.3 |
| Poland | 0.1 |
| Portugal | 4.0 |
| Slovak Republic | 0.5 |
| Spain | 3.1 |
| Sweden | 5.3 |
| Switzerland | 19.0 |
| UK | 4.5 |
| USA | 11.5 |

*Source*: data from OECD (2004c, pp. 6–7). Figures for slightly earlier years for Canada, France, Greece, Mexico and New Zealand. These are data compatibility figures: in Australia, Canada, France, Mexico, New Zealand and the USA, estimates are derived from census data; elsewhere they come from registration figures.

2002 the country receiving most refugees was Iran (with around 1.25 million) closely followed by Pakistan (UNHCR, 2003).

Table 11.2 shows the foreign populations of various OECD countries. It is assumed that these figures accurately record proportions that have not yet acquired citizenship of the country in which they now live. However, an attempt to relate these figures to some other figures on total 'foreign' population produced more or less equivalent figures for Australia, New Zealand and the USA, suggesting that the definitions of foreigners and foreign-born are the same.

Notwithstanding these data interpretation difficulties, the long-standing 'nations of immigrants' (Australia, Canada, New Zealand and the USA) still have large numbers of foreigners despite recent efforts to quell the inflow. Amongst the European nations only Switzerland stands comparison with them. There is then a group of western and northern European nations that have quite significant numbers of foreigners. Here there does seem to have been a precise distinction made between 'foreigners' and 'foreign-born'; there are OECD data on the latter showing that this group comprises 10 per cent of the population in France, 9.8 per cent of the population in the Netherlands and 11.8 per cent of the population in Sweden.

In terms of social policy it may make a difference where the foreigners come from. There are reciprocal arrangements between many of the OECD countries about the transfer of social benefit rights, and within the EU there are quite specific rules on this designed not to disadvantage migrant workers. The story EU statistics tell on the division of foreign populations between nationals of another EU state and nationals of states outside the EU is therefore of interest (table 11.3).

The supposition is that, in addition to the fact that they will not benefit from the special forms of protection for EU nationals, issues about the delivery of social policies will be more complex (and the likelihood of discrimination greater) for people from nations that are more different culturally. Whilst in some countries, perhaps particularly the UK and Ireland, many of these foreign nationals will be from culturally similar nations, in most cases they will be from societies with very different languages and religions. For example, in the Netherlands the largest group of foreign nationals is from Surinam and there are groups nearly as large from Turkey, Indonesia and Morocco (OECD, 2002).

## Citizenship

Given all this evidence on foreign nationals in various countries, it is useful to return to the concept of citizenship discussed briefly in chapter 9 (see pp. 187–8). In relation to ethnic groups, issues about the denial of citizenship in the formal sense are very salient. Systems of institutionalised and legalised discrimination deny full citizenship. It

**Table 11.3** Foreign nationals in the European Union, 2000

| Country | Number of foreign nationals from outside the EU (thousands) | People from outside the EU as a percentage of foreign nationals |
|---|---|---|
| Austria | 654 | 87 |
| Belgium | 290 | 32 |
| Denmark | 203 | 79 |
| Finland | 71 | 81 |
| France | 2068 | 63 |
| Germany | 5485 | 75 |
| Greece | 116 | 72 |
| Ireland | 34 | 27 |
| Italy | 1122 | 88 |
| Netherlands | 456 | 70 |
| Portugal | 138 | 72 |
| Spain | 489 | 61 |
| Sweden | 310 | 64 |
| UK | 1439 | 63 |

*Source*: European Commission (2003, p. 115).

is important to recognise, as stressed in the earlier discussion, the importance of social rights. The denial of these rights does not merely occur in societies with substantial formal systems of official discrimination. In many societies the rights of minorities are undermined by measures controlling immigration and denying full citizenship to new entrants from other countries (Layton-Henry, 1992). They may also be affected, more subtly, where social policies prioritise some cultural patterns relative to others, or fail to recognise the salience of some cultural characteristics and culturally determined needs (perhaps deliberately, perhaps not). This is an issue that is getting increasing attention in relation to the presence of Islamic people in many European countries.

These forms of discrimination contribute to the creation of situations in which denials of full citizenship tend to reinforce economic, particularly job market, disadvantages. Further, there are some particular ways in which migrants are pushed into exceptionally exploited positions. One of these is where entry is allowed only to perform some particularly menial and ill-rewarded task. The recruitment of domestic workers in many societies falls into this category, linking gender roles and ethnic disadvantages in a particularly exploitative way (see

Ungerson in Evers et al., 1994, chapter 3). A perhaps even more disturbing situation arises with illegal migrants, vulnerable to exploitation and blackmail from those who provide employment and housing.

The advanced industrial countries have nearly all encountered substantial amounts of recent immigration. This is likely to have been related to labour shortages and to a search for new work opportunities by people from less prosperous economies. But it has also been affected by previous imperial connections, the extent to which countries like the UK and France spread their culture within their colonies and created an image of a 'mother country' to which people from those colonies could turn for work or education, ironically called, in the title of one book on British race relations, 'the empire strikes back' (Centre for Contemporary Cultural Studies, 1982).

The issue about citizenship that connects social policy with social stratification concerns the social rights which immigrant workers are given. The concept of the 'guest worker' (particularly evident in Germany and Switzerland) is of an immigrant who comes to the country simply to work. That worker's long-run security may be regarded as no concern of the 'host' country; it may well be happy for the worker to pay taxes and social security contributions but not to make demands on the benefit and care systems which these pay for. The worker's family obligations – to provide for and educate children, to support other adults, and so on – may likewise be regarded as of no concern of the 'host', who may indeed sometimes make it difficult for migrant workers to bring 'dependants' with them (Castles and Kosack, 1973; Castles, 1984; Castles and Miller, 1993, 2003). Within the EU, human rights concerns have modified the worst aspects of these practices.

This is an extreme form of the denial of social citizenship. Others may be a little less malign. Immigration to work may lead to the granting of rights after a period of stay in the country. The countries that boasted of their paternalistic stance towards their colonies were perhaps more readily shamed into enabling immigrants to become full citizens. The treatment of refugees, unable to look back to their place of origin, also demands (if human rights pledges are to be honoured) progression towards citizenship in the new country (Joly and Cohen, 1990).

As far as social rights are concerned, it is important to bear in mind the variety of ways in which ostensible equality may be denied in practice. Here are some examples.

• If income maintenance benefits depend on past contributions, most newcomers to a country may be disadvantaged by late entrance.

- The late entrance problem may also undermine opportunities to gain access to other benefits where waiting times are used to regulate access to resources, for example with social housing.
- If a society contains both people from a specific ethnic group who are formally supposed to have full citizenship rights and others who do not, officials may discriminate against and stigmatise the first group whenever they may be confused with the second (there is a special issue here about purges against illegal immigrants, which are likely to catch legitimate ones in the 'coarse nets' used to deal with the problem).
- Conflict between societies in the world may engender situations in which groups of people living outside their country of origin are seen to contain members who are deemed to be a security threat; authorities find it difficult to distinguish such people with consequences that disadvantage the whole group (as in the case of many people from Islamic countries living in Europe).
- The state may be suspicious of claimed dependants, particularly where this is associated with cultural patterns strange to the dominant society. Hence efforts to get wives, children and other dependent relatives into the country may be difficult, and obligations to send money back to them may be disregarded by income maintenance systems (Gordon and Newnham, 1985; Gordon, 1986; Castles and Miller, 2003, pp. 231–6).

## Ethnicity and culture

The last point in this list leads on to a larger issue about ethnic minorities and social policy. This concerns the way in which cultural differences are dealt with in the delivery of services: health, social care and education. There is an often-proffered 'liberal' solution to this, which is flawed (even in its own terms). This is the view that such services should be ethnicity 'blind', with all people treated the same regardless of race, creed or language. This, it is argued, is what an equal rights policy requires. However, there are a number of problems with this policy.

- It is a line of argument offered to resist scrutiny by officials who are actually discriminating. One cannot be confident about an egalitarian policy without collecting evidence to ensure that it is in operation (Henderson and Karn, 1987).
- To operate without regard to people's actual needs and preferences may be discriminatory. Supplying houses or income maintenance

benefits that do not enable people to meet their actual social obligations may severely disadvantage them. Supplying services which violate very deeply held beliefs and feelings (disregard of religious practices and holidays, medical services that have no regard to family cultural practices, education that imposes instruction in an alien religion) may alienate and lead to underuse of badly needed services.

- More complicatedly, induction into full citizenship requires acceptance that the history, the traditions, the culture and the language of the individual has a value along with that of the dominant society. To do anything less is to send the message that many of the things that create the individual's own sense of identity are not important, an implicit way of making him or her feel a second-class citizen (Stone, 1981).

The last of these considerations has important but difficult implications for education. It is arguable that the child of an immigrant has the best prospects in the new society if he or she concentrates on imbibing the new culture and of course language. But the price to pay for doing this is alienation from family and other roots. If this painful process is undergone (as various poignant autobiographical accounts testify), there is no guarantee that the dominant society will accept the individual as fully assimilated (particularly if he or she has a different skin colour). In the face of discrimination a person may cope better with a pride in their 'roots' than if they have undergone a process that has systematically undermined that.

In this sense it is important to recognise the dynamic nature of culture. Individuals are not choosing between the culture from which they come and the one that offers assimilation. Both are changing:

> The dynamic nature of culture lies in its capacity to link a group's history and traditions with the actual situation in the migratory process. Migrant or minority cultures are constantly recreated on the basis of the needs and experiences of the group and its interaction with the actual social environment. (Castles and Miller, 1993, pp. 33–4)

In any effort to accommodate the conflicting demands of the new culture and the old one, there is a difficult line to be drawn between the extreme outlined above and an opposite extreme of providing a separate socialisation process for a separate people. This will be one that reinforces separation and tends to pass on disadvantages. People will then tend to remain separate whether they like it or not.

This is an issue about which there are strong feelings. There is a view taken by radical elements within some discriminated against groups that the prospects for the liberal model are so poor that separate institutions are preferable. Castles and Miller (2003) argue:

> Culture is becoming increasingly politicised ... As ideas of racial superiority lose their ideological strength, exclusionary practices against minorities increasingly focus on issues of cultural difference. At the same time, the politics of minority resistance crystallise more and more around cultural symbols. Yet these symbols are only partially based on imported forms of ethnicity. Their main power as definers of community and identity comes from the incorporation of new experiences of ethnic minority groups in the immigration country. (ibid., p. 40)

Language differences pose particular problems inasmuch as failure to gain proficiency in a dominant language often leads to severe economic disadvantages. Bilingualism offers a solution, though dominant groups are rarely as ready to learn the less important language as subordinate groups are to learn theirs (a point that should not be lost on all those who, like myself, have the special advantage of having one of the world's dominant languages as their native tongue).

There are also some very difficult issues where cultural differences involve beliefs and practices about which there are deeply held values on either side. A central example here is family practices, involving different perceptions on appropriate relationships and behaviour between men, women and children.

## The Implications of Ethnicity for the Social Divisions Model

Any class analysis of society will need to take into account barriers to the upward mobility of ethnic groups. These barriers may take a variety of forms, from explicit arrangements to deny full citizenship through to more subtle phenomena that perhaps reflect the impact of past institutions. These are going to have an impact on the representation of disadvantaged ethnic groups within the three groups, in ways that do not need spelling out in any more detail. But then, what role do social policies play? There are perhaps two key points to make.

First, with regard to the first two groups, earlier discussions (see pp. 188–90 and 208–11) have made the distinction that those in 'group'

1 tend to be the main users of private systems (pensions, schools and health-care systems, in particular) whereas those in 'group' 2 are the mainstream users and beneficiaries of state services. Ironically, if there are tendencies for the needs of an ethnic minority to be disregarded within the state system, then those relatively successful in economic terms may be more likely to use private systems than their counterparts in the majority group. Private schools set up to meet cultural and linguistic needs and health services which have regard to minority beliefs and practices may have a particular appeal to this group.

Second, for many of the less successful within an ethnic minority there may be particularly strong forces which tend to ensure that these people are found within 'group' 3 rather than 'group' 2. Reference has already been made to insurance rules that may disadvantage migrant workers and people who arrive in a new society partway through their working life. Forms of discrimination will limit people to less well paid and less secure work, and this will be reflected in disproportionate representation amongst the unemployed. Residential segregation, whether the result of explicit discrimination or produced by a combination of low 'market power' and the selection of areas where security and the availability of appropriate institutions (places of worship, voluntary organisations, etc.), may have an impact on choice of houses, schools and health services.

Theories about the 'underclass' (Murray, 1984), or an earlier variation on this same theme about the 'culture of poverty' (Lewis, 1968), are expressed in terms which involve implicit allusions to ethnic minorities. Behaviour that is a response to, and even perhaps a way of coping with, disadvantage, when manifested by a minority ethnic group, is regarded in these theories as a natural characteristic of that group. In societies where explicit racism is taboo, at least in intellectual or journalistic analyses of social problems, talk about the 'underclass' or the 'problems of the inner cities' and so on may be a covert kind of racist rhetoric (see Moore's analysis of this in Coenen and Leisink, 1993). This may then encourage variations in official responses, based upon whether or not 'deviants' belong to minority ethnic groups.

Alternatively, positive discrimination in social policy may involve an attempt to add to efforts to avoid simple discrimination by recognising that the impact of earlier discrimination will have imposed economic and cultural disadvantages on a minority group. Positive discrimination may involve quotas to bring the representation of certain groups within an occupation or educational institution up to their proportion in the population. Such actions thus implicitly involve discrimination against better-qualified members of the defined majority group(s). Fierce philosophical arguments have raged about the justifiability of this approach (Edwards, 1987). It is comparatively rarely practised – a belief that it is widespread features in the fantasies of racist rhetoric in societies where cautious efforts are being made to outlaw simple discrimination.

In principle it ought to be possible to compare and perhaps classify countries in terms of the way in which minority groups are treated or affected by social policy; in practice comparative data on this complex subject are limited. Castles and Miller (2003, p. 234) suggest 'a rough classification of social policy responses'.

- Active social policies with a 'basic assumption . . . that such policies do not lead to separatism but, on the contrary, form the precondition for successful integration' (ibid.) (e.g. Australia, Canada, Sweden, the Netherlands).
- The rejection of special social policies in a context within which there are nevertheless equal opportunities, anti-discrimination and affirmative action measures (e.g. the USA and, to some extent, the UK).
- The former 'guest-worker' recruiters whose policies have been inconsistent, but who have shown increasing concern about social exclusion (e.g. Germany and Switzerland).

However, Castles and Miller also give attention to the peculiarities of the French response (which they had described as the 'republican model' in the 1993 edition of their book), embodying a strong emphasis on equal social rights but a strong emphasis on assimilation. Clearly, policy debates centre around the attention that should be paid to cultural differences, as highlighted by some of the issues concerning the education of Muslim children. Here, an interesting contrast arises between the French approach, the 'republican' tradition banning all special clothing prescribed by religion (with an impact on Muslim girls who want to wear some form of veil and Sikhs boys who want to wear turbans), and an English court case that overruled a head-teacher's efforts to ban Muslim dress. Of course, there is a much greater range of issues about acceptance of multiculturalism than these; however, they are symbolic of a division between a policy stance that demands a degree of conformity as the price of equal treatment and one that countenances differences at a price that may undermine equality of treatment.

Finally, some comment is appropriate to follow up on the suggestion in chapter 9 that the discussion of stratification should to some extent extend to a recognition of global divisions between nations. Much of contemporary migration (particularly economic migration) needs to be seen as a reflection of an economic relationship in which many of the advantages of some are rooted in the vulnerable situations of others. Migration may make a contribution to redressing the balance, in terms of new opportunities for those who move and the remittances back to their families. Inasmuch as social policies are conceived solely in terms of national interests, the implications of these interrelationships tend to be disregarded.

## Conclusions

This chapter has endeavoured to generalise about ethnic stratification across modern industrial societies. In doing so it has inevitably mixed together a variety of phenomena (which may or may not arise in combination): divisions arising in the context of migration and the according of limited 'guest-worker' status, longer-standing divisions in a society, racial divisions (in which physical differences facilitate discrimination), language differences and religious differences. These variations obviously influence the social divisions in societies and the ways in which social policies respond to them or reflect them.

It is useful to return to the concept of 'citizenship', asking to what extent particular situations involve one of the following:

- the total denial of formal citizenship rights ('apartheid' or the 'guest-worker' phenomenon);
- a variety of limitations on full participation, because of the impact of length of residence (as in social insurance) or culture (as in education) on full participation;
- discrimination that is officially taboo but widely practised (inside public services as well as in the private sector);
- disadvantage that is a difficult-to-eradicate legacy of earlier denials of full citizenship.

It is important not to be fooled by official statements which suggest that only the last applies, look very closely at the way institutions work in practice. In doing so, bear in mind that social policy is used to control and channel as well as respond to emergent divisions in societies and in the world.

## GUIDE TO FURTHER READING

As is evident from the chapter, issues about the impact of ethnicity on experience of social policy have had little attention by comparison with the vast literature on gender. Castles and Miller (1993, 2003) is a key source. A number of recent books give specific attention to issues about migration. Amongst these, Geddes (2003) is recommended. Moore's essay in Coenen and Leisink (1993), recommended at the end of chapter 9, deals well with some of the issues about ethnicity, citizenship and the underclass perspective.

# CHAPTER 12

# AGEING SOCIETIES

## Introduction: Identifying the Issues

Throughout the world, and most particularly in the more developed nations, societies are ageing inasmuch as the average age is rising with falling death rates and falling birth rates. The only exceptions to this are societies where premature death remains a very common occurrence, for example in the societies of Southern Africa where AIDS is rampant. Even in many societies where early death is still common, for example Russia, low birth rates are contributing to the overall ageing of the society. This chapter discusses the implications of societal ageing for social policy, recognising that where this is significantly shifting the age profile of a nation it must be having some impact, crucial for the future of social policy; however, I also provide a critique of the rather hysterical analysis of this which talks of a 'demographic time bomb', with dramatic effects.

To obtain a balanced picture of the impact of societal ageing on social policy, there is a need to examine the process of demographic change and its relationship to economic policy rather carefully before going on to look at its direct impact on social policy. It is important to make this a comparative analysis since even in the societies where this ageing process is quite marked there are different rates of change, with potentially different implications.

The first section of the chapter examines the demographic evidence, i.e. the nature and rate of change, unpicking the respective influences of changing birth rates and changing death rates and acknowledging that migration may also have an impact on a country's demographic profile. The second section explores some of the economic aspects of demographic change, namely its impact on economic growth and on the labour force. I suggest that there is a tendency for analyses to forget that whilst demographic projections may be comparatively easily made, economic ones are very difficult. In predicting the future it may be that the latter are much more important than the former. The third section analyses the key social policy implication of ageing in a society, namely the increased need for pensions. I relate this topic to the economic issues discussed in the previous section, exploring how pensions are paid for and providing a critique of the widespread argument that there needs to be increased pre-funding of pensions in ageing societies. The fourth section takes a wider view of the social policy implications of ageing, exploring the extent to which it implies increased need for health and social care but recognising that to some extent the increased needs of the elderly may be traded off against the decreased needs of the young. This leads on finally to some discussion of the role of the family in care.

## The Demographic Evidence

It is most appropriate to start this analysis of how societies are ageing with some data on what has already happened. Table 12.1 looks at the growth of the population over 65 between 1960 and 2003 in the OECD member countries. This and table 12.2, taken together, are clear evidence of the significance of the ageing of the population throughout the OECD area. However, there are wide variations in the pattern of ageing. There are some nations, all European, with relatively high proportions of elderly people before 1960; in some of these the increases in those proportions were quite slight between 1960 and 2003. There is also a group with quite low proportions of elderly in 1960 that have experienced little change (notably Austria and Belgium). The most dramatic changes are in those nations where the proportion of elderly people has risen very fast from a low starting point in 1960, above all Korea and Japan, but to a lesser extent also some of the southern European nations together with Finland and Poland.

The next question is where are the big changes still occurring? A comparison of the old age dependency ratio for 2000 with a projection for 2050 is set out in table 12.2 for almost all the countries listed in table 12.1. This looks at over-65s relative to people aged 20–64. Looking at the issue in this relative way highlights the 'dependency ratios' that figure in predictions of the problems associated with these changes. It is interesting to note that, on the whole, the European nations that already had quite a high elderly population in 1960 tend to be expected to experience less growth in the elderly population in the fifty years after 2000.

**Table 12.1** Numbers of elderly people in various countries, 1960 and 2003

| Country | Percentage over 65 in 1960 | Percentage over 65 in 2003 | 2003 data as percentage of 1960 |
|---|---|---|---|
| Australia | 8.5 | 12.8 | 151 |
| Austria | 7.9 | 8.8 | 111 |
| Belgium | 8.2 | 9.0 | 110 |
| Canada | 7.6 | 12.8 | 168 |
| Czech Republic | 9.6 | 13.9 | 145 |
| Denmark | 10.6 | 14.9 | 141 |
| Finland | 7.3 | 15.5 | 212 |
| France | 11.6 | 16.2 | 138 |
| Germany | 10.8 | 16.6 | 154 |
| Greece | 8.1 | 16.8 | 207 |
| Hungary | 9.0 | 15.3 | 170 |
| Ireland | 10.9 | 11.1 | 102 |
| Italy | 9.0 | 18.2 | 202 |
| Japan | 5.7 | 19.0 | 333 |
| Korea | 2.9 | 8.3 | 286 |
| Netherlands | 9.0 | 13.8 | 153 |
| New Zealand | 8.7 | 11.9 | 137 |
| Norway | 10.9 | 14.8 | 136 |
| Poland | 5.8 | 12.9 | 222 |
| Slovak Republic | 8.9 | 11.5 | 129 |
| Spain | 8.2 | 16.9 | 206 |
| Sweden | 11.8 | 17.2 | 146 |
| Switzerland | 10.7 | 16.0 | 150 |
| UK | 11.7 | 15.6 | 133 |
| USA | 9.2 | 12.3 | 134 |

*Source*: data from OECD (2004c, pp. 6–7).

Population change is affected by death rates, birth rates and migration rates. Death rates are relatively easy to predict over the long run. In countries like those featuring in tables 12.1 and 12.2, life expectancies will probably increase over the next 50 years but by relatively small amounts. These countries have already experienced dramatic falls in death rates. Hence predictions of the numbers of elderly people in 2050 will be reasonably accurate. The people about whom these predictions are made are already born. The other sides of the equation

**Table 12.2** Estimated ratios of over-65s to 20–64-year-olds in 2000 and 2050

| Country | Ratio of over-65s to 20–64-year-olds in 2000 | Ratio of over-65s to 20–64-year-olds in 2050 | 2050 data as a percentage of 2000 |
|---|---|---|---|
| Australia | 18 | 40 | 222 |
| Austria | 23 | 55 | 239 |
| Belgium | 26 | 42 | 180 |
| Canada | 19 | 44 | 232 |
| Czech Republic | 20 | 59 | 295 |
| Denmark | 23 | 42 | 183 |
| Finland | 22 | 46 | 209 |
| France | 25 | 46 | 184 |
| Germany | 24 | 49 | 204 |
| Hungary | 21 | 50 | 238 |
| Ireland | 18 | 40 | 222 |
| Italy | 27 | 66 | 244 |
| Japan | 25 | 72 | 288 |
| Korea | 10 | 55 | 550 |
| Netherlands | 20 | 42 | 210 |
| New Zealand | 18 | 38 | 211 |
| Norway | 24 | 44 | 183 |
| Poland | 18 | 50 | 278 |
| Spain | 25 | 68 | 272 |
| Sweden | 27 | 27 | 174 |
| Switzerland | 24 | 55 | 229 |
| UK | 24 | 39 | 163 |
| USA | 19 | 32 | 168 |

*Source*: data from United Nations (2003).

are more difficult. Table 12.2 ignores the very young in the calculation of the ratio, but nevertheless anyone born between 2000 and 2030 will feature on the youthful side of the equation for 2050. Predictions of the numbers in this group therefore involve some rather complicated arithmetic, taking into account the numbers of potential parents and their predicted reproductive behaviour. The latter is based on reproductive behaviour as observed in the present – so significant changes in the latter could upset the prediction. In this respect it should be noted that there are nations in the tables that are experiencing dramatic social changes. Several countries are emerging from the long period of Russian domination in Eastern Europe. There are also countries experiencing strong economic growth. The nations of southern Europe are experiencing changes that could take their birth rates in either direction; growth may be a positive influence on them but, alternatively, the demise of the traditional family may be a negative one. The two East Asian countries are deeply worried about their demographic changes and actively debating policies that will reverse their low birth rate.

Perhaps the biggest unknown is migration. Typically, migration involves young adults at or close to child-producing age. So high rates of emigration will increase the ratio of old to young and high rates of immigration will operate in the other direction. If there is a significant population shift from Eastern to Western Europe in the next few years, this will increase the ageing of the former group of countries and decrease that of the latter. We also need to recognise the substantial flow of migrants from non-OECD countries to OECD ones (as shown in chapter 11). In addition, there may be growth of a less typical form of migration that has not been seen in the past very much, namely migration of elderly people. If Spain and Greece, for example, continue to attract retired people from northern Europe, this will undermine even the predictions of the numbers of old people there and in the exporting nations.

## Demography and Economics

The discussion of migration in the last section suggested economic factors that might vitiate demographic predictions. We turn now to some much more complicated questions about the relationship between demographic trends and economic ones. The official literature on ageing populations is dominated by concerns about the cost of the elderly and the extent to which their pensions and care are charges upon the economically active. It is therefore very important to ask:

- whether figures on the relationship between the numbers of old and the numbers of younger adults (as set out in table 12.2) provide a realistic picture of the extent of 'dependency' now or in the future;
- whether the dependent/non-dependent relationship within a nation is determined by demography or by economics;
- what in either case is meant by 'dependent';
- whether those identified as dependent are a source of costs for a nation;

- whether nations with high numbers of dependents, however estimated, are necessarily disadvantaged relative to others;
- whether it matters overall that there are high levels of economic dependency.

These questions are listed in order from the easiest to answer to the hardest. At the bottom of the list are encountered what are largely philosophical debating points, confronting the strong productivist logic of much conventional thinking. At the top there are issues on which it is possible to assemble some telling comparative evidence against the conventional 'demographic time bomb' thesis.

The exploration of issues about dependency used in the demographic predictions employ age as the defining variable. However, if it is defined instead in terms of labour market participation, the picture may be very different. Table 5.1 showed that no country has much over 80 per cent of the population aged between 15 and 64 (the OECD preferred definition of the 'working age population') in the labour force and that there are many countries where the percentage is around two-thirds. Many of the countries particularly worried about demographic change have quite a lot of scope for increasing the size of the labour force. Note for example the fact that Korea, where the demographic changes are predicted to be particularly massive, has only 66 per cent of the working age population in the labour force.

However, the simple statistical measure of the size of the labour force masks a variety of phenomena:

- low labour market participation by the young because they are still in the education system;
- low labour market participation by people engaged in caring tasks, particularly women who are caring for children;
- low labour market participation because of premature withdrawal from the labour force, either because of ill health or because of the unavailability of work.

The issue of early withdrawal from the labour force is obviously the phenomenon that deserves particular attention here. Table 12.3 uses OECD labour force statistics to analyse employment rates of males aged between 55 and 64. Alongside data for 2000, figures for 1970 have been added (from those countries for which data are available). The contrast between these two years shows how much less common early withdrawal from the labour force was 30 years ago, despite the fact that people are now living longer. There are some remarkably low

**Table 12.3** Employment rates of males aged 55–64 in 2000 and 1970

| Country | 2000 | 1970 |
|---|---|---|
| Canada | 58 | 79 |
| Finland | 44 | 73 |
| France | 38 | 74 |
| Germany | 48 | 79 |
| Italy | 30 | 48 |
| Japan | 78 | 85 |
| Netherlands | 50 | 79 |
| Norway | 73 | 83 |
| Spain | 55 | 83 |
| Sweden | 68 | 84 |
| USA | 66 | 81 |

*Source*: data from Casey et al. (2003, table 7).

employment rates listed, particularly in Finland, France and Italy. In every case for which data are available these rates are below those of 1970, even slightly so in Japan despite the story its demographic data tells. The issue of early withdrawal from the labour force is securing increasing attention in many societies, after a period in which some governments actually gave it official encouragement as a measure to combat unemployment and enhance opportunities for the young.

The questions about the extent to which nations have scope to increase labour market participation amongst other groups are more complicated (and controversial). It has been shown in chapter 10 that there are wide variations in female labour market participation. Obviously many nations could increase this, though then questions arise about the impact of this on the birth rate in the absence of new public policies on child care. As far as the labour market participation of the young is concerned, the trend in many countries has been to increase the length of periods in education; it may questioned whether reversing this is desirable, but the point of the argument here is that in the face of a need for more workers it would be feasible to reverse it.

Then there is the issue about labour market participation by people over pension age. Significantly, in many European countries this has fallen since the labour-hungry days of the 1950s and 1960s despite the fact that the population is getting fitter. Not surprisingly, therefore, countries are examining ways to increase this participation, including the possibility of raising the age points at which pension entitlement starts.

To sum up the argument so far: the group of people who may be able to change their status from economically inactive is substantial, therefore offering a challenge to predictions about an exceptionally unfavourable ratio of dependent to non-dependent people based on a crude demographic analysis; but this has the wider implication that labour demand may be a much bigger influence on labour market participation and non-participation than labour supply. That last point therefore needs further amplification. It is odd how at the same time as the demographic time bomb thesis was being developed, there were other futurologists making predictions about the difficulties future economic systems would have in generating jobs. If they are right, then the issues about support for 'dependents' has nothing to do with the age distribution of the population. As was noted in chapter 5, there were massive changes in the world of work during the second half of the twentieth century. These changes are likely to continue; that alone makes predicting employment patterns in 2050 difficult. But in reality there are many other changes occurring in the world that make it very likely that employment patterns will be very different in 2050: the dramatic changes in economic activity in countries like China, the coming depletion of fossil fuel stocks, climate change, and so on. Hence there are very good reasons for expecting that 'dependency' will be determined by the availability of work not the age or health status or gender of the workforce.

We may go further than this, since there are other problems about a thesis that classifies the population into two groups, one dependent on the other. Much of the argument sees that dependency as being based on transfer of cash resources from the incomes of earners to non-earners. Clearly, however, any dependency relationship may take a form in which it is not a cash transfer that is involved but rather services.

There is a problem here about conventional economic thinking that counts only monetised transactions. GDP, an index of the prosperity of a nation that has been much used in this book, is defined as the total value of goods and services produced within that nation in the course of a defined period (usually a year). It does not count non-monetary productive activity and transactions. It therefore undercounts economic activity in countries where there is high use of the informal economy and of productive activity within the family. It has been ironically pointed out that if, within a household, one member starts to formally employ another to do domestic work, national GDP increases! To return directly to elderly people then, many allegedly 'dependent' or 'non-productive' people make substantial contributions to the welfare (and thus surely the 'wealth') of the nation through care activities (for children or other elderly people) and through voluntary activities.

There are essentially three ways in which care tasks may be undertaken, each of which has very different implications for the roles of family, market and state and accordingly very different implications for the way we count the cost of these activities.

1 The tasks may simply be absorbed within the family: in this case the costs do not feature in public accounts, people who might be active labour market participants are instead engaged in unremunerated 'employment', and largely unrecognised within-family 'transfers' occur.
2 They may be the subject of market transactions in which care is purchased, employment is generated and conventional accounting systems recognise them as being part of the economy.
3 They may be undertaken by the state, in which case employment is created but the general tendency of accounting systems is to see this as a cost to the private economy.

We are talking here once again about alternative approaches to 'decommodification' within the welfare state. From this perspective there are alternative questions to be addressed about the way changing demographic balances will be approached in different societies. If the state is prepared to take on a large role as the provider and subsidiser of care (this in effect has been a feature of the Scandinavian model of welfare provision), then as care needs increase so too will employment increase. If this is a matter to be left to the market, then the key issue for the creation of employment may be about putting those in need of care services in the best position to be able to purchase them, ironically a case for the very policy of pension enhancement that is seen as most threatened by demographic change. But if the issue is seen as one to be left to families, then surely data on labour market participation (and also market consumption data) will become a less and less adequate measure of the amount of actual *work* being done.

For those who stress the health and social care needs that may increase as a result of an increasingly elderly population, while much of the debate may be about resources to pay for services, the under-lying problem is the increased need for services however provided. The extent to which an ageing population is also a population in greater need is an issue to which we will return.

A final note is needed on the last two questions in the list at the beginning of this section, i.e. whether nations with high numbers of dependents, however estimated, are necessarily disadvantaged relative to others and whether it matters overall that there are high levels of economic dependency. The first point refers to a complex issue of macro-economics, about the conditions for economic growth. It may be argued that to have a large section of the population who are, at least in the economic terms implied in the productivist thinking outlined above, consumers but not producers engenders a situation in which economic activity is damped down and there is a strong tendency for imports to be sucked in from other countries. Whilst it may again be questioned whether this phenomenon may simply be blamed on the ageing of the population, there are certainly concerns about the political consequences of low-growth scenarios for individual countries (or indeed blocs of countries, like the EU). The first of the two questions repeated above raises this complex economic issue – I do not explore it further but it would be wrong for a discussion of this topic to ignore it altogether. The second raises perhaps a more fundamental philosophical question about the case for resisting the productivist and growth obsession. Ageing people have to come to terms with ageing, perhaps ageing nations have to do so as well.

## Meeting the Costs of Dependency

The range of points made in the last section may seem to some to have argued away the so-called problem of dependency altogether. This was not intended. The case was strongly made because so much of the drift of contemporary argument (called 'apocalyptic demography' in a Canadian critique by Gee and Gutman, 2000) runs so forcefully the other way, seeing anyone over a certain defined age (and often quite a young age like 65) as dependent on the rest of the adult population. However, there does remain a need to look at two key questions:

- the extent to which the concept of retirement does imply a signific-ant shift of national resources from the economically active to the inactive, a shift that may either have negative economic consequences or may be resisted by the economically active;

- the extent to which there are extensive health and social problems amongst the elderly population, to which substantial national resources need to be applied.

These two topics are explored in separate sections.

## Paying for Pensions

The conventional device for providing incomes to those who have left the workforce is the pension. Pension schemes originated in the era of the growth of formal, largely manufacturing, work between the middle of the nineteenth and the middle of the twentieth centuries when employers looked for ways of off-loading their older and (probably) less productive workers. Providing for someone to enjoy retirement – as opposed to struggling on with work, or being forced to claim support because of sickness, or being driven into inadequately supported unemployment – can be seen as a humane way of dealing with ageing in a workforce. In the discussion of the meaning of dependency above, more might have been made of conventional distinctions between retirement as an acceptable form of dependency and less acceptable forms (the test of acceptability of course depending on the attitudes of those required to pay for it). There is opinion poll evidence that spending on pensions is seen as much more acceptable than spending on unemployment benefits (Taylor-Gooby, 1985).

However, when many pension schemes originated, life expectancy was low so that this form of dependency would often not last very long. Now life expectancy is much longer, and there is obviously something to be said for a review of the ages at which pension schemes start. So one relatively uncontroversial aspect of the contemporary policy debate concerns the qualifying age for pensions. The only further point to make on this now is to refer back to the last section: if employers are often in fact discharging workers below qualifying pension age, this measure will simply shift costs to the individuals concerned.

However, this discussion will concentrate on another facet of the debate about the implications of ageing. Many pension schemes (as noted in chapter 4, pp. 78–83) are in some sense contributory (though not necessarily involving an exact equivalence between what goes into a scheme and what comes out). The conventional response to the evidence that the number of pensioners is growing has been to demand that more of the cost of pensions must be pre-funded. There has however been a tendency to see this issue as essentially a problem for state-financed pensions, using pay-as-you-go financing arrangements. Hence encouragement of the development of funded private pensions has been seen as a solution to the problem.

Certainly private pensions lift the burden directly off the public exchequer, but such funded pensions are just as much transfers between the generations as unfunded ones. Much of the alarmist literature on the future burden of public pay-as-you-go schemes disregards the fact that 'funding' implies saving and investment, and therefore correspondingly 'disinvestment' with implications for the workers and savers of the future (and, at worst, implications for the ultimate value of the money) when that money is drawn out to meet needs (see Barr, 2001, 2002 for lucid discussions of the economic issues here). This point is even endorsed in one of the earlier of a number of influential OECD reports on the issues being explored here.

> reducing the costs of ageing populations cannot be met by merely changing the balance of responsibility. The real costs are appropriately measured by the current-period consumption they support, and only reducing the consumption of the elderly from all sources – public and private – reduces their costs to society. The means of financing, advance-funding versus pay-as-you-go methods does not change those costs. (OECD, 1994b, pp. 14–15)

Barr puts the point more succinctly: 'individuals must exchange current production for a claim on future production', hence 'both funded and pay-as-you-go plans are claims on future output, and they are of no use to retirees if the country is not producing enough goods and services to meet those claims' (Barr, 2002, p. 4).

Myles (2002) argues that the best approach to the issue of a fair deal between the generations is, assuming present relativities between the income flow to the old and the pension contributions (both public and private) being made by the workforce, a formula that changes both pensions and contributions over time to maintain those relativities. Hence if we reach a time when the size of the dependent generation rises rapidly, then the cost of that can be proportionately shared between those who pay and those who receive benefits. He goes on to argue that this solution will be the easiest for governments to adopt, given the pressures on them to both minimise tax increases and minimise pension cuts.

The important part of Myles' argument for the issues being considered here is that, where pension schemes are substantially privatised, although the direct political problems for governments may be less, there may be very acute problems of equity as market forces affect different groups differently. He argues that 'in a totally privatised system based on advance funding and other personal assets' problems of cost allocation between the generations would be solved 'by producing lucky and less lucky generations'. Hence: 'Some cohorts and individuals would benefit from favourable wage histories and returns to their capital and so be in a position to retire early. Other cohorts and individuals would be less fortunate and be required to work longer to avoid an impoverished retirement' (Myles, 2002, p. 139). It may be argued that the uncertainties of the investment market actually make the benefits of any funded approach to future provision very hard to predict.

The point of Myles' analysis is that what may emerge is a situation where, whilst the poorest have state protection, those who depend on the market but are not in a particularly privileged position in relation to it may find that they gain very little from extensive pension contributions, and are indeed forced to retire on very poor pensions or to work much longer. This is likely to be a particularly important issue for women, since they are often in less well-paid jobs and not able to participate in the labour force as long as men.

There is of course another aspect to this argument: there may be grounds for the encouragement of funded pensions (either private or public) based on a need for more investment *now*. The arguments about this take the discussion into complex aspects of macro-economic policy. It may be argued in defence of funding through the private market that individuals contribute to the growth of the economy, thereby creating a richer society that is more able to afford transfers to them in their later years. There is something to be said for this argument, but only if there will actually be an investment shortfall if individuals do not pay into pension funds. This proposition is disputed by Blackburn (2002), who draws attention to the complex relationship between the pensions and insurance market on the one hand and the wider economy on the other. This gets us into some complex issues beyond the scope of this book. But there is a related point that is very pertinent to comparative social policy. The World Bank (1994) draws attention to the clear need for investment in developing economies and sees funded pension schemes as a valuable resource. The problem about this solution is that economies are so open in the modern world that it is very difficult to retain investments in the country in which they are made. While at the same time evading the overall problem, the World Bank does indeed acknowledge a paradox that the best way to protect an individual's contributions may often be to invest them outside the weak economy of the country in which they are made. A further paradoxical implication of this, which may be an argument in favour of private investment from the individual's point of view, is that a pension funded by overseas investment may be more secure than a pay-as-you-go promise made by an insecure government.

Returning to Myles' analysis of the alleged 'crisis' for pensions, he divides the nations into those which have good state-supported pension schemes, like Germany, Sweden and Austria, that will have to be adjusted to balance the conflicting pressures between contributors and beneficiaries and a group of nations he calls the 'latecomers', within which (with some qualifications) he includes the UK. He says of these 'latecomers' that 'by adopting advance funding and (typically) defined contribution designs [they] have avoided the public finance problems induced by population ageing but not the larger economic challenge' (Myles, 2002, p. 151). He stresses that 'ensuring intergenerational fairness or maintaining solidarity within generations cannot be achieved without considering the retirement income system as a whole (the public and the private side of the ledger)' (ibid., p. 152).

Nations differ in the extent to which these issues of future pension provisions are on the agenda. Politicians have on the whole very short time frames and are thus likely to want to pay attention to the needs of those already at or close to pension age. The extent to which they look further forward may then be heavily influenced by the extent to which there are strong future-oriented lobbies. The most obvious of these is the private pensions industry, whose future orientation stems from a need to sell their product in the present. Notwithstanding these considerations there are some nations where extensive attention is being given to the longer-run arithmetic of pension arrangements both public and private. South Korea is perhaps remarkable in this respect. Choi and Bae (2005, p. 142) report proposals 'to stabilize the National Pension funds by deferring the expected year of their insolvency from 2047 to after 2070'. Over that period even the demographic predictions will be very inaccurate, let alone any economic ones. Additionally, this shows a remarkable faith in the political future (given that South Korea is a state formed out of a divided nation, with the other half an unpredictable neighbour).

## The Increased Need for Health and Social Care

Much of the discussion so far has stressed the roles of people aged over 65 as actual and potential contributors to society on a scale much greater than the 'demographic time bomb scenario' suggests. This ignores the fact that there is within this large group of people some who make much heavier demands on social policy systems. These people are today generally described as the old elderly, identified as those over 75 or 80 or 85 (the statistics vary with respect to the defining age). In the 15 countries of the pre-2004 EU, 18% of the population is aged between 60 and 79 and 3.7% is aged over 80. The variations between countries are quite slight as far as the over-80s are concerned, with a high of 4.5% in Sweden and a low of 2.5% in Ireland (European Commission, 2004, p. 178).

A growth of 48% in the numbers of the over-80s in this group of EU countries is predicted to be likely by 2015 (ibid.). A study by Casey and his colleagues looks further ahead. It suggests that whereas 22 per cent of over-65s are over 80 now, 35 per cent will be over 80 in 2050 across the sample of countries examined (Casey et al., 2003, p. 34). This study suggests:

> Looking forward, spending is expected to increase further as the share of the elderly increases. This reflects the fact that the per capita consumption of health-care services by the elderly is three to five times higher than for younger groups. This will affect both 'normal' health care (hospital and ambulatory care and pharmaceuticals) and care services for the frail elderly. For the 19 countries where this information is available, the projections indicate an average increase in health and long-term care spending of around 3–3½ percentage points of GDP over the 2000–2050 period. (ibid., p. 9)

As far as health care is concerned, the more medicine can do to prolong life, the more it has to cope with high demands on its services in that extra period it has added to people's lives. However, a great deal depends on what progress can be made with the avoidance of chronic illness. In many respects, as far as acute illness is concerned, the expense is concentrated in the last months of life. With the lengthening of life, this does not necessarily increase. In respect of chronic illness it may be that there will be dramatic changes both because of medical advances and because people give more attention to their lifestyles. It may be that national differences can be detected in respect of the latter.

The authors of the study cited above note wide between-country variations, particularly in respect of social care. This takes us back to (1) issues about the balance between public and private care discussed in chapter 7 and (2) issues discussed earlier in this chapter (and also in chapter 10) about where the costs of care really fall. Clearly, public-sector interventions tend to concentrate on shifting these costs away from the public purse.

There is an important interaction here with the issues about pensions: inasmuch as the incomes of the elderly are increasing, so are their capacities to pay their care costs themselves. This is important in the context of the diminishing capacity of the family, the other alternative to the state, to take on these costs in the context of falling family size and increased female labour market participation. Wealthy pensioners can more easily be independent of both the state and their families. There is a case for arguing for an 'individual' model of pensioner welfare in the same way as feminists argue for such a model for the welfare of women.

Finally, it is worth mentioning another largely unexplored issue. A considerable number of elderly people are income poor but asset rich. This is particularly the case where the asset in question is ownership of a house. There are interesting variations between European societies in this respect. Table 12.4 provides data on owner occupation in Europe; unfortunately this source does not provide any information about the ages of owners.

What is important about owner occupation by the elderly is that even when loans have been needed to buy houses in the first place, those loans are likely to have been repaid and the houses are likely to be owned outright (see Fahey, Nolan and Mâitre, 2004, who also

**Table 12.4**   Percentage of European Union households owning their own accommodation

| | |
|---|---|
| Spain | 82 |
| Ireland | 75 |
| Greece | 74 |
| Belgium | 71 |
| Italy | 71 |
| Luxembourg | 70 |
| UK | 69 |
| Portugal | 66 |
| Finland | 64 |
| Sweden | 59 |
| Denmark | 56 |
| France | 53 |
| Netherlands | 51 |
| Austria | 51 |
| Germany | 41 |
| EU15 | 59 |

*Source*: data from European Commission (2004, p. 193).

argue that this owner occupation is an important source of poverty reduction for the elderly). Clearly, then, a very elderly person with a house is likely to be going, very soon, to pass on either a free house or a significant sum of money to descendants. The policy question that thus arises is: what should happen when a person with a low income but an owned house secures expensive care services from the state? This is a particularly relevant point when that expensive care is in an institution, in circumstances in which the house will be left behind unoccupied. Typically, governments apply means-tests to determine what should be charged for social care. Such means-tests pay attention to the ownership of assets. Where this occurs it is implicitly the case that relatives have in the long run to contribute to the costs of care inasmuch as their inheritances are reduced. We have thus an example of a tax on relatives whose impact is varied and haphazard, being influenced by the complex preceding circumstances: the extent of need for care, the availability of housing property assets, the use of that property by others and the rules applied by specific means-testing systems. In relation to these complexities, it is interesting to note the high levels of people over 80 living with other family members in some of the countries with very high levels of owner occupation: Spain, Portugal and Ireland. Is it too much to speculate that the sharing of the asset contributes to the sharing of care (or indeed vice versa)? There are some interesting comparative questions here about the impact of housing arrangements in societies on family care systems.

This brings the discussion back to the wider issue that has been the concern of this chapter, the so-called rising burden of elderly populations. The discussion of pensions suggested that private pensions are 'assets' that involve claims on current production when they are cashed. This is not the case with housing wealth. Inasmuch as they own fully paid-for housing, people take a pre-funded asset into their elderly years. They may realise this asset if they 'trade down' to cheaper smaller accommodation or take advantage of marketed equity release schemes. They may be forced to realise the asset by means-tests. Or they may pass on the asset to the next generation. In all cases they are reducing the burden on the next generation in ways that have been given very little attention in discussions of the impact of so-called dependency.

## Conclusions

This chapter has explored the issues concerning the extensive demographic changes occurring in the world, which have the effect of producing a much increased ratio of old people to younger people. I have shown how this is widely explored as a set of problems about 'dependency', a large inactive population becoming dependent on an economically active population rapidly diminishing in size. This is conventionally seen as posing problems for both pension policies and care policies.

However, many of the assumptions within this conventional literature have been challenged within the chapter. I have argued that it is important to recognise that it is the pattern of labour market participation rather than the demographic profile in each country that needs primary attention. Furthermore, even use of this more accurate index of dependency can lead us into economistic thinking where only people who are economically active are perceived as making contributions to society.

This discussion then leads on to consideration of issues about pension systems, where pre-funding is increasingly advocated as necessary to cope with the requirements of a large pensioner genera-tion. I have suggested that this argument often disregards the fact that this involves, in macro-economic terms, just as much a 'burden' on producers as pay-as-you-go state-managed transfer systems and has highly unpredictable and inegalitarian characteristics. Lastly, I have examined the implications of ageing for care systems, accepting that there are some important issues to be addressed but that even here there is a need to be much more precise in identifying where the need comes from and how it is met.

This chapter has been concerned with one of the dominant issues in discussions of the future of social policy, and its implications have to be examined together with the other dominant issue, the impact of global economic change (the main concern of the next chapter).

GUIDE TO FURTHER READING

The conventional case for concern about ageing is made in a good com-parative data survey by Casey et al. (2003). In *The Overselling of Population Ageing*, Gee and Gutman (2000) provide a critique of the demographic time-bomb thesis using Canadian data. The arguments for pension investments is developed in a World Bank report (1994). A criticism of this can be found in Beattie and McGillivray (1995). Barr (2002; see also 2001, part 3) provides a good summary of economic pros and cons of the various approaches to pension provision, while Myles (2002) sets out how pay-as-you-go pensions can be protected and argues for their underlying egalitarian potential.

# CHAPTER 13

# CONCLUSIONS: SOCIAL POLICY CONVERGENCE AND GLOBALISM

## Introduction: Identifying the Issues

In chapter 2, early comparative theory was criticised for its simplistic emphasis on policy convergence, whereas regime theory was presented as superior because it emphasises and tries to explain diversity. Yet the questions about convergence will not go away, given both the evidence of shared demographic change (as explored in the last chapter) and arguments about the impact of global economic, cultural and political developments.

In this chapter the aim is explore to what extent it is true that social policy systems are converging in the modern world, what that convergence implies (particularly whether it is convergence 'downward' under strong market forces or 'upwards' towards universal social policy ideals, or indeed some combination of the two) and to what extent any observed trends may be explained.

This then leads on to a final section, concluding the book as a whole, that highlighs continuing evidence of social policy diversity and the strengths and weaknesses of attempts to explain that using comparative theory.

## Globalism and Comparative Theory

Early comparative social policy analyses which suggested that social policy development was a largely unidimensional growth in which rising GDP would inevitably bring with it growing state expenditure on social policy involved what was, in a sense, a globalist proposition. This was that welfare systems will converge as nations grow. This idea of convergence is still around. However, much of the contemporary preoccupation is with an argument that convergence will be rather more in a downwards direction under pressure from the global economy.

The exploration of convergence in social policy is inevitably mainly addressed in terms of national expenditure data. Convergence can be a combination of a variety of different developments, some nations going one way, others going the opposite way. It will be seen as essential to tease out of this discussion some evaluation of what Castles calls 'the race to the bottom hypothesis':

> Where countries are engaged in international trade and where enterprises cannot be prevented from relocating to countries in which costs are lower, governments are seen as having little option but to accede to the demands of capital for lower taxes, a more flexible labour market, and less 'red tape' around health, safety and environmental issues. (Castles, 2004, p. 21)

There is then a second hypothesis, potentially but not necessarily entirely competitive with the first one, that catching up on the part of less-developed nations (the concern of early comparative theory) involves a movement upwards rather than downwards in certain nations. These two processes may of course both be occurring.

We need to move on from there to explain what is actually happening. What will be shown is that convergence is limited and the behaviour of some nations offers reasons to question both of the hypotheses stated above. Hence there are some important questions about what conditions enable nations to resist global pressures on their social policy-making. Related to this are questions about the extent to which global forces have very different implications for different nations, and particularly questions about the extent to which the issues for the less-developed nations are very different from those for the developed ones. This last discussion raises questions about the need to analyse power globally, and to recognise that so-called economic inevitability may be simply a dominant ideology.

Finally, there are some important questions to be posed about the consequences of autonomous policy-making. The economistic hypothesis may thus partly be supported, inasmuch as there may be evidence that global pressures are resisted at a price, namely lowered competitive capacity within those nations that resist it. This is the theme that came to the fore in the 1980s in the debate about the 'crisis of the welfare state', suggesting that the massive growth of social policy in the period 1950–1980 had to stop. This leads to empirical questions about the extent to which those nations that have tried to resist global pressures have paid a price in terms of arrested economic development. This will lead to some conclusions about this perspective, asking to what extent the panic about the future of the welfare state has been rooted in the recognition of some really problematic consequences of ignoring the dominant warning.

The analysis of policy developments within nation states needs to be seen in a global context. That is undisputed. What is more controversial is the extent to which global influences should be seen as imposing constraints on national policy decision-making or, to put it even more strongly, superimposing a global system in place of individual systems.

## Globalist Theory

Globalist theory embodies various themes: the development of global financial markets, the cross-national diffusion of technology, the emergence of trans-national or global corporations (and the increasing economic pressure on large corporations to 'think globally') and the emergence of global cultural flows. All these trends offer challenges to state autonomy and stimulate new political formations beyond the nation state. However, it has been argued that there is nothing really new about globalism: complex supra-national economic developments and the transmission of culture between nations have a long history (Hirst and Thompson, 1992). It may be simply the speed of modern communications, and the ways in which the media can expose us to developments elsewhere in the world, that heightens awareness of the phenomena. Whilst ultimately global development needs to be seen as a whole, it is pertinent here to distinguish the economic aspects of globalist theory from the cultural aspects. They offer rather different perspectives on what is happening to policy decision processes.

Much of the theory about economic globalism is determinist in character. It stresses the openness of world markets and the impact this has on the choices available within nation states. But is it saying that here are a series of structural developments about which politicians can do little? Or is it merely saying that issues about the power of economic interests need to be analysed in supra-national terms? In other words, this is not so much a determinist point of view as one which emphasises *either* that national policy-makers must increasingly be able to deal with interests organised outside their country *or* that effective policy processes need to be supra-national too (Hirst and Thompson, 1992). The latter position may lead to a pessimistic stance on the feasibility of achieving solutions to political problems in the face of institutional complexity, but it is not ultimately a determinist stance. However, Hay suggests that it is determinist inasmuch as 'Whether the globalist thesis is "true" or not may matter far less than whether it is *deemed* to be true – or, quite possibly, just useful – by those employing it (Hay, 2002, p. 258). Hence he argues that decision-makers may alternatively believe that there is no alternative but to respond to perceived global economic forces or that globalisation 'may provide a most convenient alibi, allowing politicians to escape the responsibility they would otherwise bear for reforms which might otherwise be rather difficult to legitimate' (ibid., p. 259).

On the other hand, the cultural perspective on globalism stresses the extent to which ideas are shared between nations. This is very well brought out by George and Wilding (2002). They suggest that whilst much of the argument has been about the development of a global economy, a full examination of globalisation has to embrace a whole range of political and cultural phenomena. It has to be recognised that what is involved is almost all aspects of modern life. Hence whilst much of the evidence about economic change tends to inculcate a deterministic pessimism, when it is identified that there are many important issues about the opening of communications between people and the spread of ideas, a more balanced picture of both opportunities and problems emerges.

This leads to two points. First, the communication of ideas does not of course involve the dissemination of one point of view but rather a variety of perspectives. The economistic arguments about globalism coming from the USA and from international organisations like the World Bank are disputed by European states where welfare institutions are stronger and by other international organisations. The conflict between perspectives generates space for choice between alternatives, preserving the at least partial autonomy of national decision-makers. Second, there are signs of efforts to develop 'global social policy', which will set aspirations for national policy-making, not just impose constraints on it. George and Wilding set out evidence of developments of this kind in chapter 7 of their book.

A lot of the debate about globalism is set out in terms of the 'good' and 'bad' things that come with it. For analysts of social policy much of this can be seen as involving a contrast between the 'pessimists' who see welfare development greatly constrained by the world economy and the 'optimists' who, like George and Wilding, suggest that international social policy goals can be set out in defiance of narrow economistic points of view.

## Evidence of Convergence

The OECD is the only comprehensive data source for information on expenditure trends over a relatively long period. It has inevitably been mined by others interested in this theme, whose observations will be brought into this discussion. The data are not very good before 1980, and in going back that far some modern members of OECD will have to be left out because they were not members then, notably Korea and the Eastern European nations. The case for ignoring pre-1980 data is not merely a pragmatic one; it is also the case that the view that the welfare state costs too much was just beginning to be expressed widely at that time (for discussions see Mishra, 1984; Berthoud, 1985). It may be noted that governments committed to rolling back the welfare state had been elected in 1979 in the UK and 1980 in the USA. Table 13.1 compares social policy expenditure in 1980 and 2001 in the OECD nations for which data are available. It adds education expenditure into the OECD 'social expenditure' category, therefore inevitably providing a slightly different picture to that provided by those who simply use the latter. This is consistent with this book's examination of education policy and with the expenditure figures provided in table 2.1, from which the second column is taken. The countries are listed in order of public social expenditure as a proportion of GDP from the highest in 1980 downwards.

Table 13.1 suggests that there is some convergence between 1980 and 2001. In 1980, the gap between the highest (Sweden) and the lowest (Greece) was 24 percentage points; in 2001, this gap was only 17.8 (between Denmark and Ireland). There is something very special about Ireland, perhaps confusing the overall picture. Across the period being examined, Ireland enjoyed a massive growth in GDP, something like three times that of the growth in the OECD group as a whole (which was 49 per cent) (see table 13.3). In these special circumstances it might be expected that, in a country with comparatively conservative governments, social expenditure growth might lag behind this dramatic economic growth. The interesting point about convergence within the group of nations shown in table 13.1 is that if Ireland is excluded, the convergence *within Europe* is quite striking. The gap between the

**Table 13.1** Social policy expenditure, 1980 and 2001

| Country | Public social expenditure (including education) as percentage of GDP, 1980 | Public social expenditure (including education) as percentage of GDP, 2001 | Change, 1980–2001 |
|---|---|---|---|
| Sweden | 37.8 | 35.2 | –2.6 |
| Denmark | 35.7 | 35.7 | 0 |
| Netherlands | 34.6 | 26.7 | –7.9 |
| Belgium | 29.9 | 32.3 | 2.4 |
| Austria | 28.0 | 31.4 | 3.4 |
| Germany | 28.0 | 31.7 | 3.7 |
| France | 26.2 | 34.2 | 8.0 |
| Norway | 24.8 | 29.7 | 4.9 |
| Finland | 23.7 | 30.3 | 6.6 |
| Ireland | 23.4 | 17.9 | –5.5 |
| New Zealand | 22.9 | 24.3 | 1.4 |
| UK | 22.9[a] | 25.3 | 2.4 |
| Italy | 22.8 | 28.9 | 6.1 |
| Canada | 21.1 | 23.0 | 1.9 |
| Switzerland | 19.4 | 31.7 | 12.3 |
| USA | 18.1 | 19.6 | 1.5 |
| Australia | 16.7 | 22.6 | 5.9 |
| Japan | 16.1 | 20.4 | 4.3 |
| Portugal | 15.1 | 26.7 | 11.6 |
| Greece | 13.8 | 28.0 | 14.2 |

[a] Education element estimated from 1984 figure.

*Source*: data from OECD (2004e) with education expenditure figures for 1980 taken from OECD (1990, p. 87).

highest and the lowest spender, in proportion to GDP, reduced from 24 to 10.4 (between Denmark and the UK).

Castles (2004) carried out a similar analysis of convergence, with 1998 rather than 2001 as the last year in his comparison and with education expenditure excluded from the analysis. His results are very similar, except that he shows a little less convergence. This demonstrates how sensitive these broad statistical comparisons are to choice of years, choice of indices and sometimes (though not in this case) choice of nations. The inclusion of education in the comparison here seems significant. In the context of decreasing numbers of children,

**Table 13.2** Changes in social expenditure (excluding education) as a percentage of GDP, 1998–2001

| Country | Rate of change in social expenditure (as defined by OECD and by Castles) between 1998 and 2001 |
|---|---|
| Australia | 0.2 |
| Austria | 0.3 |
| Belgium | −0.3 |
| Canada | −0.6 |
| Denmark | −1.0 |
| Finland | −1.7 |
| France | −0.5 |
| Germany | 0 |
| Greece | 1.5 |
| Ireland | −1.8 |
| Italy | 0.7 |
| Japan | 2.4 |
| Netherlands | 1.2 |
| New Zealand | −1.5 |
| Norway | −1.8 |
| Portugal | 2.0 |
| Sweden | −1.5 |
| Switzerland | −0.5 |
| UK | 0.3 |
| USA | 0.3 |

*Source*: data calculated from OECD (2004e) and Castles (2004).

education expenditure growth is perhaps easier to curb than growth in other social expenditure, where ageing has a big impact. The other point about the differences between the two sets of results is the way in which the inclusion of three extra years makes a difference. Table 13.2 sets out the rates of change between 1998 and 2001 in the social expenditure figures used by Castles, for the sample of countries featured in table 13.1.

These figures are interesting in that they show continuing convergence between the end of Castles' study period and 2001, with a lot of countries showing declines in relative expenditure. They support Castles' generalisation about convergence towards a 'steady-state' welfare state, 'with a number of expenditure laggards substantially increasing their spending and some previous expenditure leaders making significant, but somewhat smaller, spending cuts' (Castles, 2004, p. 168). He describes this as a consequence of two processes:

> The first was a process of catch-up by countries that adopted expenditure programmes later than others. The second involved corrections for expenditure overshoot in countries where predicted expenditure outcomes had been premised on levels of economic growth greater than later turned out to be the case. (ibid.)

Castles examines the extent to which there is a particular convergence within the European nations, something suggested by the data in table 13.1. His analysis goes much more deeply into the different components within the overall expenditure patterns, suggesting that while there is aggregate convergence there is divergence in specific spending patterns. He suggests in particular divergence in pension provision and in the attention being given to social care (this latter being salient in the Scandinavian countries). The implicit warning in Castles' more complex work of being cautious about generalisation based on observation of broad expenditure patterns is supported by Taylor-Gooby's work (2001, 2002) in which he contrasts quantitative analyses of change with the evidence from qualitative studies. He argues:

> In general, most recent accounts see welfare systems as surprisingly resilient to the pressures that confront them. . . . [An examination of pension reform suggests that] different analyses tend to lead to rather different conclusions: quantitative analysis tends to stress continuity and stability, while case studies present a picture that allows greater weight to differences in national political processes and to the instability of current settlements. Quantitative approaches tend to predominate in the literature, because of the availability of statistical data and because of the technical difficulties in carrying out adequate cross-nationally comparative case studies. The outcome may be a tendency to over-emphasise stability, just at a point when radical changes are on the cards. (Taylor-Gooby, 2002, p. 619)

It must be stressed that the evidence shown here supports the convergence hypothesis but not the 'race to the bottom' one. 'Catching up' is much more significant than down-sizing in this convergence process. Table 13.1 shows that social expenditure as a proportion of GDP grew in all but three nations. It is also very important to bear in mind that these statistics are about social expenditure as a *share* of GDP, in a context in which there has been substantial GDP growth. In this sense even the three nations that have reduced social expenditure in relative terms have increased it substantially in absolute terms.

## The Economic Implications of the Absence of a Race to the Bottom

In considering the lack of evidence for a 'race to the bottom' it is worth going back to what writers were saying about the 'crisis' or 'impending crisis' for the welfare state in the 1970s and 1980s. In the 1970s, the sharp oil price rise was unsettling to many economies. It came at a time when deflationary monetarist policies were beginning to become the conventional economic wisdom. These identified public expenditure control, and particularly public borrowing control, as key 'cures' to economic problems. For countries like the UK, Australia and New Zealand where balance of payment problems loomed large as part of the crisis, the international economic 'doctors' were quick to prescribe public expenditure cuts. Political shifts to the Right reinforced receptiveness to these ideas.

Marxist analyses of the development of the welfare state have seen it as playing a role in postponing the arrival of the 'crisis' within capitalism (see chapter 2), but then facing tensions that undermine its ameliorative effect (O'Connor, 1973; Gough, 1979; Offe, 1984). These writers argue that, over time, the price to be paid for the achievement of social and industrial peace through social policy expenditure tends to rise. This follows logically from their argument that such measures postpone rather than abolish the realisation of the capitalist crisis (see also Wolfe, 1977). In particular, the role of social policy in 'legitimising' an unequal and exploitative society – dealing with the casualties of market processes and offering social benefits to buy off proletariat discontent – becomes increasingly expensive. Here then, it is suggested, is a force which drives welfare expenditure ever upwards. This imposes costs on production that will undermine competitive efficiency and will tend to be resisted by the bourgeoisie. A conflict arises, these theorists argue, that cannot be resolved through normal political processes in a capitalist society. If political decisions are made to cut costs, they intensify discontent; yet if cuts are not made, increasing public sector costs undermine enterprise.

There is an equivalent to the Marxist theory of crisis to be found in theories particularly linked with the opposite side of the political spectrum. The 'economic theory of democracy' has suggested that politics involves an auction in which party competition to win elections drives up social expenditure, particularly when the costs can be hidden, delayed or spread (see Tullock, 1976; Brittan, 1977). The rising expectations of citizens fuel these political demands, and so long as politicians respond to them this has a feedback effect to produce more demands.

Echoing the work of neo-Marxist theorists like O'Connor, New Right theorists argue that welfare expenditure is unproductive, dependent on the productive part of the economy. The imposition of increasing welfare costs is seen as threatening economic efficiency and competitiveness within economies. It is suggested that social policy places demands on state investment which tend to crowd out investment in productive enterprise (Bacon and Eltis, 1976). There is also concern about the levels of taxation required to support social policies. These are seen as damaging the productive sector, deterring entrepreneurial risk-taking and reducing work efforts.

While Marxist theory postulates the development of a conflict that cannot be resolved without radical, perhaps revolutionary change, New Right theory argues that there is a way forward. This requires political elites to resist the demands on them. This seems to involve a conflict between the needs of capitalism and the demands of democracy (see Brittan, 1977). Some writers have suggested, moreover, that limitations on the taxing or spending powers of governments should be enshrined in constitutions (Buchanan and Wagner, 1977). Alternatively, it may be argued merely that elites have a duty to educate electorates to accept the damage that unreasonable demands for expenditure will do to the economy.

Whether this New Right theory should be called 'crisis theory' is debatable. Unlike Marxist theory it specifies a non-revolutionary way forward. However, some exponents of this view have sought to specify levels of public expenditure that they identify as a crisis point, where economic disaster will follow if nothing is done. There are nevertheless grounds for doubt as to whether identifying such points is feasible. These doubts rest principally upon ambiguities embedded in the data upon which such judgements are based.

New Right crisis theories either focus on the relationship between productive and unproductive activities or on the relationship between private and public sectors (with these two often treated as synonymous, despite the fact that the latter may be a source of production and the former includes private services of all kinds). A particularly popular version of this argument looks at public expenditure as a proportion of GDP in a society, suggesting that there is some threshold at which the former is dangerously high.

There are various problems about these judgements. There are difficulties in measuring GDP accurately, and serious difficulties about defining some activities as productive and others as unproductive. Why should the manufacturing of drugs and medical equipment be defined as productive whereas the tax-provided resources consumed during their use by state health services be considered as unproductive? There is much productive activity with consequences positively damaging to societies: take your pick of weapons, tobacco, addictive drugs, pornographic videos, etc. It seems odd to have a theory which sees these as 'good' for society and publicly provided caring services as bad! The classification of private services sold to fellow nationals as contributing to GDP but public tax-supported services as drains upon it has some validity if your concern is levels of taxation but little if you are dealing with allegations about a lack of national productivity.

On the public expenditure side, a number of writers have pointed to a confusion in the arguments between public sector consumption and the organisation by the public sector of transfer payments. It is argued that the provision of income maintenance benefits and other kinds of cash subsidies involve merely the state shifting money from one group of citizens (tax-payers) to others (Hill and Bramley, 1986). It was shown in chapter 3 (table 3.2) that these are large elements in welfare state expenditure. They have been particularly prominent in the growth of public expenditure. If they are deducted from the proportion of GDP 'consumed', the result is figures that are much less alarming, in either absolute or growth terms.

The overall point is that some comparatively arbitrary definitions are used to arrive at figures that have been treated with great reverence in the debate about the 'burden' of social policy. However, it is important not to take the scepticism expressed in the last two paragraphs too far. The theories that are particularly suspect are those which rest on concerns about productivity and investment. The suggestions above do not provide a basis for refuting concerns about effects of public expenditure on competitiveness between countries or about the impact of the 'burden' of taxation on individuals.

These ingredients in the crisis debate can be evaluated by looking again at social expenditure data trends. The basic proposition in the crisis literature is that nations that do not take these economic considerations seriously will, in a context of global competition, experience economic decline. Two simple tests of that are offered:

- by relating social policy expenditure growth to economic growth over the period since the crisis theory began to be taken seriously (around 1980);
- by looking at social policy levels in 1980 (assuming that if they were high they would impose particular constraints) and relating them to economic growth since then.

**Table 13.3** Social policy growth related to economic growth, 1980–2001

| Country | Public social expenditure change, 1980–2001 | Social policy expenditure as percentage of GDP, 1980 | GDP growth, 1980–2001 |
|---|---|---|---|
| Greece | 14.2 | 13.8 | 26 |
| Switzerland | 12.3 | 19.4 | 22 |
| Portugal | 11.6 | 15.1 | 75 |
| France | 8.0 | 26.2 | 42 |
| Finland | 6.6 | 23.7 | 51 |
| Italy | 6.1 | 22.8 | 45 |
| Australia | 5.9 | 16.7 | 51 |
| Norway | 4.9 | 24.8 | 73 |
| Japan | 4.3 | 16.1 | 57 |
| Germany | 3.7 | 28.0 | 46 |
| Austria | 3.4 | 28.0 | 52 |
| Belgium | 2.4 | 29.9 | 46 |
| UK | 2.4 | 22.9 | 61 |
| Canada | 1.9 | 21.1 | 41 |
| USA | 1.5 | 18.1 | 53 |
| New Zealand | 1.4 | 22.9 | 32 |
| Denmark | 0 | 35.7 | 43 |
| Sweden | −2.6 | 37.8 | 43 |
| Ireland | −5.5 | 23.4 | 167 |
| Netherlands | −7.9 | 34.6 | 49 |

*Source*: social policy growth rate as set out in table 13.1. Economic growth per head calculated from data in OECD (2005a), relating countries in terms of purchasing power parities at 2001 prices.

Table 13.3 does this. As far as the relative growth rates are concerned, whilst there are some extreme cases of low growth and high expenditure increases (Greece and Switzerland) and one extreme case of high growth and low expenditure increases, i.e. proportionately negative (Ireland), there is really no clear evidence that high social policy growth has had any impact on economic growth.

Table 13.4 adopts two arbitrary yardsticks to evaluate national performance in relation to 1980 expenditure levels. It counts high social spenders in 1980 as those spending over 25% of GDP on social policy and low social spenders as those spending below that ratio. The table

**Table 13.4** Relationship between social policy spending in 1980 and GDP growth

|  | Growth at or below average | Growth above average |
|---|---|---|
| Spending in 1980 below 25% of GDP | Greece, Switzerland, Italy, Canada, New Zealand | Australia, Portugal, Finland, Norway, Ireland, Japan, UK, USA |
| Spending in 1980 above 25% of GDP | France, Germany, Belgium, Denmark, Sweden, Netherlands | Austria |

suggests that only one of the early high spenders had an above-average economic growth rate (Austria), whereas several of the lower spenders in 1980 have enjoyed high rates of economic growth.

Taking the two indicators of allegedly problematical social spending together it may be argued that starting high and staying high has not been disastrous for nations, even though starting high may have put countries at a slight disadvantage. On the other hand, the economic experience of the nations that started low and caught up on social spending during the period examined has been very mixed: very positive in the case of Portugal (and to some extent Norway), very negative in the cases of Greece and Switzerland. Using the Irish example to generalise an argument for keeping social policy expenditure low would involve making a great deal too much of one small special case.

However, many more economic indicators need to be used for a full evaluation of the arguments about the relationship between social policy and the fate of the economy. Particularly important for the assessment of arguments about globalism is consideration of the openness of the economy (e.g. the extent of the dependence on exports) and the nature of the economy (to what extent economic activities are vulnerable to international competition on wage costs and related grounds). Various studies have struggled with these variables to try to get a better understanding of the impact of social policy over time than that offered here.

A book called *Can the Welfare State Compete?* (Pfaller, Gough and Therborn, 1991), though now rather old, provides a systematic examination of the impact of social policy on economic policy, combining a

review of correlations between quantitative indices of economic performance and social policy expenditure indices with some single-
country case studies. The quantitative review ends with the following
cautious suggestion that there seems to be some evidence of problems
about the competitiveness of the welfare state:

> Our analysis cannot show in a consistent fashion that welfare states
> are less competitive than other industrialised capitalist countries.
> Nonetheless, taken together our findings add a certain support to the
> view that in international comparison welfare statism has come to
> undermine economic performance and has, thus, turned into a com-
> petitive disadvantage. If we take correlation coefficients above 0.35
> as moderately significant, we have discovered nine of these and all of
> them are negative. Of these seven apply to the 1980s. . . . they comprise
> negative associations between several measures of welfare statism and
> rates of economic growth, and between tax levels and export growth
> and productivity growth in manufacturing. There are no even modestly
> positive correlations between our measures of welfare statism and
> economic competitiveness in the 1980s. On the other hand, the signi-
> ficantly negative correlations amount to only seven out of many and
> all the others are inconclusive. Nevertheless, there is reason to expect
> that international competition is putting pressure on the welfare state.
> (ibid., pp. 40–1)

Kite (2004) explores the impact of globalisation on social policy and
the implications of political resistance to it. She develops a classification
of states in terms of whether their economies are open or closed and in
terms of whether the need for retrenchment is accepted or rejected.
This implies problems for the open system if retrenchment is resisted,
much as crisis theory suggests. But Kite's results do not point clearly
in this direction:

> The evidence presented here is consistent with a modified globalization
> argument with regard to cross-national variation in retrenchment. More
> open states are more prone to retrenchment, but domestic resistance
> potential plays an important role in limiting it. At the same time, it is
> also possible to reject arguments that non-retrenchers are punished in
> the form of poorer economic performance. At best there is some indica-
> tion that they might experience somewhat lower growth rates, but even
> this is not entirely clear. There is no evidence that they suffer higher
> levels of inflation or unemployment. Moreover, if economic equality is
> used as a measure of performance, then the non-retrenchers perform
> considerably better. (ibid., p. 233)

Castles (2004) explores the impact of the extent to which economies are open (using two indices, the extent of overseas trade and the amount of foreign direct investment) and suggests that there is a significant relationship between these variables and lower welfare expenditure growth. But he goes on to show that his results are very sensitive to strong individual country effects, that a full analysis of this issue requires attention to be given to changes in the internal economies of countries, and that the relationship between 'prior expenditure levels and subsequent expenditure change' needs to be taken into account (ibid., p. 113).

To say that sophisticated efforts to model economic effects do not offer significantly greater insights into this issue should not be read as a belittling comment in respect of this work. Rather it demonstrates the need to go beyond explanations of responses to social policy expenditure change in terms of economics. In fact most contemporary analyses use both political and economic variables in their models.

## Explaining Variation in Change in Political Terms

Paul Pierson (2001) brings together essays on variations in the ways in which nations have responded to the pressures for welfare state retrenchment. Within this book, Swank's quantitative study offers crucial empirical evidence on the various influences on this. He indicates the extent to which economic pressures towards social policy retrenchment are in practice affected by the following.

- The presence or absence of strong social policy support coalitions: here he is principally drawing on the same kinds of variables, particularly support for political parties of 'left' or 'right', that Esping-Andersen used in developing his regime model.
- Institutional arrangements that affect the likelihood of institutional change (political systems that inhibit or facilitate policy change).

Whilst in some respects these two groups of political variables are interrelated, they have been given different degrees of emphasis in more qualitative accounts of policy change. For some writers (e.g. Pierson, 1994; Hinrichs, 2000; Béland, 2001) it is the presence or absence of strong support coalitions that are crucial. This argument is important for explaining why, within some countries, some policies are resistant to change (where they benefit significant and powerful groups within the population) and why some countries have more deeply embedded systems inasmuch as they provide 'universal' benefits. Both of these issues have been explored to some extent in chapter 9 with reference to 'social divisions'.

However, for other writers it is the more specific institutional embeddedness of systems that is emphasised. Institutional arrangements, it is argued, contribute to policy inertia. Once embarked on particular policy pathways, countries are unlikely to shift significantly away from them. Whilst this approach has much in common with the other one (stressing the way interest groups protect institutional arrangements that favour them), it depends a lot less on what we may call 'political arithmetic', the assessment of the relative size of coalitions for or against policies, and rather more on the way in which formal arrangements are hard to alter (Immergut, 1998; Pierson, 2000). Closely related to this are issues about the way political institutions work. Coalitions for change are easier to assemble in some systems, for example the politically simple majoritarian 'Westminster-style' democracies, than in others.

The really interesting feature of this work is the way it shows that the protection of social policies has not necessarily been 'punished' by irresistible economic forces. Nations may make choices, influenced by domestic politics, and if they choose to defend welfare institutions they can 'get away with it'. This shifts the discussion of globalism back to the notion that what is significant is the dissemination of ideas. A group of countries accepted the neo-liberal implications of the crisis theory and responded accordingly (we are talking here in many respects of the dissemination of an American ideology). Other countries (largely European) have welfare institutions that are more deeply embedded and have also chosen to resist the international dissemination of neo-liberal theory.

This distinction between responses brings us back to regime theory. Esping-Andersen, Pierson and others have suggested that responses to global economic change can be predicted from regime analysis. This cannot be demonstrated through a simple analysis of expenditure change (such as in table 13.1). The important point is not that, for example, Sweden and Denmark have limited their expenditure growth but that they have not shifted dramatically away from the very high levels of expenditure they had already established by 1980.

Castles makes the interesting point that there is to some extent a particular convergence process within the 'families' of nations identified in Esping-Andersen's regime theory. There is some evidence for this (notably the relative rise of social expenditure in Switzerland as well as the southern European nations to make the original 'conservative' group rather more homogeneous, as well as convergence in the social democratic group). Taylor-Gooby (2001) similarly suggests that the nature of the response to economic pressure has very much depended on the 'regime' already established. Hence it has been argued that Scandinavian 'social democratic regimes' and continental European regimes have been less susceptible to these new pressures than 'liberal' ones like the UK and Ireland. But a fuller analysis of this topic requires attention to be given not merely to expenditure levels but also to the forms which social policy expenditure take (something that has of course been explored throughout this book).

What Esping-Andersen also does is go beyond this notion, that different regimes have the autonomy to behave differently, to suggest reasons why the social democratic and conservative regimes have been able to resist the predicted 'crisis'. His argument embodies several propositions:

- that the 'corporatist' model of economic relationships makes possible the negotiation of responses to economic pressure in which valued social protection systems can be preserved;
- that inasmuch as social protection systems contribute to social harmony they generate a commitment to national problem-solving;
- that where the neo-liberal model suggests that competitiveness can be achieved only through the driving down of wages and the removal of social protection there is an alternative that involves a focus on preserving a highly trained and adaptable labour force;
- that since the welfare state is a system for the socialisation of costs, then where it is absent the costs of economic change fall elsewhere with possibly more damaging consequences for the society (a key example here is of course the existence of high crime rates). Hence the economic equation is not as simple as neo-liberal theory suggests.

These elements are loosely derived from Esping-Andersen's more recent work (1996, 1999, 2002).

Of course Esping-Andersen's theory embodies three regime types, and is thus not simply contrasting the liberal alternative with the rest. In fact he sees problems within the conservative approach inasmuch as strongly corporatist systems may prevent flexibility, treating the support of existing workers, even in doomed industries, as of over-riding importance. He also see the excessive dependence on the family as a protective institution as problematical in the conservative regime. Although he argues for new approaches that go beyond it, he leaves little doubt that the social democratic model has advantages:

Another strategy, evident in Scandinavia, consists in shifting welfare
state resources from passive income maintenance to employment and
family promotion. The era of public employment growth has clearly
ended and, instead, policy is directed to active labour market measures,
such as training and mobility, and wage subsidies. Scandinavia appears
now to have accepted that greater inequalities are unavoidable but seeks
to build in guarantees against these being concentrated in any particular
stratum, or becoming permanent across people's life courses. In this
regard, the Nordic welfare states may be said to spearhead a social
investment strategy. They have clearly not escaped high unemployment,
or the necessity for significant cuts in social benefit levels. Yet, their
unemployment record must be gauged against the backdrop of record
high activity rates and, contrary to continental Europe, very modest
degrees of social marginalization, exclusion, and youth unemployment.
(Esping-Andersen, 1996, p. 25)

There seems to be an optimistic message here: nations can ride out
global economic change and largely preserve welfare institutions. But
does this lead to the nice prescription: follow Sweden's example and
all will be well? Surely it does not, and the reason it does not is itself
embodied in regime theory and all the modern political and institutional theory that has been influenced by it. In many respects such
theory rejects economic determinism but puts a kind of political determinism in its place. Nations are running along one of three pathways,
but can they shift easily from one to another? Esping-Andersen's
answer is surely 'no' – there are strong forces that tend to keep them
on the same pathway. On the other hand, this book has made much of
the limitations of the notion of three distinct regimes; much evidence
of borderline cases and mixed situations has been produced. However, it is important to recognise how much social policy change is a
slow and incremental process so that dramatic shifts of direction are
difficult. Here the economic **determinism** argument also returns. It is
one thing to be a 'resister' of economic forces in the context of already-
strong social policy institutions, but it is quite another to try to change
institutions in the face of those forces. This brings us to some crucial
issues about nations outside, or on the margins, of the OECD member
group examined so far.

## Latecomers to the World of Welfare

The long-standing members of OECD have been shown as responding
to the pressures that come with economic globalisation in ways that

are to a degree under their control. Cultural globalism has been seen as a process that enables exchange of ideas between them, and may support either the reinforcement of a market-oriented response to economic globalism or a measure of resistance to it. The question is: if this is the situation within this rich 'club' of nations, to what extent does it apply to latecomers to that club or those outside it? The analysis in the last section suggested that the welfare state ideal is preserved by some members of the club, even if it is challenged by others (notably the USA). The implication is that nations can still bring the conditions by which they operate their social welfare systems largely under their control. But can every nation aspire to this, or is it a privileged position reserved to the early starters down the welfare road?

Clearly, some nations have managed to arrive late and achieve quite substantial social policy systems. Three figure amongst the nations discussed above: Greece and Portugal; a third, Spain, is only missing because of a lack of useable data. The much larger list of OECD nations used for table 2.1 featured some others that seem to be moving in the same direction: the Czech Republic, Hungary, Poland, the Slovak Republic and South Korea. However, it is very important to bear in mind that all in the first list of nations have been EU members for some time, and all but Korea in the second list joined the EU in 2004. Around the fringe of the original core EU members there have been opportunities to join in a shared European development process; candidate membership and now full membership enhance that process.

Korea is interesting since there is an academic debate about where it (and Taiwan) may be placed in the families of nations used in various versions of regime theory (see chapter 2, pp. 32–4). Ramesh (2004, p. 199 citing Kuhnle, 2002) notes 'one veteran observer is of the opinion that at least Korea is on its way to becoming a social democratic welfare state'. Shin (2003) portrays Korea as moving from a 'minimalist' approach to social policy, through a 'residualist' welfare system to an 'enterprise-centred regulator welfare system' and is now undergoing transition to an 'institutional welfare system'. Others, as was noted in chapter 2, see Korea and Taiwan as essentially 'productivist' welfare states, involving state intervention in the economy in ways untypical of liberal regimes but nevertheless needing to be very mindful of the power of global economic forces. So an examination of these borderline cases suggests a need for caution about the extent they can achieve a high measure of liberation from the constraints provided by the global economy. It would be very optimistic to suggest that the privileged club could enlarge indefinitely on these terms.

In addition, there are two things that it is particularly important not to forget when trying to take a view on the prospects for future developments:

- that contemporary globalism (like imperialism before it) is a system in which some players are advantaged precisely because others are disadvantaged;
- that a core argument used to explain why some nations have been able to resist processes by which international competition drives down wages is that they have developed niche activities whereby high value-added work by a highly educated workforce protects them (see chapter 5).

When we look at the nations outside the rich club, we are looking at the underside of these developing countries in which poorly remunerated economic activities are being carried out in a global context largely controlled by that club. What this suggests then is that there is a case for seeing comparative studies not as comparing nation states but as analysing a global 'division of welfare'. In this case the migration flows analysed in chapter 11 need attention, with the rich countries benefiting from inflows of labour to help to run their welfare states and the poor countries depending on cash flow back from the earning of those workers.

If the observations set out in the list above are true, then globalism does not imply a world that is in some sense homogenising, forming 'one world' in a potentially egalitarian sense. Whilst the neo-liberal formula for state development is contested within the rich club, it still plays a very important role in the way in which the club as a whole relates to outsiders. Hence the suggestion is that globalism as an economic influence on social welfare development is much more significant for those countries where efforts are still being made to develop social welfare institutions than it is for the established systems. This sort of proposition is much more difficult to test quantitatively than some of those about the developed systems.

## Conclusions on Globalism

Without analysing the underlying theoretical work in any depth, this chapter has explored the complex implications of globalism for social policy. Globalism is seen as comprising a set of economic pressures on welfare systems, hypothesised to work largely in an anti-social policy direction, and also a variety of cultural influences that may be either negative or positive in this respect. I have explored evidence on convergence within the social policy systems of the developed nations, suggesting that this reflects both limited elements of downward pressure on policy growth in the countries where strong institutions were developed comparatively early and a catching-up process on the part of later developers. In this sense the economic dimension within globalism has been seen, at least in relation to social policy, as overstated.

I have explored the factors that explain the limited degree of convergence, and particularly the absence of the sort of 'race to the bottom' that welfare state crisis theory suggests, indicating ways in which nations may have been able to retain the capacity to make choices about their social policies, notwithstanding probably some restraints shared by all. This has taken the discussion back to regime theory, exploring the extent to which the regime alternatives define options for strategic choice by nations or (less positively) indicate political and institutional paths which cannot easily be changed.

I have ended by exploring to what extent the choice process is still going on, even amongst much later arrivals in the rich group of nations, and have suggested reasons why this is getting harder and probably cannot go on indefinitely.

## Conclusions to the Book as a Whole

It has been noted that one of the key concerns of regime theory is to stress that national social policy systems will not necessarily converge but may cluster in 'families of nations' with similar characteristics. Throughout the book versions of regime theory have been used to explore issues about how nations cluster and to offer an approach to some of the broader questions about social divisions of welfare and about 'universalism' in social policy. Several observations can be drawn from the evidence presented.

1  In many ways, as was suggested in chapter 2, many of the most interesting comparative questions arise when attention is given either to nations who do not fit the generalisations very well or to situations where it is found that nations which might be expected to have much in common differ on particular policies or policy issues. In this sense, examining 'families' or regimes' can be a useful starting point for more intensive exploration.

2 Since social security indices dominated the empirical work to establish regime theory, it is not surprising that when other policy areas are examined or even when social security expenditure is separated into its component parts other ways of grouping nations emerge.

3 Nevertheless, one division emerges over and over again in comparative work: between nations using liberal economic approaches to the organisation of both the market and the social policy system and those where state management of the system (often in collaboration with 'social partners' drawn from both sides of industry) is more salient.

4 However, even the distinctiveness of the liberal nations is only clear relative to the northern European conservatives and social democratic nations but not when compared with the southern Europeans. Moreover, within them a distinction needs to be drawn in terms of commitment to public services and the targeting of benefits towards the poor. This tends to separate the clear liberal group from another group sometimes called 'radical'. In some cases this leaves the USA as the solitary liberal nation.

5 The Eastern European nations are interesting in sharing with the southern European nations low levels of expenditure but having apparently rather higher commitments to public services and poverty reduction that place them, perhaps, as moving towards the northern European conservative model.

6 The two East Asian nations are near the bottom on all the available indices. They do not figure, as might be expected from the productivist thesis, as high public spenders on education (but note the word 'public' here). A sample of two does not however constitute a satisfactory basis for a regime category, and the non-OECD nations in that part of the world show varied patterns of development. An impressive and rapidly growing body of work analysing developments in these nations suggests that the Eurocentric regime labels need to be used with caution.

7 There is a need to bear in mind the extent to which the nations that have secured little attention in this analysis, namely those outside the OECD, may be seen as having very mixed, largely non-state-based, patterns of welfare provision. The extent to which the OECD nations provide a context of both positive and negative influences on welfare in these countries, within a global 'social division on welfare', also needs to be recognised.

8 The shift in attention, towards the end of the book, to social divisions further highlights complications for generalisations about nation states. Pertinent here is an emergent body of work that makes a dis-

tinction between 'old' and 'new' social risks. Where the old concerns were with ensuring an 'income stream to the male breadwinner' (Bonoli, 2005, p. 432) in a context in which industrial employment was dominant, the new 'risks' are seen as (a) reconciling work and family life, (b) single parenthood, (c) having a frail relative, (d) possessing low or obsolete skills and (e) insufficient social security coverage (in a context of less secure labour market participation) (ibid., pp. 433–5). The essence of new social risk theory (see also Taylor-Gooby, 2004b) is that the politics of welfare in respect of such issues is likely to diverge from that highlighted in traditional regime theory inasmuch as those particularly likely to be exposed to risks (such as workers in what was described in chapter 9 as group 3), women and ethnic minorities have limited power resources and need to form alliances to advance their causes.

This book has stressed that the analysis of social policy in the modern world can involve an approach that sets aside the recognised unique characteristic of national systems and explores instead the things nations have in common and the broad ways in which they may be grouped and compared. One of the most important arguments for comparative work is that it invites us to think both about how our nation compares with others and about the extent to which we share common concerns and problems. Whilst the issues highlighted in this and the previous chapter (i.e. globalism and demographic change) secure particularly widespread attention in this respect, those about social divisions (examined in the previous three chapters) must not be forgotten. The central concern of a great deal of analytical and philosophical writing on social policy concerns the role of social policy in reducing social divisions. Comparative analysis is very important for that concern.

### GUIDE TO FURTHER READING

George and Wilding's *Globalisation and Human Welfare* (2002) offers an excellent overview of the issues about the impact of globalisation on social policy. Esping-Andersen has been involved in the debate about the impact of globalism and related changes, editing two important collections on this theme (1996, 2002). Paul Pierson's book *The New Politics of the Welfare State* (2001) explores data on contemporary change in social policy, his overview and Swank's essay being particularly recommended. Castles (2004) provides a good review of OECD data in a book already recommended earlier in this one.

# GLOSSARY

Note that *The Blackwell Dictionary of Social Policy* (Alcock, Erskine and May, 2002) offers further clarification of many of these terms.

**bureaucracy**   Formal organisation involving a hierarchy.

**conservative**   Used in the context of **regime theory** to describe nations where social policy has been state led but not egalitarian.

**convergence theory**   Suggests that national social policies will become similar as a consequence of shared social, economic and political development trends.

**corporatism**   Governmental arrangements in which key interests (particularly representatives of employers and employees) are involved in close collaboration with government.

**cost-sharing**   Provisions to make recipients pay some part of a service cost (e.g. prescription charges).

**cyclical unemployment**   Unemployment that occurs when there is insufficient purchasing power, or demand, to stimulate production and employ all those who want work.

**decommodification**   Development of social policies delivering extensive social support without making labour market attachment a crucial qualifying condition. This is the key index for Esping-Andersen's regime theory.

**determinism**   Theory that sees policy development as directly determined by economic and social change, thereby ignoring elements of political choice that may be involved (*see also* **functionalist theory**).

**direct taxation**   Where individuals are assessed for tax contributions based on their income (cf. **indirect taxation**).

**divisions of welfare**   Divisions in a social welfare system that reflect, and may reinforce, social divisions in society. Originally used by writers who drew attention to the way tax reliefs and untaxed fringe benefits may convey privileges to some, largely better-off, people.

**federalism**   State systems where sub-national units have protected rights and prerogatives enshrined in a constitution (as in the USA, Canada, Germany and Australia).

**frictional unemployment**   Temporary unemployment resulting from time-lags and information gaps in the market as individuals search for or move jobs and employers seek new staff.

**functionalist theory**   Suggests that policy developments can be directly explained by social or economic developments.

**globalisation**   Development of economic, cultural or political interdependencies across the world, often linked with predictions about policy convergence.

**gross domestic product (GDP)**   Value of goods and services produced by residents of a country (usually within a year). The methodology for calculating this is complex and depends on the identification of monetary transactions.

**human capital theory**   Examines activities (particularly education) in terms of the extent to which they contribute to earning power. This may be applied to both individuals and, with more difficulty, societies.

**ideal types**   Categories devised for analytical purposes that may draw on the characteristics of a number of cases but may not exactly correspond to any specific case. The categories used in **regime theory** are ideal types.

**indirect taxation**   Where tax is paid as additions to the price of goods and services (cf. **direct taxation**).

**infant mortality**   Death within the first year of life.

**informal economy**   Economic activity that evades official recognition, and thus taxation.

**inputs**   Resources to pay for policies (the crucial point here is that much of this data is input information, giving no indication on how that income is actually used) (cf. **outputs** and **outcomes**).

**institutional theory**   Stresses the way in which pre-existing institutions influence subsequent policy decisions (often described in terms of notions of national 'pathways' conditioned by existing institutional arrangements).

**International Labour Organisation (ILO)**    An international organisation set up to promote and protects the interests of workers.

**labour market participation**    Participation within the paid labour force (including unemployed people who are seeking to enter it). This rather awkward expression is preferable to talking of the working population, since that implies that only paid work is really work.

**liberal**    Used in the context of regime theory to describe nations where social policy has involved strong concern for the preservation of market systems.

**Marxism, Marxist theory**    Directly attributes political developments to the conflict between capital and labour.

**means-test**    Requirement that applicants for a benefit or service have to provide evidence of low income or capital in order to secure it.

**mixed economy of welfare**    Describes the way in which benefits and services are provided and funded in diverse ways, involving combinations of the public sector, the private and voluntary sectors and family or informal care.

**OECD (Organisation for Economic Cooperation and Development)**    International organisation representing nations committed to democracy and the market economy (broadly the world's wealthy nations).

**outcomes**    Results of service or benefit expenditure (poverty reduction, health improvement, etc.).

**outputs**    Actual service provided or money spent (compare **inputs**).

**pay-as-you-go**    Provision of social security benefits out of current-year tax and contribution income (cf. **pre-funding**).

**poverty**    A level of living below that regarded as acceptable (unacceptable inequality). Clearly this is a contestable matter. In practice, comparative studies tend to use a simple yardstick that defines poverty as income substantially below any national (as opposed to international) average (e.g. below 50 or 60 per cent of the median, as shown in tables in chapter 9).

**poverty trap**    When earned incomes rise, means-tested benefits are cut; if this adjustment is more than marginal, it may operate as a disincentive to increase earnings.

**pre-funding**   Establishment of an invested fund to provide for a future contingency, an approach particularly applied to pensions (cf. **pay-as-you-go**).

**primary care**   Health-care arrangements where individuals have initial access to a doctor, who may then refer them on to more intensive forms of care.

**radical**   Used in relation to a variant of regime theory that identifies a group of nations that have developed redistributive policies without the universalist characteristic of social democratic regimes.

**regime theory**   Suggests that national social policy systems can be classified into a finite number of regime types, characterised by similar political or economic or institutional configurations.

**secondary care**   Health-care arrangements where more intensive or complex services are provided to people referred on from **primary care**. Generally, therefore, hospitals are seen as key providers of secondary care.

**social assistance**   Systems of cash benefits regulated by means-tests.

**social democratic**   Used in the context of regime theory to describe nations where social policy has been state led, universalist and egalitarian.

**social insurance**   Systems of cash benefits where entitlements depend on past contributions.

**tax credits**   Means-tested benefits provided through the taxation system.

**territorial justice**   Principle that within a single nation state individuals should not get different services or standards of services simply as a consequence of where they live. This principle offers a challenge to lower-level autonomy in federal systems and may be applied to entities like the European Union or even worldwide.

**transfer payments**   Applied to situations where the role of government involves taking from some people and giving to others. It is readily apparent in social security systems but also applies to phenomena like agricultural subsidies.

**underclass**   A term used by some writers to characterise a group of people outside the main social stratification system.

**universalism**   Provision of a single, relatively uniform service for all citizens regardless of income or class.

# REFERENCES

Alcock, P. (2003) *Social Policy in Britain*, 2nd edn. Basingstoke: Palgrave Macmillan.

Alcock, P. and Craig, G. (eds) (2001) *International Social Policy*. Basingstoke: Palgrave Macmillan.

Alcock, P., Erskine, A. and May, M. (eds) (2002) *The Blackwell Dictionary of Social Policy*. Oxford: Blackwell.

Alcock, P., Erskine, A. and May, M. (eds) (2003) *The Student's Companion to Social Policy*. Oxford: Blackwell.

Alcock, P., Glennerster, H., Oakley, A. and Sinfield, A. (eds) (2001) *Welfare and Wellbeing: Richard Titmuss's Contribution to Social Policy*. Bristol: Policy Press.

Alexander, R., Broadfoot, P. and Phillips, D. (eds) (1999) *Learning from Comparing*. Wallingford: Symposium Books.

Almond, G.A., Powell, G.B. Jr, Strøm, K. and Dalton, R.J. (2004) *Comparative Politics Today*, 8th edn. New York: Pearson, Longman.

Ambler, J.S. (ed.) (1991) *The French Welfare State*. New York: New York University Press.

Andersen, J.G. and Jensen, J.B. (2002) Employment and unemployment in Europe: overview and new trends. In J.G. Andersen, J. Clasen, W. van Oorschot and K. Halvorsen (eds) *Europe's New State of Welfare: Unemployment, Employment Policies and Citizenship*. Bristol: Policy Press.

Anheier, H.K. and Salomon, H.K. (2001) *Volunteering in Cross-national Perspective: Initial Comparisons*. Civil Society Working Paper 10. London: London School of Economics.

Anttonen, A. and Sipilä, J. (1996) European social care services: is it possible to identify models? *Journal of European Social Policy* 6(2), 87–100.

Anttonen, A., Baldock, J. and Sipilä, J. (eds.) (2003) *The Young, the Old and the State*. Cheltenham: Edward Elgar.

Archer, M. (1979) *The Social Origins of Educational Systems*. Beverly Hills: Sage.

Arts, W. and Gelissen, J. (2002) Three worlds of welfare capitalism or more? *Journal of European Social Policy* 12(2), 137–58.

Ashford, D.E. (1986) *The Emergence of the Welfare States*. Oxford: Blackwell.

Auer, P. and Cazes, S. (2003) *Employment Stability in an Age of Flexibility.* Geneva: International Labour Office.

Bacon, R. and Eltis, W. (1976) *Britain's Economic Problem: Too Few Producers.* London: Macmillan.

Bahle, T. (2003) The changing institutionalisation of social services in England and Wales, France and Germany: is the welfare state on retreat? *Journal of European Social Policy* 13(1), 5–20.

Bailey, J. (ed.) (1992) *Social Europe.* London: Longman.

Baldwin, P. (1990) *The Politics of Social Solidarity.* Cambridge: Cambridge University Press.

Ball, M., Harloe, M. and Martens, M. (1988) *Housing and Social Change in Europe and the USA.* London: Routledge.

Ball, S.J. (1990) *Politics and Policy Making in Education.* London: Routledge.

Bambra, C. (2005a) Worlds of welfare and the health care discrepancy. *Social Policy and Society* 4(1), 31–41.

Bambra, C. (2005b) Cash versus services: 'worlds of welfare' and the decommodification of cash benefits and health care services. *Journal of Social Policy* 34(2), 195–214.

Barr, N. (2001) *The Welfare State as Piggy Bank.* Oxford: Oxford University Press.

Barr, N. (2002) *The Pension Puzzle.* Economic Issues 29. New York: International Monetary Fund.

Barrett, M. (1980) *Women's Oppression Today.* London: Verso

Bartholomew, J. (2004) *The Welfare State We're In.* London: Politico.

Beattie, R. and McGillivray, W. (1995) A risky strategy: reflections on the World Bank report, averting the old age crisis. *International Social Security Review* 48(3/4), 5–22.

Beck, U. (1992) *Risk Society: Towards a New Modernity.* London: Sage.

Becker, G. (1964) *Human Capital: A Theoretical and Empirical Analysis with Special Reference to Education.* New York: Columbia University Press.

Béland, D. (2001) Does labor matter? Institutions, labor unions, and pension reform in France and the United States. *Journal of Public Policy* 21(2), 153–72.

Bell, D.N.F., Gaj, A., Hart, R., Hubler, O. and Schwerdt, W. (2001) *Unpaid Work in the Workplace: A Comparison of Germany and the UK.* London: Anglo-German Foundation.

Bendix, R. and Lipset, S.M. (eds) (1967) *Class, Status and Power,* 2nd edn. London: Routledge.

Berthoud, R. (ed.) (1985) *Challenges to Social Policy.* Aldershot: Gower.

Bettio, F. and Plantenga, J. (2004) Comparing care regimes in Europe. *Feminist Economics* 10(1), 85–113.

Blackburn, R. (2002) *Banking on Death.* London: Verso.

Blair, T. and Schroder, G. (1999) Europe: the third way/die neute mitte. *The Spokesman* 66, 27–37.

Blank, R. and Burau, V. (2004) *Comparative Health Policy.* Basingstoke: Palgrave Macmillan.

Blaug, M. (1970) *The Economics of Education*. Harmondsworth: Penguin Books.

Bolderson, H. and Mabbett, D. (1991) *Social Policy and Social Security in Australia, Britain and the USA*. Aldershot: Ashgate.

Bonoli, G. (1997) Classifying welfare states: a two-dimensional approach. *Journal of Social Policy* 26(3), 351–72.

Bonoli, G. (2005) The politics of the new social policies: providing coverage against new social risks in mature welfare states. *Policy and Politics* 33(3), 431–50.

Bonoli, G. and Sarfati, H. (2002) Conclusion. In H. Sarfati and G. Bonoli (eds) *Labour Market and Social Protection Reforms in International Perspective*. Aldershot: Ashgate.

Bonoli, G. and Shinkawa, T. (eds) (2005) *Ageing and Pension Reform Around the World*. Cheltenham: Edward Elgar.

Borschorst, A. (1994) Welfare state regimes: women's interests and the EC. In D. Sainsbury (ed.) *Gendering Welfare States*. London: Sage.

Bovens, M., 't Hart, P. and Peters, B.G. (eds.) (2001) *Success and Failure in Public Governance*. Cheltenham: Edward Elgar.

Bowles, S. and Gintis, H. (1976) *Schooling in Capitalist America*. New York: Basic Books.

Boyle, P., Curtis, S., Graham, E. and Moore, E. (eds) (2004) *The Geography of Health Inequalities in the Developed World*. Aldershot: Ashgate.

Bradshaw, J. and Chen, J.-R. (1997) Poverty in the UK. A comparison with nineteen other countries. *Benefits* 18, 13–17.

Bradshaw, J. and Finch, N. (2002) *A Comparison of Child Benefit Packages in 22 Countries*. Department of Work and Pensions Research Report 174. Leeds: Department of Work and Pensions.

Bradshaw, J., Ditch, J., Holmes, H. and Whiteford, P. (1993) *Support for Children*. Department of Social Security Research Report 21. London: HMSO.

Brittan, S. (1977) *The Economic Consequences of Democracy*. London: Temple Smith.

Brownmiller, S. (1975) *Against Our Will: Men, Women and Rape*. New York: Simon and Schuster.

Bryson, A. (2003) From welfare to workfare. In J. Millar (ed.) *Understanding Social Security*. Bristol: Policy Press, pp. 77–101.

Bryson, L. (1992) *Welfare and the State*. Basingstoke: Macmillan.

Buchanan, J.M. and Wagner, R.E. (1977) *Democracy in Deficit*. New York: Academic Press.

Bussemaker, J. and van Kersbergen, K. (1994) Gender and welfare states: some theoretical reflections. In D. Sainsbury (ed.) *Gendering Welfare States*. London: Sage.

Cahill, M. and Fitzpatrick, T. (2002) *Environmental Issues and Social Welfare*. Oxford: Blackwell.

Cappelli, C. (1999) *The New Deal at Work*. Boston, MA: Harvard University Press.

Casey, B., Oxley, H., Whitehouse, E., Antolin, P., Duval, R. and Leibfritz, W. (2003) *Policies for an Ageing Society: Recent Measures and Areas for Further Reform*. Economics Department Working Paper 369. Paris: OECD.

Castles, F.G. (1982) *The Impact of Parties: Politics and Policies in Democratic Capitalist States*. London: Sage.

Castles, F.G. (1985) *The Working Class and Welfare*. Sydney: Allen and Unwin.

Castles, F.G. (2004) *The Future of the Welfare State*. Oxford: Oxford University Press.

Castles, F.G. and Mitchell, D. (1992) Identifying welfare state regimes: the links between politics, instruments and outcomes. *Governance* 5(1), 1–26.

Castles, S. (1984) *Here for Good: Western Europe's New Ethnic Minorities*. London: Pluto.

Castles, S. and Kosack, G. (1973) *Immigrant Workers and the Class Structure in Western Europe*. Oxford: Oxford University Press.

Castles, S. and Miller, M.J. (1993) *The Age of Migration*. Basingstoke: Macmillan.

Castles, S. and Miller, M.J. (2003) *The Age of Migration*, 3rd edn. Basingstoke: Macmillan.

Centre for Contemporary Cultural Studies (1982) *The Empire Strikes Back*. London: Hutchinson.

Chisholm, L. (1992) A crazy quilt: education, training and social change in Europe. In J. Bailey (ed.) *Social Europe*. London: Longman.

Choi, S.-J. and Bae, S.-H. (2005) National policies on ageing in South Korea. In J. Doling, C. Jones Finer and T. Maltby (eds) *Ageing Matters*. Aldershot: Ashgate.

Christopher, K., England, P., McLanahan, S., Ross, K. and Smeeding, T.M. (2001) Gender inequality in poverty in affluent nations: the role of single motherhood and the state. In K. Vlemininckx and T.M. Smeeding (eds) *Child Well-being, Child Poverty and Child Policy in Modern Nations*. Bristol: Policy Press.

Clasen, J. (ed.) (1997) *Social Insurance in Europe*. Bristol: Policy Press.

Clasen, J. (ed.) (1999) *Comparative Social Policy: Concepts, Theories and Methods*. Oxford: Blackwell.

Clasen, J. (2000) Motives, means and opportunities: reforming unemployment compensation in the 1990s. *West European Politics* 23(2), 89–112.

Clasen, J. and Freeman, R. (eds) (1994) *Social Policy in Germany*. Hemel Hempstead: Harvester Wheatsheaf.

Clasen, J. and van Oorschot, W. (2002) Work, welfare and citizenship: diversity and variation within European (un)employment policy. In J.G. Andersen, J. Clasen, W. van Oorschot and K. Halvorsen (eds) *Europe's New State of Welfare: Unemployment, Employment Policies and Citizenship*. Bristol: Policy Press.

Coates, D. (ed.) (2005) *Varieties of Capitalism: Varieties of Approaches*. Basingstoke: Palgrave Macmillan.

Coates, D. (2005) *An Agenda for Work: The Work Foundation's Challenge to Policy Makers*. London: The Work Foundation.

Cochrane, A., Clarke, J. and Gewirtz, S. (eds) (2001) *Comparing Welfare States*. London: Sage.

Coenen, H. and Leisink, P. (eds) (1993) *Work and Citizenship in the New Europe*. Aldershot: Edward Elgar.

Commission on Social Justice (1994) *Social Justice: Strategies for National Renewal*. London: Vintage.

Coons, J. and Sugarman, S. (1978) *Education by Choice: The Case for Family Control*. Berkeley: University of California Press.

Crain, R.L. (1968) *The Politics of School Desegregation*. Chicago: Aldine.

Creemers, B. and Scheerens, J. (eds) (1989) Developments in school effectiveness research. *International Journal of Educational Research* 37 (special issue), 685–825.

Croissant, A. (2004) Changing welfare regimes in East and Southeast Asia: crisis, change and challenge. *Social Policy and Administration* 38(5), 504–24.

Crompton, R. (1993) *Class and Stratification*. Cambridge: Polity Press.

Dahrendorf, R. (1959) *Class and Class Conflict in Industrial Society*. London: Routledge.

Dale, J. and Foster, P. (1986) *Feminists and State Welfare*. London: Routledge and Kegan Paul.

Daly, M. (2000) *The Gender Division of Welfare*. Cambridge: Cambridge University Press.

Daly, M. (2002) Care as a good for social policy. *Journal of Social Policy* 31(2), 251–70.

Daly, M. and Rake, K. (2003) *Gender and the Welfare State*. Cambridge: Polity.

Deacon, B. (1997) *Global Social Policy*. London: Sage.

Deakin, N. (1994) *The Politics of Welfare: Continuities and Change*. Hemel Hempstead: Harvester Wheatsheaf.

Deakin, S. (2001) The changing concept of the 'employer' in labour law. *Industrial Law Journal* 23, 289–310.

Deber, R. (1993) Canadian Medicare: can it work in the United States? Will it survive in Canada. *American Journal of Law and Medicine* XIX(1/2), 75–93.

Deleek, H., Van Den Bosch, K. and De Lathouver, K. (1992) *Poverty and the Adequacy of Social Security in the European Community*. Aldershot: Avebury.

Delphy, C. (1984) *Close to Home: A Materialist Analysis of Women's Oppression*. London: Hutchinson.

Department of Social Security (1993) *Households Below Average Income, 1979–1990/91*. London: HMSO.

De Swaan, A. (1988) *In Care of the State: Health Care, Education and Welfare in Europe and the USA in the Modern Era*. Cambridge: Polity Press.

Dewey, J. (1976) *Democracy and Education*. New York: Free Press.

Dierkes, M., Weiler, H.N. and Antal, A.B. (eds) (1987) *Comparative Policy Research: Learning from Experience*. Aldershot: Gower.

Dixon, J. and Scheurell, P. (eds) (1989) *Social Welfare in Developed Market Economies*. London: Routledge.

Donnison, D. (1982) *The Politics of Poverty*. Oxford: Martin Robertson.

Doyal, L. and Gough, I. (1991) *A Theory of Human Need*. Basingstoke: Macmillan.

Durkheim, E. (ed. S. Lukes) (1982) *The Rules of Sociological Method and Selected Texts on Sociology and its Method*. London: Macmillan.

Dworkin, R. (1977) *Taking Rights Seriously*. London: Duckworth.

Dyson, K.H.F. (1980) *The State Tradition in Western Europe: A Study of an Idea and Institution*. New York: Oxford University Press.

Eardley, T., Bradshaw, J., Ditch, J., Gough, I. and Whiteford, P. (1996) *Social Assistance in OECD Countries: Synthesis Report*. Department of Social Security Research Report No. 46. London: HMSO.

Edwards, J. (1987) *Positive Discrimination, Social Justice and Social Policy*. London: Tavistock.

Eisenstein, Z. (1984) *Feminism and Sexual Equality: Crisis in Liberal America*. New York: Monthly Review Press.

Esping-Andersen, G. (1990) *Three Worlds of Welfare Capitalism*. Cambridge: Polity Press.

Esping-Andersen, G. (ed.) (1996) *Welfare States in Transition*. London: UNRISD/ Sage.

Esping-Andersen G. (1999) *Social Foundations of Post-industrial Economies*. Oxford: Oxford University Press.

Esping-Andersen G. (ed.) (2002) *Why We Need a New Welfare State*. Oxford: Oxford University Press.

Etzioni, A. (1961) *A Comparative Analysis of Complex Organisations*. New York: Free Press.

European Commission (2003) *The Social Situation in the European Union 2003*. Luxembourg: European Commission.

European Commission (2004) *The Social Situation in the European Union 2004*. Luxembourg: European Commission.

European Commission (2005) *Social Agenda*, 11. Brussels: European Commission.

Evers, A., Pijl, M. and Ungerson, C. (1994) *Payments for Care: A Comparative Overview*. Aldershot: Avebury.

Fahey, T., Nolan, B. and Mâitre, B. (2004) Housing expenditures and income poverty in EU countries. *Journal of Social Policy* 33(3), 437–54.

Farnham, D. (1999) Human resource management and employment relations. In D. Farnham and S. Horton (eds) *Public Management in Britain*. Basingstoke: Macmillan, pp. 107–27.

Ferrara, M. (1996) The 'southern model' of welfare in social Europe. *Journal of European Social Policy* 6(1), 17–37.

Field, F. (1989) *Losing Out: The Emergence of Britain's Underclass*. Oxford: Blackwell.

Finch, J. (1989) *Family Obligations and Social Change*. Cambridge: Polity.

Finch, J. and Groves, D. (eds) (1983) *A Labour of Love: Women, Work and Caring*. London: Routledge.

Finch, J. and Mason, J. (1993) *Negotiating Family Responsibilities*. London: Routledge.

Flora, P. (ed.) (1986) *Growth to Limits: The Western European Welfare States Since World War II*. Berlin: De Gruyter.

Flora, P. and Heidenheimer, A.J. (eds) (1981) *The Development of Welfare States in Europe and America*. New Brunswick, NJ: Transaction Books.

Furniss, N. and Tilton, T. (1977) *The Case for the Welfare State*. Bloomington: Indiana University Press.

Geddes, A. (2003) *The Politics of Migration and Immigration in Europe*. London: Sage.

Gee, E.M. and Gutman, G.M. (eds) (2000) *The Overselling of Population Ageing*. Don Mills, Ontario: Oxford University Press.

George, V. and Wilding, P. (2002) *Globalisation and Human Welfare*. Basingstoke: Palgrave Macmillan.

Giddens, A. (1973) *The Class Structure of the Advanced Societies*. London: Hutchinson.

Giddens, A. and Held, D. (eds) (1982) *Classes, Power and Conflict*. London: Macmillan.

Ginsberg, N. (1992) *Divisions of Welfare*. London: Sage.

Glazer, N. and Moynihan, D.P. (eds) (1975) *Ethnicity*. Cambridge, MA: Harvard University Press.

Glendinning, C. and Millar, J. (1992) *Women and Poverty in Britain: The 1990s*. Hemel Hempstead: Harvester Wheatsheaf.

Glennerster, H. (1992) *Paying for Welfare in the 1990s*. Hemel Hempstead: Harvester Wheatsheaf.

Glennerster, H. (2003) *Understanding the Finance of Welfare*. Bristol: Policy Press.

Goldthorpe, J.H. (1980) *Social Mobility and Class Structure in Modern Britain*. Oxford: Clarendon Press.

Goldthorpe, J.H. (1983) Women and class analysis: in defence of the conventional view. *Sociology* 17(4), 465–88.

Goodin, R. and Le Grand, J. (eds.) (1987) *Not Only the Poor: The Middle Classes and the Welfare State*. London: Allen and Unwin.

Goodin, R.E., Headey, B., Muffels, R. and Dirven, H.-J. (1999) *The Real Worlds of Welfare Capitalism*. Cambridge: Cambridge University Press.

Gordon, P. (1986) Racism and social security. *Critical Social Policy* 17, 23–40.

Gordon, P. and Newnham, A. (1985) *Passport to Benefits*. London: Child Poverty Action Group.

Gorz, A. (1982) *Farewell to the Working Class*. London: Pluto.

Gough, I. (1979) *The Political Economy of the Welfare State*. London: Macmillan.

Gough, I. and Wood, G. (eds) (2004) *Insecurity and Welfare Regimes in Asia, Africa and Latin America: Social Policy in Development Contexts*. Cambridge: Cambridge University Press.

Gough, I., Bradshaw, J., Ditch, J., Eardley, T. and Whiteford, P. (1997) Social assistance in OECD countries. *Journal of European Social Policy* 7(1), 17–43.

Gould, A. (1993) *Capitalist Welfare Systems: A Comparison of Japan, Britain and Sweden*. London: Longman.

Green, A. (1990) *Education and State Formation*. Basingstoke: Macmillan.

Green, D. (1999) *An End to Welfare Rights: The Rediscovery of Independence*. London: Institute of Economic Affairs.

Gregg, P. and Wadsworth, J. (1998) *Unemployment and Non-employment: Unpacking Economic Inactivity*. London: Employment Policy Institute.

Greve, B. (1994) The hidden welfare state: tax expenditure and social policy. *Scandinavian Journal of Social Welfare* 4, 203–11.

Groves, D. (1992) Occupational pension provision and women's poverty in old age. In C. Glendinning and J. Millar (eds) *Women and Poverty in Britain: The 1990s*. Hemel Hempstead: Harvester Wheatsheaf.

Gustafsson, S. (1994) Childcare and types of welfare states. In D. Sainsbury (ed.) *Gendering Welfare States*. London: Sage, chapter 4.

Hakim, C. (2003) *Models of the Family in Modern Societies: Ideals and Realities*. Aldershot: Ashgate.

Hall, P.A. and Soskice, D. (2001) *Varieties of Capitalism: The Institutional Foundations of Comparative Advantage*. Oxford: Oxford University Press.

Ham, C., Robinson, R. and Benzeval, M. (1990) *Health Check: Health Care Reforms in an International Context*. London: King's Fund Institute.

Handy, C. (1994) *The Empty Raincoat: Making Sense of the Future*. London: Hutchinson.

Hantrais, L. (2004) *Family Policy Matters*. Bristol: Policy Press.

Harasty, C. (ed.) (2004) *Successful Employment and Labour Market Policies in Europe, Asia and the Pacific*. Geneva: International Labour Organisation.

Harrison, R. and Kessels, J. (2004) *HRD in a Knowledge Economy: An Organisational View*. Basingstoke: Palgrave Macmillan.

Harrysson, L. and Petersson, J. (2004) Revealing the traits of workfare: the Swedish example. In P. Littlewood, I. Glorieux and I. Jonsson (eds) *The Future of Work in Europe*. Aldershot: Ashgate, pp. 83–102.

Hartmann, H. (1979) The unhappy marriage of Marxism and feminism. *Capital and Class* 8, 1–33.

Hatland, A. (1984) *The Future of Norwegian Social Insurance*. Oslo: Universitetforlaget.

Hay, C. (2002) *Political Analysis: A Critical Introduction*. Basingstoke: Palgrave.

Henderson, J.W. and Karn, V.A. (1987) *Race, Class and State Housing*. Aldershot: Gower.

Hernes, H. (1987) *Welfare State and Women Power*. Oslo: Norwegian University Press.

Higgins, J. (1981) *States of Welfare*. Oxford: Blackwell.

Hill, M. (2003) *Understanding Social Policy*, 7th edn. Oxford: Blackwell.

Hill, M. (2005) *The Public Policy Process*. Harlow: Pearson Education.

Hill, M. and Bramley, G. (1986) *Analysing Social Policy*. Oxford: Blackwell.

Hill, M. and Hupe, P. (2002) *Implementing Public Policy*. London: Sage.

Hills, J. (1993) *The Future of Welfare: A Guide to the Debate*. York: Joseph Rowntree Foundation.

Hinrichs, K. (2000) Elephants on the move. *European Review* 8(4), 353–78.

Hirst, P. and Thompson, G. (1992) The problem of 'globalisation': international economic relations, national economic management and the formation of trading blocs. *Economy and Society* 21(4), 355–96.

H.M. Treasury (2004) *Opportunity for All: The Strength to Take the Long-term Decisions for Britain*. Pre-Budget Report, Cm 6408. London: The Stationery Office.

Hobson, B. (1994) Solo mothers, social policy regimes and the logics of gender. In D. Sainsbury (ed.) *Gendering Welfare States*. London: Sage, chapter 11.

Holliday, I. (2000) Productivist welfare capitalism: social policy in East Asia. *Political Studies* 48, 706–23.

Holliday, I. (2005) East Asian social policy in the wake of the financial crisis: farewell to productivism? *Policy and Politics* 33(1), 145–62.

Holliday, I. and Wilding, P. (eds) (2003) *Welfare Capitalism in East Asia: Social Policy in the Tiger Economies*. Basingstoke: Palgrave Macmillan.

Holmes, B. (ed.) (1985) *Equality and Freedom in Education*. London: Routledge.

Hudson, B. (1994) *Making Sense of Markets in Health and Social Care*. Sunderland: Business Education Publishers.

Hüfner, K., Meyer, J.W. and Naumann, J. (1987) Comparative education policy research: a world society perspective. In M. Dierkes, H.N. Weiler and A.B. Antal (eds) *Comparative Policy Research: Learning from Experience*. Aldershot: Gower.

Hurst, P. (1981) Education and development in the third world: a critical appraisal of aid policies. *Comparative Education* 17(2), 115–255.

Hutton, W. (1995) *The State We're In*. London: Cape.

Hutton, W. (2002) *The World We're In*. London: Little, Brown.

Hyman, R. (2004) Varieties of capitalism, national industrial relations systems and transnational challenges. In A.-W. Harzing and J.V. Ruysseveldt (eds) *International Human Resource Management*. London: Sage.

Illich, I. (1977) *Limits to Medicine*. Harmondsworth: Penguin.

ILO (2005) *Global Employment Trends Brief*. Geneva: International Labour Organisation.

Immergut, E.M. (1993) *Health Policy, Interests and Institutions in Western Europe*. Cambridge: Cambridge University Press.

Immergut, E.M. (1998) The theoretical core of the new institutionalism. *Politics and Society* 26(1), 5–34.

Jahoda, M., Lazarsfeld, P.F. and Zeisel, H. (1972) *Marienthal: The Sociography of an Unemployed Community*. London: Tavistock.

Jenkins, C. and Sherman, B. (1979) *The Collapse of Work*. London: Eyre Methuen.

Joly, D. and Cohen, R. (eds) (1990) *Reluctant Hosts: Europe and its Refugees*. Aldershot: Avebury.

Jones, C. (1985) *Patterns of Social Policy: An Introduction to Comparative Analysis*. London: Tavistock.

Jones, C. (ed.) (1993) *New Perspectives on the Welfare State in Europe*. London: Routledge.

Joumard, I. and Kongsrud, P.M. (2003) Fiscal relations across government levels. *OECD Economic Studies* 36, 156–229.

Kaim-Caudle, P. (1973) *Comparative Social Policy and Social Security: A Ten Country Study*. London: Martin Robertson.

Kangas, O. (1994) The politics of social security: on regressions, qualitative comparisons and cluster analysis. In T. Janoski and A.M. Hicks (eds) *The Comparative Political Economy of the Welfare State*. Cambridge: Cambridge University Press.

Kasza, G.J. (2002) The illusion of welfare regimes. *Journal of Social Policy* 31(2), 271–89.

Katzenstein, P. (1977) Conclusion: domestic structures and strategies of foreign economic policy. *International Organisation* 31(4), 879–920.

Kautto, M. (2002) Investing in services in West European welfare states. *Journal of European Social Policy* 12(1), 53–65.

Kelly, A. (ed.) (1981) *The Missing Half*. Manchester: Manchester University Press.

Kemp, P. (1990) Income-related assistance with housing costs: a cross-national comparison. *Urban Studies* 27(6), 795–808.

Kennett, P. (2001) *Comparative Social Policy: Theory and Research*. Buckingham: Open University Press.

Keynes, J.M. (1936) *The General Theory of Employment, Interest and Money*. London: Macmillan.

Kite, C. (2004) The stability of the globalized welfare state. In B. Södersten (ed.) *Globalization and the Welfare State*. Basingstoke: Palgrave Macmillan.

Klant, J.J. (1984) *The Rules of the Game: The Logical Structure of Economic Theories*. Cambridge: Cambridge University Press.

Kleinman, M. (2002) *A European Welfare State?* Basingstoke: Palgrave Macmillan.

Kogan, M. (1979) *Education Policies in Perspective*. Paris: OECD.

Korpi, W. and Palme, J. (1998) The paradox of redistribution: welfare state institutions and poverty in the western countries. *American Sociological Review* 63(5), 661–87.

Krugman, P. (1987) Slow growth in Europe: conceptual issues. In R. Laurence and C. Schultze (eds) *Barriers to European Growth*. Washington, DC: The Brookings Institution.

Ku, Y.-W. (1997) *Welfare Capitalism in Taiwan: State, Economy and Social Policy*. Basingstoke: Macmillan.

Kuhnle, S. (2002) Productive welfare in Korea: towards a European welfare state type? Presented at The Welfare State Pros and Cons ECPR Workshop, Torino.

Kvist, J. and Sinfield, A. (1997) Comparing tax welfare states. In M. May, E. Brunsdon and G. Craig (eds) *Social Policy Review 9*. London: Social Policy Association.

Kwon, H.-J. (1997) Beyond European welfare systems: comparative perspectives on East Asian welfare systems. *Journal of Social Policy* 26(4), 467–84.

Kwon, H.-J. (1999) *The Welfare State in Korea: The Politics of Legitimation*. New York: St Martin's Press.

Kwon, H.-J. (2004) (ed.) *Transforming the Developmental Welfare State in East Asia*. Basingstoke: Palgrave Macmillan.

Land, H. and Rose, H. (1985) Compulsory altruism for some or an altruistic society for all. In P. Bean, J. Ferris and D. Whynes (eds) *In Defence of Welfare*. London: Tavistock.

Langan, M. and Ostner, I. (1991) Gender and welfare towards a comparative framework. In G. Room (ed.) *Towards a European Welfare State?* Bristol: School for Advanced Urban Studies.

Lau, L.J. (1986) *Models of Development: A Comparative Study of Economic Growth in South Korea and Taiwan*. San Francisco: Institute for Contemporary Studies.

Layton-Henry, Z. (1992) *The Politics of Immigration*. Oxford: Blackwell.

Le Grand, J. (1982) *The Strategy of Equality*. London: Allen and Unwin.

Le Grand, J. (1990) *Quasi-markets and Social Policy*. Bristol: School for Advanced Urban Studies.

Leibfried, S. (1992) Towards a European welfare state? On integrating policy regimes into the European Community. In Z. Ferge and J.E. Kolberg (eds) *Social Policy in a Changing Europe*. Frankfurt am Main: Campus Verlag.

Lemaitre, G. (2005) The comparability of international migration statistics. *OECD Statistics Brief 9*.

Leon, D.A., Vägerö, D. and Olausson, P. (1992) Social class differences in infant mortality in Sweden: a comparison with England and Wales. *British Medical Journal* 305, 687–91.

Leung, J. (1994) Dismantling the 'iron rice bowl': welfare reforms in the People's Republic of China. *Journal of Social Policy* 23(3), 341–62.

Lewis, J. (1992) Gender and the development of welfare regimes. *Journal of European Social Policy* 2(3), 159–73.

Lewis, J. (ed.) (1993) *Women and Social Policies in Europe: Work, Family and the State*. Aldershot: Edward Elgar.

Lewis, J. (ed.) (1997a) *Lone Mothers in European Welfare Regimes*. London: Jessica Kingsley.

Lewis, J. (1997b) Gender and welfare regimes: further thoughts. *Social Politics*, Summer, 160–77.

Lewis, J. and Ostner, I. (1994) *Gender and the Evolution of European Social Policies*. Bremen: University of Bremen Centre for Social Policy Research.

Lewis, O. (1968) *A Study of Slum Culture: Backgrounds for La Vida*. New York: Random House.

Lijphart, A. (1975) *The Politics of Accommodation: Pluralism and Democracy in the Netherlands*. Berkeley: University of California Press.

Lijphart, A. (1999) *Patterns of Democracy*. New Haven: Yale University Press.

Lister, R. (2004) The third way's social investment state. In J. Lewis and R. Surender (eds) *Welfare State Change: Towards a Third Way?* Oxford: Oxford University Press.

Lodemel, I. and Trickey, H. (eds) (2001) *An Offer You Can't Refuse: Workfare in International Perspective*. Bristol: Policy Press.

Lukes, S. (2004) *Power: A Radical View*, 2nd edn. London: Macmillan.

Lundström, T. and Svedberg, L. (2003) The voluntary sector in a social democratic welfare state: the case of Sweden. *Journal of Social Policy* 32(2), 217–38.

MacKay, R. (1999) Work and nonwork: a more difficult labour market. *Environment and Planning* 31, 1919–34.

McKeown, T. (1980) *The Role of Medicine*. Oxford: Blackwell.

Mahler, V. and Jesuit, D. (2004) *State Redistribution in Comparative Perspective: A Cross-national Analysis of the Developed Countries*. Syracuse, NY: Syracuse University Maxwell School of Citizenship and Public Affairs, Working Paper 392.

Maltby, T., De Vroom, B., Mirabile, M.L. and Overbye, E. (2004) *Ageing and the Transition to Retirement: A Comparative Analysis of European Welfare States*. Aldershot: Ashgate.

Mann, K. (1992) *The Making of an English 'Underclass'*. Buckingham: Open University Press.

Mann, K. (1994) Watching the defectives: observers of the underclass in the USA, Britain and Australia. *Critical Social Policy* 41(2), 79–99.

Marsden, D. (1999) *A Theory of Employment Systems*. Oxford: Oxford University Press.

Marshall, T.H. (1963) Citizenship and social class. In *Sociology at the Crossroads*. London: Heinemann.

May M. (2003) The role of comparative study. In P. Alcock, A. Erskine and M. May (eds) *The Student's Companion to Social Policy*. Oxford: Blackwell.

May, M. and Brunsdon, E. (in press) Occupational welfare. In M. Powell (ed.) *The Mixed Economy of Welfare*. Bristol: Policy Press.

Maynard, A. (1975) *Experiment with Choice in Education*. London: Institute of Economic Affairs.

Messere, K. (ed.) (1998) *The Tax System in Industrialised Countries*. Oxford: Oxford University Press.

Messere, K., Heady, C. and de Kam F. (eds) (2003) *Tax Policy Theory and Practice in OECD Countries*. Oxford: Oxford University Press.

Millet, K. (1970) *Sexual Politics*. New York: Avon Books.

Milward, H.B. and Provan, K.G. (1999) How networks are governed. Unpublished paper.

Mishra, R. (1977) *Society and Social Policy*. London: Macmillan.

Mishra, R. (1984) *The Welfare State in Crisis*. Brighton: Wheatsheaf.

MISSOC (1998) *Social Protection in the Member States of the Community*. Brussels: Commission of the European Communities.

Mitchell, D. (1991) *Income Transfers in Ten Welfare States*. Aldershot: Avebury.

Mitchie, J. and Sheehan-Quinn, M. (2001) Labour market flexibility, human resource management and corporate performance. *British Journal of Management* 12, 287–306.

Moore, R. (1993) Citizenship and the underclass. In H. Coenen and P. Leisink (eds) *Work and Citizenship in the New Europe*. Aldershot: Edward Elgar.

Murray, C. (1984) *Losing Ground*. New York: Basic Books.

Murray, C. (1990) *The Emerging British Underclass*. London: IEA.

Myles, J. (2002) A new social contract for the elderly? In G. Esping-Andersen (ed.) *Why We Need a New Welfare State*. Oxford: Oxford University Press.

Myrdal, G. (1962) *Challenge to Affluence*. New York: Pantheon.

Nolan, P. and Slater, G. (2003) The labour market: history, structure and prospects. In P.K. Edwards (ed.) *Industrial Relations: Theory and Practice*. Oxford: Blackwell.

Obinger, H., Leibfried, S. and Castles, F.G. (eds) (2005) *Federalism and the Welfare State*. Cambridge: Cambridge University Press.

O'Connor, J. (1973) *The Fiscal Crisis of the State*. New York: St Martin's Press.

O'Connor, J.S. (1996) From women in the welfare state to gendering welfare state regimes. *Current Sociology* 44(2), special issue.

OECD (1990) *Education in OECD Countries*. Paris: OECD.

OECD (1994a) *Caring for Frail Elderly People*. Paris: OECD.

OECD (1994b) *New Orientations for Social Policy*. Paris: OECD.

OECD (1994c) *The Jobs Study*. Paris: OECD.

OECD (2001) *Starting Strong*. Paris: OECD.

OECD (2002) *Trends in International Migration*. Paris: OECD.

OECD (2003) *Revenue Statistics, 1965–2001*. Paris: OECD.

OECD (2004a) *Education at a Glance*. Paris: OECD.

OECD (2004b) *Health Data, 2004*. Paris: OECD.

OECD (2004c) *OECD in Figures, 2004*. Paris: OECD.

OECD (2004d) *National Accounts of OECD Countries*. Paris: OECD.

OECD (2004e) *Social Expenditure Database*. Paris: OECD.

OECD (2004f) *Working Party on Estimating Expenditure on Long-term Care*. Paris: OECD.

OECD (2005a) *Economic Outlook*. Paris: OECD.

OECD (2005b) *Health Data, 2004*. Paris: OECD.

Offe, C. (1984) *Contradictions of the Welfare State*. London: Hutchinson.

Offe, C. (1996) Full employment: asking the wrong question. In E.E. Oddvar and J. Lofyager (eds) *The Rationality of the Welfare State*. Oslo: Scandinavian University Press, pp. 120–33.

Orloff, A.S. (1993) Gender and the social rights of citizenship: state policies and gender relations in comparative research. *American Sociological Review* 58(3), 303–28.

Pacolet, J., Bouten, R., Lanoye, H. and Versieck, K. (1999) *Social Protection for Dependency in Old Age in the 15 EU Member States and Norway*. Luxembourg: European Commission.

Pahl, J. (1988) Earning, sharing, spending: married couples and their money. In R. Walker and G. Parker (eds) *Money Matters*. London: Sage.

Palier, B. (1997) A 'liberal' dynamic in the transformation of the French welfare system. In J. Clasen (ed.) *Social Insurance in Europe*. Bristol: Policy Press.

Palmer, G.R. and Short, S.D. (1994) *Health Care and Public Policy: An Australian Analysis*, 2nd edn. South Melbourne: Macmillan.

Pampel, F.C. and Williamson, J.B. (1989) *Age, Class, Politics and the Welfare State*. Cambridge: Cambridge University Press.

Pedersen, S. (1993) *Family, Dependence and the Origins of the Welfare State*. Cambridge: Cambridge University Press.

Perraton, J. and Cliff, B. (eds) (2004) *Where are National Capitalisms Now?* Basingstoke: Palgrave Macmillan.

Pfaller, A., Gough, I. and Therborn, G. (1991) *Can the Welfare State Compete?* Basingstoke: Macmillan.

Pfeffer, J. (1998) *The Human Equation.* Boston: Harvard Business School Press.

Piachaud, D. and Sutherland, H. (2001) Child poverty and the New Labour Government. *Journal of Social Policy* 30(1), 95–118.

Pierson, P. (1994) *Dismantling the Welfare State.* Cambridge: Cambridge University Press.

Pierson, P. (2000) Increasing returns, path dependence and the study of politics. *American Political Science Review* 94(2), 251–67.

Pierson, P. (ed.) (2001) *The New Politics of the Welfare State.* Oxford: Oxford University Press.

Piven, F.F. and Cloward, R. (1993) *Regulating the Poor: The Functions of Public Welfare*, 2nd edn. New York: Vintage Books.

Pollock, A. (2004) *NHS plc.* London: Verso.

Porter, M. (1990) *The Competitive Advantage of Nations.* Basingstoke: Macmillan.

Powell, M. (ed.) (in press) *Understanding the Mixed Economy of Welfare.* Bristol: Policy Press.

Ramesh, M. (2004) *Social Policy in East and Southeast Asia: Education, Health, Housing and Income Maintenance.* London: RoutledgeCurzon.

Ranade, W. (ed.) (1998) *Markets and Health Care.* London: Longman.

Rank, M.R. (1994) *Living on the Edge: The Realities of Welfare in America.* New York: Columbia University Press.

Raywid, M.A. (1985) Family choice arrangements in public schools: a review of the literature. *Review of Educational Research* 55, 435–67.

Reich, R.B. (1991) *The Work of Nations: Preparing Ourselves for 21st Century Capitalism.* New York: Simon and Schuster.

Reich, R.B. (2004) *Reason Why Liberals Will Win the Battle for America.* New York: Alfred A. Knopf.

Rex, J. (1986) *Race and Ethnicity.* Milton Keynes: Open University Press.

Richardson, J. (ed.) (1982) *Policy Styles in Western Europe.* London: Allen and Unwin.

Rifkin, J. (1995) *The End of Work: The Decline of the Global Workforce and Dawn of the Post-market Era.* New York: Putman.

Rimlinger, G. (1971) *Welfare Policy and Industrialisation in Europe, America and Russia.* New York: Wiley.

Roberts, H. (ed.) (1981) *Women, Health and Reproduction.* London: Routledge.

Robinson, P. (1999) The tyranny of league tables: international comparisons of educational attainment and economic performance. In R. Alexander, P. Broadfoot and D. Phillips (eds) *Learning from Comparing.* Wallingford: Symposium Books.

Rodgers, B., Greve, J. and Morgan, J. (1968) *Comparative Social Administration.* London: Allen and Unwin.

Rothstein, B. (1998) *Just Institutions Matter: The Moral and Political Logic of the Universal Welfare State*. Cambridge: Cambridge University Press.

Royal Commission on Long-Term Care (1999) *With Respect to Old Age*. Cm 4192. London: HMSO.

Rubery, J. and Grimshaw, D. (2003) *The Organisation of Employment: An International Perspective*. Basingstoke: Palgrave Macmillan

Sainsbury, D. (1993) Dual welfare and sex segregation of access to social benefits: income maintenance policies in the UK, the US, the Netherlands and Sweden. *Journal of Social Policy* 22(1), 69–98.

Sainsbury, D. (ed.) (1994) *Gendering Welfare States*. London: Sage.

Sainsbury, D. (1996) *Gender Equality and Welfare States*. Cambridge: Cambridge University Press.

Saltman, R. (1998) Health reform in Sweden: the road beyond cost containment. In Ranade, W. (ed.) *Markets and Health Care*. London: Longman.

Saltman, R.B. and von Otter, C. (1992) *Planned Markets and Public Competition*. Buckingham: Open University Press.

Sarfarti, H. (2002) Labour markets and social protection policies: linkages and interactions. In H. Sarfarti and G. Bonoli (eds) *Labour Market and Social Protection Reforms in International Perspective*. Aldershot: Ashgate.

Scharpf, F. (2001) The viability of advanced welfare states in the international economy: vulnerabilities and options. In S. Leibfried (ed.) *Welfare State Futures*. Cambridge: Cambridge University Press.

Segalman, R. (1986) *The Swiss Way of Welfare*. New York: Praeger.

Shin, D.-M. (2003) *Social and Economic Policies in Korea: Ideas, Networks and Linkages*. London: RoutledgeCurzon.

Siaroff, A. (1994) Work, welfare and gender equality: a new typology. In D. Sainsbury (ed.) *Gendering Welfare States*. London: Sage, chapter 6.

Sinfield, A. (1978) Analysis in the social division of welfare. *Journal of Social Policy* 7(2), 129–56.

Sinfield, A. (1998) Social protection versus tax benefits. *European Institute for Social Security Yearbook 1997*, 111–52.

Sinfield, A. (2000) Tax benefits in non-state pensions. *European Journal of Social Security* 2(2) 137–67.

Smeeding, T.M., O'Higgins, M. and Rainwater, L. (1990) *Poverty, Inequality and Income Distribution in Comparative Perspective*. Hemel Hempstead: Harvester Wheatsheaf.

Smith, J.G. (2005) *There is a Better Way: A New Economic Agenda for Labour*. London: Anthem Press.

Södersten, B. (ed.) (2004) *Globalization and the Welfare State*. Basingstoke: Palgrave Macmillan.

Spender, D. and Sarah, E. (1980) *Learning to Lose: Sexism and Education*. London: The Women's Press.

Stacey, M. (1988) *The Sociology of Health and Healing*. London: Unwin Hyman.

Stone, M. (1981) *The Education of the Black Child in Britain*. Glasgow: Fontana.

Swank, D. (2001) Political institutions and welfare state restructuring: the impact of institutions on social policy change in developed democracies. In P. Pierson (ed.) *The New Politics of the Welfare State*. Oxford: Oxford University Press.

Taylor, R. (2002) *Britain's World of Work: Myths and Realities*. Swindon: ESRC.

Taylor-Gooby, P. (1985) *Public Opinion, Ideology and State Welfare*. London: Routledge.

Taylor-Gooby, P. (ed.) (2001) *European Welfare States under Pressure*. London: Sage.

Taylor-Gooby, P. (2002) The silver age of the welfare state: perspectives on resilience. *Journal of Social Policy* 31(4), 597–622.

Taylor-Gooby, P. (ed.) (2004a) *Making a European Welfare State?* Oxford: Blackwell.

Taylor-Gooby, P. (ed.) (2004b) *New Risks, New Welfare: The Transformation of the European Welfare State*. Oxford: Oxford University Press.

Teddlie, C. and Reynolds, D. (eds) (2000) *The International Handbook of School Effectiveness Research*. London: Falmer.

Titmuss, R.M. (1958) *Essays on the Welfare State*. London: Allen and Unwin.

Titmuss, R.M. (1974) *Social Policy: An Introduction*. London: Allen and Unwin.

Townsend, P. (ed.) (1970) *The Concept of Poverty*. London: Heinemann.

Townsend, P. (1979) *Poverty in the United Kingdom*. Harmondsworth: Penguin Books.

Townsend, P. (1993) *The International Analysis of Poverty*. Hemel Hempstead: Harvester Wheatsheaf.

Townsend, P., Davidson, N. and Whitehead, M. (eds) (1988) *Inequalities in Health*. Harmondsworth: Penguin Books.

Trifilletti, R. (1999) Southern European welfare regimes and the worsening position of women. *Journal of European Social Policy* 9(1), 49–64.

Tullock, G. (1976) *The Vote Motive*. London: Institute of Economic Affairs.

Twigg, J. and Grand, A (1998) Contrasting legal conceptions of family obligations and financial reciprocity in the support of older people: France and England. *Ageing and Society* 18(2), 131–46.

UNDP (2004) *Human Development Report*. Available at www.hdr.undp.org/

Ungerson, C. (1994) Morals and politics in payments for care. In A. Evers, M. Pijl and C. Ungerson (eds) (1994) *Payments for Care: A Comparative Overview*. Aldershot: Avebury.

Ungerson, C. (1995) Gender, cash and informal care: European perspectives and dilemmas. *Journal of Social Policy* 24(1), 31–52.

Ungerson, C. (2000) Thinking about the production and consumption of long-term care in Britain: does gender still matter? *Journal of Social Policy* 28(4), 623–44.

UNHCR (2003) *Refugees by Numbers*. Geneva: United Nations High Commission for Refugees. Available at www.unhcr.ch

United Nations (2003) *World Population Prospects*. New York: United Nations.

United States Social Security Administration. *Social Security Programs throughout the World*. Available at www.ssa.gov/policy/docs/progdesc/ssptw/

US National Center for Health Care Statistics (2002). Available at www.cdc.gov.nchs

Van Doorselaer, E., Masseria, C. and the OECD Health Equity Research Group (2004) *Income-related Inequality in the Use of Medical Care in 21 OECD Countries*. OECD Health Working Papers 14. Paris: OECD.

Van Waarden, F. (1999) Ieder land zijn eigen trant? In W. Bakker and F. van Waarden (eds) *Ruimte rond regels: Stijlen van regulering en beleidsuitvoering vergeleken*. Amsterdam: Boom, pp. 303–39.

Visser, J. and Hemerijck, A. (1997) *'A Dutch Miracle': Job Growth, Welfare Reform and Corporatism in the Netherlands*. Amsterdam: Amsterdam University Press.

Vlemininckx, K. and Smeeding, T.M. (eds) *Child Well-being, Child Poverty and Child Policy in Modern Nations*. Bristol: Policy Press.

Wachtel, H. (1972) Capitalism and poverty in America: paradox or contradiction. *American Economic Review* 62(2), 187–94.

Wadensjo, E. (2002) Institutional change. In H. Mosley, J. O'Reilly and K. Schomann (eds) *Labour Markets, Gender and Institutional Change: Essays in Honour of Gunter Schmid*. Cheltenham: Edward Elgar.

Walker, A. and Wong, C.-K. (1996) Rethinking the western construction of the welfare state. *International Journal of Health Services* 26(1), 67–92.

Walker, A. and Wong, C.-K. (2004) The ethnocentric construction of the welfare state. In P. Kennett (ed.) *A Handbook of Comparative Social Welfare*. Cheltenham: Edward Elgar.

Walker, A. and Wong, C.-K. (eds) (2005) *East Asian Welfare Regimes in Transition*. Bristol: Policy Press.

Walker, R. (2005) *Social Security and Welfare: Concepts and Comparisons*. Maidenhead: Open University Press.

Walker, R. and Parker, G. (eds.) (1988) *Money Matters*. London: Sage.

Weir, M., Orloff, S. and Skocpol, T. (eds) (1988) *The Politics of Social Policy in the United States*. Princeton: Princeton University Press.

Welch, A.R. (1993) Class, culture and the state in comparative education: problems, perspectives and prospects. *Comparative Education* 29(1), 7–27.

Whiteley, R. (ed.) (2000) *Divergent Capitalisms: The Social Structuring and Change of Business Systems*. Oxford: Oxford University Press.

WHO (2005) *Selected Core Health Indicators*. Geneva: World Health Organisation.

Wilensky, H.L. (1975) *The Welfare State and Equality*. Berkeley: University of California Press.

Wilensky, H.L. and Lebaux, C.N. (1965) *Industrial Society and Social Welfare*. Glencoe, IL: Free Press.

Wilkinson, R.G. (1996) *Unhealthy Societies*. London: Routledge.

Williams, F. (1989) *Social Policy: A Critical Introduction*. Polity Press: Cambridge.

Wilsford, D. (1991) The continuity of crisis: patterns of health care policy making in France, 1978–88. In J.S. Ambler (ed.) *The French Welfare State*. New York: New York University Press.

Wilson, W.J. (1981) Race, class and public policy. *American Sociologist* 16(2), 125–34.

Wilson, W.J. (1987) *The Truly Disadvantaged*. Chicago: University of Chicago Press.

Wistow, G., Knapp, M., Hardy, B. and Allen, C. (1994) *Social Care in a Mixed Economy*. Buckingham: Open University Press.

Wolf, A. (2002) *Does Education Matter?* London: Penguin Books.

Wolfe, A. (1977) *The Limits of Legitimacy*. New York: The Free Press.

Wollmann, H. and Schröter, F. (eds.) (2000) *Comparing Public Sector Reform in Britain and Germany*. Aldershot: Ashgate.

World Bank (1994) *Averting the Old Age Crisis*. Oxford: Oxford University Press.

World Bank (2002) *The Little Data Book*. Washington, DC: World Bank.

Yi, I. and Lee, B.-H. (2004) Unemployment and policy responses in Taiwan: gender and family implications. In H.-J. Kwon (ed.) *Transforming the Developmental Welfare State in East Asia*. Basingstoke: Palgrave Macmillan.

*Useful websites*

www.espanet.org
www.ilo.org
www.issa.org
www.lisproject.org
www.oecd.org
www.pisa.oecd.org
www.sheffield.ac.uk/socst/ICSP
www.who.int

# INDEX